T0320043

Empirical Entrepreneurship in Europe

Empirical Entrepreneurship in Europe

New Perspectives

Edited by

Michael Dowling

University of Regensburg, Germany

Jürgen Schmude

University of Regensburg, Germany

Edward Elgar
Cheltenham, UK • Northampton, MA, USA

Published by
Edward Elgar Publishing Limited
Glensanda House
Montpellier Parade
Cheltenham
Glos GL50 1UA
UK

Edward Elgar Publishing, Inc.
William Pratt House
9 Dewey Court
Northampton
Massachusetts 01060
USA

A catalogue record for this book
is available from the British Library

Library of Congress Cataloguing in Publication Data

Interdisciplinary European Conference on Entrepreneurship Research (4th : 2006 : University of Regensburg)
    Empirical entrepreneurship in Europe : new perspectives / edited by Michael Dowling, Jürgen Schmude.
        p. cm.
    Includes bibliographical references and index.
    1. Entrepreneurship—Europe—Congresses. I. Dowling, Michael J. (Michael Joseph) II. Schmude, Jürgen, 1955- III. Title.

    HB615.I567 2007
    338'.04094—dc22

                                                        2006037090

ISBN: 978 1 84720 212 3

Printed and bound in Great Britain by MPG Books Ltd, Bodmin, Cornwall

Contents

Contributors

Andy Adcroft, University of Surrey, UK.

A. Miguel Amaral, Technical University of Lisbon, Portugal.

Rui Baptista, Technical University of Lisbon, Portugal and Max Planck Institute of Economics, Jena, Germany.

Wolfgang Bessler, Justus-Liebig-University, Giessen, Germany.

Claudia Bittelmeyer, Justus-Liebig-University, Giessen, Germany.

Spinder Dhaliwal, University of Surrey, UK.

Michael Dowling, University of Regensburg, Germany.

Riccardo Fini, University of Bologna, Italy.

Michael Fritsch, Friedrich-Schiller-University, Jena, Germany, Max Planck Institute of Economics, Jena, Germany and German Institute for Economic Research (DIW), Berlin.

Rosa Grimaldi, University of Bologna, Italy.

Tatiana Iakovleva, Bode Graduate School of Business, Norway.

Carola Jungwirth, University of Zurich, Switzerland.

Jill Kickul, Simmons School of Management, Boston, MA, USA.

Pamela Mueller, Max Planck Institute of Economics, Jena, Germany.

Michael Niese, WirtschaftsVereinigung Metalle, Berlin, Germany.

Arnis Sauka, Stockholm School of Economics, Riga, Latvia and University of Siegen, Germany.

Dirk Schilder, Technical University of Freiberg, Germany.

Jürgen Schmude, University of Regensburg, Germany.

Robert Strohmeyer, Institute for Small Business Research, University of Mannheim, Germany.

Vartuhi Tonoyan, Institute for Small Business Research and Department of International Management, University of Mannheim, Germany.

Mikki Valjakka, Lappeenranta University of Technology, Finland.

Friederike Welter, University of Siegen, Germany and Stockholm School of Economics, Riga, Latvia.

Preface

This book presents a selection of the best papers from the fourth annual Interdisciplinary European Conference on Entrepreneurship Research (IECER), held at the University of Regensburg in February 2006. As the organizers of this series of conferences, we are interested in annually bringing together researchers from all over Europe to share results from their latest empirical work. The conference included over 40 presentations from 17 different European countries and over 80 participants. IECER 2007 will be held at the Montpellier Business School in France from 28 February to 2 March 2007. It is our belief that IECER will continue to grow and become the premier forum in bringing together entrepreneurship researchers from all across Europe.

We would also like to gratefully acknowledge the generous financial support for the IECER from the Hans Lindner Institute, a private foundation created by the entrepreneur Hans Lindner and his family to support small business and entrepreneurship research in Eastern Bavaria. Additional support was provided by the EXIST programme of the German Federal Ministry of Education and Research.

1. Introduction

Michael Dowling and Jürgen Schmude

The chapters in this book are a selection of the best papers from the fourth annual Interdisciplinary European Conference on Entrepreneurship Research (IECER). We believe that these chapters demonstrate that there is a growing variety and depth of empirical entrepreneurship research in Europe. Academic researchers in different disciplines are using a number of interesting methodologies to study the phenomenon of entrepreneurship both in Europe in general and in specific country settings.

The chapters of this book can be divided into three sections. The first seven chapters deal with examining entrepreneurship issues in specific country settings from Portugal, the UK and Germany in Western Europe to Eastern European countries such as Russia and Latvia, and to Scandinavia and Finland. All of the studies are based on empirical data collected in the individual countries or across Europe. The second set of two chapters uses data from companies in Germany and Italy, but the focus is not on these individual countries but rather on the special issues of technology-based companies in Europe. The final group of two chapters deals with venture capital issues in Europe. The venture capital market has similarities to the more closely studied market in the United States, but there are interesting differences highlighted in these two chapters. Here we briefly summarize each of the chapters presented in this book.

In Chapter 2, 'Determinants of Transitions from Paid Employment into Entrepreneurship: An Empirical Study', Miguel Amaral and Rui Baptista investigate why individuals become business owners. The characteristics of business owners are studied, taking the mode of entry (start-up versus acquisition) into consideration as well as the type of transition (directly from paid employment or from non-employment to business ownership). A model incorporating a variety of factors (human capital characteristics and organizational conditions) applying a logit procedure is used to estimate the probability of an individual who leaves paid employment becoming a business owner. The study uses an extensive dataset on individuals' background, career path and flows between firms and sectors covering the

Portuguese economy from 1986 to 2000. The dataset on business owners and paid employees includes gender, age, function, tenure schooling and skills level and contains about 5 million individuals who switched to business ownership. The authors found that older and more experienced individuals were more likely to switch over to business ownership instead of seeking another position as paid employees. Highly educated individuals represent a very small percentage of those leaving paid employment. This suggests that – once in paid employment – the opportunity costs for highly educated people in switching occupations are very significant and may reduce the pool of potentially successful entrepreneurs.

In Chapter 3, 'Accurate Portrayal or Lazy Stereotype? The Changing Nature of the Asian Business Sector in the UK', Spinder Dhaliwal and Andy Adcroft analyse the longer-established, more successful enterprises of the Asian business community. The authors seek to draw out trends within this increasingly important sector of the economy and consider their economic sustainability. This chapter contradicts the traditional opinion that ethnic minority enterprises are perceived as being concentrated in low entry barrier industries with low value-added activities and limited opportunity for market expansion. The data for the empirical analyses were directly drawn from the annual wealth index produced by the *Eastern Eye* magazine in the UK. The authors find that over the past seven years (1998 to 2004) the capacity for wealth creation in the upper reaches of the Asian business sector (200 Asian wealth creators) is much higher than in the UK economy as a whole and across many sectors. The growth of this part of the Asian business sector is pushed by the lower and middle part of the sector, whereas the growth of the UK economy as a whole is dependent on a few large companies at the top. Finally Dhaliwal and Adcroft consider a change in the composition of the Asian business sector with important shifts away from the traditional sectors (for example retailing, textiles and manufacturing) towards higher-technology and higher-value activities with higher levels of economic sustainability.

Chapter 4 by Tatiana Iakovleva and Jill Kickul, entitled 'Personal and Organizational Success Factors of Women SMEs in Russia', addresses both issues of gender in entrepreneurship research and entrepreneurship in transition economies. Entrepreneurship in Russia is a particularly interesting topic as it has only been since 1990 that individual ownership of firms has been allowed and there is only very limited research on entrepreneurial companies in the Russian setting. Iakovleva and Kickul review the research that has been conducted both in general and on Russian female entrepreneurs. They then examine the literature on personality and individual competences of entrepreneurs in order to develop hypotheses for these issues in the Russian setting. Hypotheses are developed about entrepreneurial firm resources, environmental context and strategies. To test these hypotheses a sample of Russian women-led SMEs was developed and survey data were collected. Five hundred and fifty-five usable questionnaires were received, representing a large sample of women-led firms in Russia. Hypotheses were tested using a structural equation modelling approach. The analysis shows that the ability of female entrepreneurs in Russia to identify opportunities as well as the availability of financial resources and personal commitment are the crucial factors associated with superior firm performance in these firms. These findings provide not only interesting results for gender issues for entrepreneurship in general but also serve as a model for conducting similar studies in other countries in Europe, in particular in Eastern European situations.

Serial entrepreneurship is a widespread economic phenomenon in Germany. Around 18 per cent of business owners in Germany have previously gained self-employment experience. Chapter 5, 'Entrepreneurship: Only a Few are Chosen but Some are Even Chosen Twice' by Pamela Mueller and Michael Niese, distinguishes non-entrepreneurs (individuals that have never started a firm), novice entrepreneurs and serial entrepreneurs, with a special focus on the differences between novice and serial entrepreneurs. The authors try to answer to the question of whether serial entrepreneurs have a different risk attitude. The data on entrepreneurship are taken from the German Socio-Economic Panel Study (SOEP), a representative longitudinal panel study of private households in Germany which began in 1984 and is carried out annually. The analysis is restricted to those 330 respondents who switched to self-employment in 2003 and 2004 either from paid employment, unemployment, retirement or schooling. About 23 per cent of those who had previously turned to self-employment had a business and could be characterized as serial entrepreneurs. The authors found that although bankruptcy has a negative stigma, failure does not discourage serial entrepreneurs and that they hardly differ from novice entrepreneurs. An explanation for the similarities between novice and serial entrepreneurs might be that a novice entrepreneur can become a serial entrepreneur. One difference is that serial entrepreneurs have a more unstable work history which is not characterized by phases of unemployment but by a greater number of job changes compared to novice entrepreneurs. Mueller and Niese conclude that serial entrepreneurship seems to be an attitude to life rather than being driven by necessity or profitable opportunities.

In Chapter 6, 'Productive, Unproductive and Destructive Entre-preneurship in an Advanced Transition Setting: The Example of Latvian Small Enterprises', Arnis Sauka and Friederike Welter set out to explore different forms of entrepreneurship based on the example of small Latvian enterprises. A key idea in defining unproductive and destructive entrepreneurship is that not everything that is entrepreneurial is necessarily desirable. Some entrepreneurs do not make a productive contribution to the real output of an economy and in some cases they even play a destructive role. The authors believe that the extent and nature of entrepreneurial value creation affect the success of the venture and influence its contribution to the development of the economy. From the empirical side their chapter is based on 133 face-to-face interviews with owners and owner-managers of small and medium-sized enterprises (SMEs) (out of 550 contacts) conducted in Riga (Latvia) during the summer of 2005. According to the authors it is much more complicated to measure productive, unproductive and destructive entrepreneurship empirically than to define these types conceptually. Thus, the results give a first insight into tendencies regarding the contribution which conforming and deviant activities make to SME value creation on different levels. The authors find that SMEs which are less involved in deviant activities appear to perform better and that activities that bring value on the venture level also contribute to the society level. For future research Sauka and Welter postulate extending the sample and they suggest using a multivariate statistical approach to gain a more insightful and accurate picture.

Chapter 7 by Robert Strohmeyer and Vartuhi Tonoyan, 'Working Part-Time or Full-Time? On the Impact of Family Context and Institutional Arrangements on Atypical Work: A Cross-National Comparison of Female Self-Employment in Western and Eastern Europe', also addresses gender-specific issues in entrepreneurship using data in this case from all of Europe. The authors also focus on part-time employment as a form of gainful occupation. A series of hypotheses are developed based on both micro-level and macro-level perspectives. In the micro-level context the authors suggest that part-time self-employment is dependent on both the presence of small children in the household and whether or not the female entrepreneur has a partner. At the macro level the authors suggest that women's part-time self-employment will vary between different types of institutional environments across Europe. The data for this study are based on the European Labour Force Survey (Eurostat 2005) of 85 000 self-employed women in 25 Western and Eastern European countries. The dependent measures examine whether or not the respondents worked part-time or full-time. A Heckman probit model is used to test the hypotheses. The findings from these tests support most of the hypotheses developed in this chapter. At the micro level the presence of young children significantly increases the likelihood of women engaging in part-time self-employment, which was found to be stable across most countries in Western and Eastern Europe. In addition, the probability of taking on part-time self-employment is strongly associated with the presence of a partner or husband within the household. This suggests that having an economically active partner increases the likelihood of part-time self-employment positively in both Western and Eastern Europe. However, the effect of family on part-time self-employment differs between various institutional settings within Western Europe as well as between Eastern, Southern and Western European countries. The probability of part-time work was found to be strongest in the most conservative welfare states, such as Germany, Austria and the Netherlands, where there are institutional and cultural factors that support women being the primary care-givers. There are however exceptions to this general finding. In France, for example, policies fostering active female participation in the labour market are close to models in Scandinavia, which have created an institutional environment which is more supportive for women's full-time self-employment. In Eastern Germany there is also a disproportionately lower share of part-time self-employment. This may be a result of the institutional setting left over from former East Germany, where kindergarten and day nurseries were plentiful and publicly supported. There were also some interesting anomalies in the study; for example, the authors found a strong effect of family on part-time self-employment in Italy, which was quite different from other states in Southern Europe, such as Spain or Greece. The Czech Republic also showed atypical behaviour compared to other Eastern European countries. This study therefore makes important contributions to the general topic of gender-based entrepreneurship research and provides a set of findings that can be broadly applied across many European situations.

In Chapter 8, 'Is Modesty Attractive? Study of the Present and Future States of the Entrepreneurial Skills of Finnish Small and Medium-Sized Entrepreneurs', Mikki Valjakka tries to answer the question of whether modesty is attractive. The author defines entrepreneurial skills as two kinds of competency: creating value (for example ability to create good customer relationships, competency in mastering the technology and developing products or services) and enabling contingency (for example competency in directing and steering business operations, competency in developing the personnel and mastering the knowledge). The aim of his study is to shed light on entrepreneurial skills because they are one of the most important factors with regard to competitiveness. The author's perspective is centred on Finnish small and medium-sized entrepreneurs. The study follows a quantitative approach and is based on a questionnaire which was sent by e-mail to 3253 to owner-entrepreneurs with a response rate of 20 per cent (163 female and 493 male entrepreneurs). As Valjakka shows, 'planning and managing operations' and 'collaboration and communication' are the highest-ranked skills (the respondents ranked them as 'good') whereas 'languages' was the least known. None of the skills or themes was ranked 'excellent' by the respondents, but they seem to be satisfied with having only a good level of the skills and know-how commonly needed and do not want to be excellent. The author concludes that the old Finnish proverb 'Modesty is attractive' seems to be true with regard to the results of his study.

Chapter 9 by Wolfgang Bessler and Claudia Bittelmeyer, 'Performance and Survival of Technology Firms: The Impact of Intellectual Property', is a study of patenting behaviour of German firms that went public on the Neuer Markt, which was the equivalent of the NASDAQ market in the USA in the late 1990s until 2003. The objective of this empirical analysis was to see whether these technology-based firms that went public on this exchange outperformed companies with no patent technologies. Although in most studies on innovation- and technology-based firms research and development expenditure are used, there is also extensive literature using patents as an output measure of innovations. In this chapter Bessler and Bittelmeyer focus on using patents and examining daily stock price performance for firms that went public on the Neuer Markt over the period from 1997 to 2003. They identified 90 firms in their sample that filed for over 6200 patents. Performance was measured using a buy-and-hold abnormal return model. In the second part of the study Bessler and Bittelmeyer examined whether patents have an effect on the success and survival of firms that went public in this period. Their sample was divided into two groups: one of all firms that went public but then later exited the market, and a second group of all firms that went public and continued to operate through the end of the observation period. Empirically they investigated whether the two groups are different with respect to the success of the intellectual property activity. Overall their findings suggest that investment in intellectual property in the form of patents has a positive impact on the value long-run performance of these technology-based firms; in particular the abnormal performance of firms that went public with patents is positive and significantly higher that those without patented technologies. Moreover, they found empirical evidence that patenting behaviour has a significant impact on the success or bankruptcy of firms. Firms that had fewer patents and patents of lower quality had a much higher failure rate. These results provide interesting comparative findings to similar research that has been conducted on technology-based start-ups in the United States setting.

Chapter 10 by Riccardo Fini and Rosa Grimaldi, 'Academic Founders and Business Opportunity Generation: An Empirical Analysis based on Italian Academic Spin-Offs', examines the important role that academic spin-offs have in supporting economic and technological growth. Academic spin-offs are those companies that are created to exploit technological knowledge that originates within universities or other institutes of higher education. In this chapter, after reviewing the relevant literature, Fini and Grimaldi develop a framework to examine the issue of opportunity recognition in such academic spin-off companies. A descriptive empirical analysis is presented based on a database of 47 Italian academic spin-offs that originated in five different universities in Northern Italy. Data were gathered using a questionnaire sent to the academic founders. In addition to providing the descriptive analysis of the data, a factor analysis is used to examine likely sources of opportunity recognition. The findings suggest that industry experience is a relevant source for opportunity recognition. In addition, personal-level characteristics such as academics' personal ties with industrial partners and their personal investments in applied research activities have an impact. These results confirm earlier research by Shane in the United States, suggesting that the prior knowledge of markets and customer problems of how to serve a market influence the opportunity discovery process. Their findings also suggest that environmental influences play an important role. Here, again, their research confirms studies by Mowery and his colleagues in the United States that suggest the importance of environmental factors. Taken together, this chapter represents an important contribution to the growing topic of opportunity recognition in entrepreneurship research and confirms earlier research by other prominent researchers in the USA.

The final two chapters examine venture capital issues for innovative start-ups in Germany and in Switzerland. In Chapter 11 by Michael Fritsch and Dirk Schilder, 'Is There a Regional Equity Gap for Innovative Start-Ups? The Case of Germany', the authors address the issue of spatial distribution of venture capital (VC) supply and demand within Germany. It has been shown by previous research, particularly in the United States, that spatial proximity between VC firms and the location of their investments is a crucial issue. The literature suggests that the exchange of knowledge with portfolio firms requires frequent face-to-face contact and close location. This has been shown in particular in the research by Gompers and Lerner in the United States. In addition, the monitoring and advising activities often require frequent visits to the companies. If this tendency is also true in Europe, then a strong clustering of venture capital companies might lead to an undersupply of venture capital for regions where only a few VC firms are present. Fritsch and Schilder show that in Germany venture capital firms are concentrated in four major cities: Berlin, Hamburg, Frankfurt and Munich. The authors conducted a survey with 75 personal interviews with venture capital managers who were involved in start-up financing in Germany. Independent corporate VC companies, business individuals, banks, VC subsidiaries of banks and public providers of equity were included. These data show that banks, bank-dependent VC firms, public VC firms and business angels have over 75 per cent of their investments within a distance of 100 km. However, the independent venture capital firms have less than 30 per cent of their investments at such a short distance and have spread their investments all over Germany and in fact throughout Europe. Their data suggest that VC firms that have relatively distantly located investments substitute contact via telecommunication for personal meetings. One of the main reasons given by private venture capitalists for a wider geographic dispersion is that there are not enough investment opportunities in the regions close to their main offices. Another method that is used for overcoming distance barriers is syndication, that is, more than one investment company invests in a portfolio company and tries to locate a syndication partner close to the firm. The results from the study in Germany suggest that the importance of regional proximity is overstated in the literature. This may be due to the fact that most research on this topic has been conducted in the United States in very regionally focused areas such as Silicon Valley or in the Route 128 corridor around Boston, where there is a high concentration of both venture capital firms and investments. This study suggests that the venture capital industry on an international basis is more diverse and further international comparative studies are warranted.

The final chapter, Chapter 12, 'How Market Appraisal Affects Investments in Human Capital: Evidence from Austrian and Swiss Venture Capitalists' by Carola Jungwirth, examines issues of human capital as a driver of investment strategies of venture capital firms using data from firms in Switzerland and Austria. Jungwirth examines relevant literature in studying the venture capital industry in the United States and then develops two hypotheses relating issues of market potential and market size to industry-specific human capital in venture capitalist firms. To test these hypotheses she generated a database based on addresses provided by venture capital associations in Austria and Switzerland and sent questionnaires to over 100 firms. Fifty-eight usable responses were received and data were analysed using ordinary least squares regression methods. The results suggest that there were significant differences between venture capitalists' willingness to invest in human capital between Swiss and Austrian venture capital firms. The results also show that venture capitalists that believed that markets were relatively small invested less in human capital and tended to invest in later stages of the investment process and had a more diverse portfolio. On the other hand, venture capitalists that believed that markets would develop faster tended to invest in earlier-stage financing and held fewer industries in their portfolio. Although the data from the study represent a relatively small number of venture firms, they further suggest that venture capital industries have country-specific variables that impact upon investment decisions and that simply extrapolating research from the United States situation to other venture capital markets worldwide is at best problematical and at worst simply incorrect.

Taken together, we believe that the chapters in this book represent excellent examples of the growing amount of theoretically based and empirically sound interdisciplinary research on entrepreneurship in a

European setting. Several of these studies show that results from US-based research cannot simply be extrapolated to other national settings. On the other hand, in some cases research presented confirmed US findings. However, there exists a further need for developing European entrepreneurship research that takes into account environmental and market-specific differences. We hope that the IECER conferences will continue to represent an interesting opportunity for European researchers to exchange ideas and results and therefore broaden the research base for entrepreneurship research.

REFERENCES

Eurostat (2005), *LFS User Guide: Labour Force Survey: Anonymised Data Sets*, European Commission Eurostat.

Gompers, Paul A. (1995), 'Optimal investment, monitoring, and the staging of venture capital', *Journal of Finance*, **6**, 1461–89.

Lerner, Joshua (1995), 'Venture capitalists and the oversight of private firms', *Journal of Finance,* **50**, 301–18.

Mowery, D., R. Nelson, B. Sampat and A. Ziedonis (2001), 'The effects of the Bayh-Dole Act on US academic research and technology transfer', *Research Policy*, **30** (1), 99–119.

Shane, S. (2000), 'Prior knowledge and the discovery of entrepreneurial opportunities', *Organizational Science*, **11** (4), 448–69.

2. Transitions from Paid Employment into Entrepreneurship: An Empirical Study

A. Miguel Amaral and Rui Baptista*

INTRODUCTION

Entrepreneurial dynamics has become a prominent issue, mainly due to the widespread conviction about the role played by entrepreneurship in generating innovation, employment, industrial restructuring and socio-economic prosperity. The objective of the present chapter is to investigate the factors and conditions influencing the probability of entering entrepreneurship after being a paid employee. The characteristics of business owners are studied, taking into consideration the mode of entry (that is, start-up versus acquisition) and the type of transition (that is, directly from paid employment to business ownership, or with a non-employment period in-between). Transitions are analysed by looking at a variety of factors – such as human capital characteristics and organizational conditions – that have been found to influence an individual's choice to become an entrepreneur.

Even though the concept of an entrepreneur can assume diverse meanings, our analysis focuses on business owners (including the self-employed)[1] and will use the terms 'entrepreneurship', 'business ownership' and 'self-employment' interchangeably. For the purpose of this study, entrepreneurs are those who, regardless of whether they: (1) are earning a wage or salary or not; (2) have full or partial ownership of the business; (3) have employees or not; (4) work full- or part-time; and (5) have started, acquired or inherited the business, report themselves as being owners of their current businesses.[2]

Unlike most OECD countries, Portugal has experienced significant growth in (non-agricultural) self-employment in the last few decades (Blanchflower 2000, OECD 2000). Despite this idiosyncrasy, research addressing the topic of transitions into self-employment in Portugal is relatively scarce, thus making this study particularly interesting.

Why do Individuals become Business Owners?

Neoclassical economic models focus mainly on the pecuniary factors underlying the option of entering entrepreneurship. Several crucial works in this strand argue that individuals with relatively low wages are more likely to switch to self-employment (Evans and Leighton 1989, Evans and Jovanovic 1989, Blanchflower and Meyer 1992). Still, a number of empirical works show that even though independent workers receive lower wages, have lower wage growth in the long run and work more hours on average than other workers, some still prefer to be self-employed rather than employees (see, for instance, Hamilton 2000). A possible explanation for this apparent paradox is to stress the importance of non-pecuniary determinants of entrepreneurship, such as independence and flexibility (Scase and Gofee 1982, Blanchflower and Oswald 1991); desire to succeed (McCelland 1961, Chell et al. 1991), and perceived entrepreneurial ability (Taylor 1999, Burke et al. 2002).

Blanchflower et al. (2001) have found that in industrial countries entrepreneurship is motivated by large numbers of people wanting to be independent workers. In fact there is a higher proportion of people preferring to be self-employed than effectively being self-employed. Those authors justify this with the argument that latent entrepreneurs face some constraints or incentives that impact on their choice of becoming self-employed. Other authors emphasize contextual phenomena (mostly associated with the business cycle) such as unemployment push (Acs et al. 1994, Alba-Ramirez 1994, Moore and Mueller 2002), whereby people are pushed to self-employment due to the lack of a better income-generating alternative, or prosperity pull (Evans and Leighton 1989, 1990; Blanchflower and Oswald 1991), whereby people are pulled to self-employment due to a general atmosphere of optimism arising from economic growth.[3]

DETERMINANTS OF TRANSITIONS TO ENTREPRENEURSHIP

According to Parker (2004), there are at least three different empirical approaches to the study of occupational choice in the literature:
- the first focuses on the probability that individuals are entrepreneurs rather than paid employees;
- the second studies the factors affecting the decision to become an entrepreneur rather than a paid employee; and
- the third looks at individuals' decisions to leave entrepreneurship instead of remaining self-employed.

The focus of the present research is on the second approach: we look at a variety of factors that may predict an individual's choice to become an entrepreneur after being a paid employee, rather than the probability of being an entrepreneur or surviving in entrepreneurship. Such factors include demographics (such as age and gender), human capital characteristics (such as education, labour force attachment, non-employment spells, experience in the labour market) and microeconomic factors (such as size and industry characteristics associated with the firm where the individual is a paid employee). Wage is used as a pecuniary variable.[4]

This study also addresses the issue of necessity-based versus opportunity-based entrepreneurship, in which entrepreneurship is approached by contrasting entry to entrepreneurship out of non-employment (unemployment-push factor) with entry into entrepreneurship out of paid employment. Although it may not always be the case, it seems reasonable to expect that the latter entrepreneur is considerably more likely to be starting a business to exploit a discovered opportunity than the former.

The rest of this section looks at the background literature about determinants of transitions from paid employment towards entrepreneurship.

Demographics

Age is an important determinant of employment status. The literature on entrepreneurship and occupational choice suggests a wide variety of effects associated with age on the decision to become an entrepreneur. Some authors claim that the transition to self-employment is positively correlated with age (Van Praag and Van Ophen 1995). The reason for this is that older people have had more time to build better networks and to identify valuable opportunities (Calvo and Wellisz 1980) and are more likely to have accumulated capital which can be used to set up a business (Blanchflower and Oswald 1998). Still, any positive effects of age on the probability of an individual entering entrepreneurship will tend to fade as age increases, possibly disappearing as the individual reaches retirement age (Destré and Henrard 2004).

Another research stream suggests that self-employment is concentrated among young individuals because older people may be more risk averse (Miller 1984) and also because older people will be less prone to embark on the more demanding work schedules required by self-employment (Rees and Shah 1986). Some empirical evidence shows that transitions from paid employment to entrepreneurship are more frequent among individuals in mid-career – 35–44 years old (Cowling 2000, Reynolds et al. 2002) – while other empirical works suggest that the probability of becoming self-employed is independent of age and experience until a certain age: 40 years old according to Evans and Leighton (1989); 50 years old according to Evans and Jovanovic (1989).

Gender is also a prominent issue in entrepreneurship studies. In general, women have a lower likelihood of becoming entrepreneurs than males (Wagner 2005, Van Gelderen et al. 2005). In some studies it is argued that it is more difficult for female entrepreneurs to gain access to capital (Hisrich and Brush 1984, Lee-Gosselin and Grise 1990).

Human Capital

A variety of theoretical and empirical works suggest, and indeed verify, that a more educated person has a higher probability of choosing self-employment than a less well-educated person (Lucas 1978, Borjas 1986, Carrasco 1999). More educated workers tend to be better informed, implying that they are more efficient at assessing self-employment opportunities; furthermore, education increases productivity and reduces the variance of self-employment earnings (Rees and Shah 1986). However, Blanchflower (2000) underlines the fact that in most countries both the better educated and the less well educated show an above-average probability of being self-employed. A different line of reasoning claims that a high level of education deters entry into self-employment (De Wit and Van Winden 1989). Indeed, it is also possible that higher levels of education may facilitate entry into wage employment and thus reduce the likelihood of self-employment. De Witt (1993) finds a significantly negative relationship between the propensity of becoming self-employed and education. Additionally, Destré and Henrard (2004) find a negative effect of secondary and university education on the probability of switching from paid employment to self-employment.

Time spent in paid employment may provide individuals with a variety of tasks and experiences and, therefore, a wide range of skills that might influence their choice to become entrepreneurs. Lazear (2002) points out that the possession of a diversity of experiences and skills – that is, in marketing, human resources management, technology, finance – is important for someone aiming to establish and/or run a firm. Lazear (2004) and Wagner (2005) find that entrepreneurs are likely to possess a greater variety of experience and skills than non-entrepreneurs.

Microeconomic Characteristics

The kind of firm where the individual works as a paid employee may influence the probability of transition to entrepreneurship. Being a wage worker in a small firm may enhance the probability of switching to self-employment (Destré and Henrard 2004) since small firms are more likely not to survive for long (see, for instance, Mata and Portugal 1994) and pay lower wages (Brock and Evans 1989).[5]

Earnings profiles also differ across industries, as do working conditions and required specific abilities (Lazear and Moore 1984, Jovanovic 1982), thus suggesting that if differences in expected incomes play a part in motivating transitions from paid employment to entrepreneurship, the extent of incentives may differ according to the industry where the individual is employed.

Evidence is mixed with regard to the role played by earnings differentials in occupational choice decisions between paid employment and self-employment. In reviewing the empirical literature addressing this subject, Parker (2004) points out that the widespread failure of empirical studies to obtain clear and robust results with regard to the role played by relative earnings in both cross-sectional and transitional occupational choice may be a result of the variety of data sets and specifications used by researchers, but might also be simply due to the fact that pecuniary rewards are not the primary motive for choosing self-employment. The results obtained by Taylor (1996) suggest that individuals are attracted to self-employment because of higher expected earnings than in paid employment, but also by the freedom from managerial constraints that it offers. It has also been argued that the self-employed suffer from unrealistic optimism and may choose a low-return occupation because they anticipate high future profits.

DATA DESCRIPTION AND CONSTRUCTION

This study benefits from an extensive data set on individuals' backgrounds, career paths, and flows between firms and sectors, originating from a longitudinal matched employer–employee database (Quadros de Pessoal)[6] covering the Portuguese economy during the period 1986–2000. The database consists of mandatory information submitted by firms to the Portuguese Ministry of Employment and Social Security. For the purpose of this study, entrepreneurs are defined as those who report themselves as being owners of their current businesses. Yearly data on business owners and paid employees include gender, age, function, tenure, schooling and skill levels. For each firm, yearly data is available on size (employment), age, location, sector and number of establishments (including location and employment). In total, the data set accounts for about 5 million individuals who switched from paid employment to business ownership (or not) during this period.

Choice of Labour Market Status

There are basically three types of observed subjects in the database for each year:

1. Those who reported being a business owner in one or more firms.
2. Those who reported paid employment as their professional situation, including those who switched to business ownership afterwards and those who did not.
3. Those who, before or after turning up in one firm (as a business owner or paid employee), had experience of two or more years not connected to any firm (that is, out of the database).

Although these last cases may reflect different realities (for instance, unreported data by firms), we assume that for the most part they reflect frictional unemployment. This assumption is particularly important if one intends to detect cases of people entering business ownership out of necessity – that is, due to unemployment-push factors – as opposed to those who do it through the detection of market opportunities.

Backgrounds Prior to Transition of Labour Market Status

Our interest is in distinguishing the cases of people who change over from paid employment (or non-employment) to business ownership from those who do not. It is therefore necessary to compare the backgrounds of those who become entrepreneurs with the backgrounds of those who do not. To do this, we consider two moments in time: before (t-1) and after (t) people switch occupations. In order for this to be possible, only people who switch firms during the period of time under analysis can be considered in our study: some of these people switch from paid employment to business ownership in another firm; others switch from paid employment in one firm to paid employment in another firm. People who do not switch firms across the time period covered by the database (whether they remain permanently as business owners or paid employees) are therefore not considered in this study.[7]

In order to focus on differences between those who switch firms and occupation, from paid employment to entrepreneurship, and those who switch firms but remain paid employees, this study considers only those whose first professional situation (as recorded in the database) is that of paid employee. Hence, people entering business ownership directly are excluded, since there is no prior information on their backgrounds.

Exclusion of Censored Cases

In order to observe only first-time transitions from paid employment to business ownership, it is necessary to exclude cases of individuals who may have been business owners before the time span covered by the database (1986–2000). Hence, to ensure that the individuals observed are entering the database under similar conditions (that is, entering the workforce for the first time as paid employees) the following methodological aspects were taken into account:

1. Since some values are missing for certain one-year spells – which usually points to non-response by firms – it was decided that all 1986 and 1987 observations should be filtered out in order to make reasonably sure that the first time an individual is observed in the database does in fact correspond to the year he or she enters the labour force for the first time.
2. In order to provide an additional control, only people entering the data set aged 25 years or under are included, since younger people are considerably less likely to have had prior labour force experience, whether entrepreneurial or otherwise.

Selection of Cohorts

Since one of the goals of this study is to determine the probability of switching to entrepreneurship, it is important to account for the possibility of length-biased sampling. For example, an individual who enters the labour market as a paid employee in 1998 may not have had sufficient time or experience to switch to business ownership, an outcome that might occur after the period of time covered by the database in the future. Thus, a bias may occur due to the existence of right censored cases. In order to avoid this potential bias, the data were divided into two entry cohorts, distinguishing people who entered the database as paid employees for the first time before 1995 from people who entered the database as paid employees for the first time after 1995 (that is, Cohort 1: entry observed in 1988–95; Cohort 2: entry observed in 1996–2000). For this study, only the first cohort is used to examine whether individuals move from paid employment to entrepreneurship. This allows us to track forward individuals' decisions after entering the labour force up to at least five years after entry.

Modes of Entry and Exit

This study examines the mode of entry of paid employees into entrepreneurship by cross-checking the year of the individuals' entry into business ownership with the year of the firm's entry in the market, hence differentiating between 'starters' and 'acquirers'. If an individual enters a firm for the first time and that same firm is new in the market (that is, the founding year is the same as the year of entry into business ownership), the firm is deemed a start-up, otherwise we assume that it has been acquired (or inherited) by the business owner. In the same fashion, it is also possible to determine whether the individual's exit from his or her previous occupation coincides with the extinction of the firm (mode of exit).

After data cleansing in accordance with all the issues referred to above, we are left with a representative sample where entrepreneurs and non-entrepreneurs are categorized following the types of labour market transitions presented in Table 2.1.

Table 2.1   Groups and Types of Transitions Studied

Type of Transition	Frequency	%
(1) If an individual is a paid employee in t-1 and becomes a paid employee again in a different firm in t	17 499	79.7
(2) If an individual is a paid employee in t-1 and becomes a business owner of a different firm in t	3 197	14.6
(3) If an individual is a paid employee in t-1 and becomes a business owner of a new firm in t+k (k>1), that is, he or she registers a non-employment spell of two or more years in-between	1 258	5.7
Total	21 954	100

Hence, our final data set (Cohort 1) accounts for a total of 21 954 individuals, of whom 4455 switched firms and occupation, from paid employment to business ownership during 1988-1995 in Portugal, and 17 499 individuals who switched firms but remained as paid employees.

THE MODEL

In order to investigate why individuals who switch firms choose entrepreneurship instead of paid employment, we use a discrete choice model, in line with those proposed by Evans and Jovanovic (1989), Evans and

Leighton (1989) and Taylor (1996), in which occupational choice is determined by the expected utility from each different occupation. There are two possible occupations (j), here denoted by E (entrepreneur) and P (paid employee). Each individual (i) has a vector X of observed characteristics and derives utility $U_{ij} = U(X,j) + u_{ij}$ if they work in a j specific occupation (E or P), where $U(X,j)$ is observable utility and u_{ij} is unobserved utility:

$$E(U_j) = f(D, H, P, O)$$

Expected utility from being a paid employee or an entrepreneur [$E(U_j)$] is a function of a series of variables: (D) = demographic characteristics, (H) = Human capital and experience, (P) = pecuniary incentive, and (O) = organizational features. We assume that individuals receive no utility from non-employment and thus seek an occupation permanently.

An individual will prefer entrepreneurship if: $E(U_E) > E(U_P)$; in addition, he or she will exit self-employment if: $E(U_E) < E(U_P)$. We can define the observable indicator variable z_i* as:

$$z_i* = E(U_E) - E(U_P) - u_{iE} + u_{iP.}$$
$$z_i* = \alpha + \beta' E(U_E) + v_i,$$

where z_i equals 1 if $z_i* \geq 0$ (that is, individual i is observed in E) and z_i equals 0 if $z_i* \leq 0$ (that is, individual i is observed in P), being $\Pr(z_i = 1) = \Pr(z_i* \geq 0)$. A model of the determinants of transition is then estimated using a binomial logit procedure to assess how the probabilities of job transitions are affected by the different variables.

Dependent Variables

The variable SWITCH allows us to analyse different types of labour market transitions to entrepreneurship, with a binomial response, distinguishing between:

- $d0$ = those who, having entered the labour force as paid employees in 1988–95, do not enter entrepreneurship until 2000;
- $d1$ = those who, having entered the labour force as paid employees in 1988–95, switch to business ownership before 2000.

A series of different models are estimated. First, the cases of those who entered entrepreneurship directly from paid employment are separated from those who entered business ownership after having experienced a spell of non-employment between occupations. This was done in order to determine whether there are significant differences in the determinants of transitions to business ownership between people who become entrepreneurs following a non-employment spell (possible unemployment-push effect), and people who leave their current job to become entrepreneurs (more likely to do so because of opportunity discovery). Second, we separate the cases of people who become entrepreneurs by starting a new firm (starters) from those who become entrepreneurs by acquiring (or inheriting) an existing firm (acquirers).

Independent Variables

The vector of variables influencing the choice between switching from paid employment in one firm to business ownership in a different firm, and switching from paid employment in one firm to paid employment in a different firm, reflect the determinants of occupational choice discussed above. These variables are:

1. Demographics: dummy variable for GENDER (1 = female); and AGE at the moment of entry into the labour force.
2. Human capital: dummy variables for EDUCATION (secondary and tertiary) versus no schooling or primary education; professional QUALIFICATION (1 = high-level);[8] EXPERIENCE as an employee (number of years as paid employee); and dummy variable for MODE OF EXIT from previous occupation (1 = exit from previous occupation and firm extinction are simultaneous).
3. Pecuniary: wage prior to exiting paid employment, given by LOGWAGE (logarithm of the individuals' monthly draw).
4. Organizational: dummy variables for more technology-intensive activities – TECH INDUSTRY and TECH SERVICES (1 = technology intensive activities);[9] and size, given by LOGSIZE (logarithm of the number of workers).

Descriptive statistics for these variables are presented in Table 2.2 (for those individuals who switch to paid employment in a different firm) and Table 2.3 (for those individuals who switch to business ownership in a different firm). Both tables also present descriptive statistics for the proportion of individuals who go through a spell of two or more years in-between occupations (NON-EMPLOYMENT SPELL). Table 2.3 also presents descriptive statistics for a variable measuring whether people switching to business ownership do so by creating a new firm (START-UP) versus acquiring or inheriting an existing firm.

Table 2.2   Descriptive Statistics Prior to Transition to Paid Employment

Variables	N	Mean	Standard deviation
GENDER	17 499	0.426539	0.494588
AGE	17 499	20.91731	2.344091
AGE^2	17 499	443.0283	99.60207
EDUCATION (SECONDARY)	17 499	0.579005	0.493733
EDUCATION (TERTIARY)	17 499	0.010972	0.104174
QUALIFICATION (HIGH-LEVEL)	17 499	0.002629	0.051205
EXPERIENCE IN EMPLOYMENT	17 499	1.660152	1.328833
EXPERIENCE IN EMPLOYMT. ^2	17 499	4.521801	10.83667
MODE OF EXIT	17 499	0.796846	0.402358
TECH SERVICE	17 499	0.002057	0.045312
TECH INDUSTRY	17 499	0.049146	0.216178
LOGSIZE	17 334	3.830139	1.874664
LOGWAGE	17 499	40926.41	37541.82
NON-EMPLOYMENT SPELL	17 499	0.169724	0.375401

Table 2.3   Descriptive Statistics Prior to Transition to Entrepreneurship

Variables	N	Mean	Standard deviation
GENDER	4455	0.293603	0.455463
AGE	4455	21.9165	2.263955
AGE^2	4455	485.4572	97.92398
EDUCATION (SECONDARY)	4455	0.628507	0.483258
EDUCATION (TERTIARY)	4455	0.011448	0.106392
QUALIFICATION (HIGH-LEVEL)	4455	0.008081	0.089539
EXPERIENCE IN EMPLOYMENT	4455	1.814366	1.289093
EXPERIENCE IN EMPLOYMENT^2	4455	4.953311	7.879285
MODE OF EXIT	4455	0.769024	0.421505
TECH SERVICE	4455	0.002245	0.04733
TECH INDUSTRY	4455	0.041975	0.200555
LOGSIZE	4455	3.061009	1.752646
LOGWAGE	4455	42340.97	33359.39
NON-EMPLOYMENT SPELL	4455	0.282379	0.450208
START-UP	4455	0.510887	0.499938

RESULTS

Estimation results for binomial logit models of the probability of transition from paid employment to entrepreneurship are presented in Table 2.4. Separate models were estimated for direct transitions from the first to the second occupation, and for indirect transitions (with at least a two-year period of non-employment in-between occupations). For each group, estimations are presented for the probability of transition to entrepreneurship for all kinds of new business owners, and then separately for acquirers or inheritors and starters.

In accordance with most empirical evidence available on this subject, we find a significant and statistically negative coefficient for female entrepreneurship. All models estimated show that the probability of switching from paid employment to entrepreneurship is very significantly and positively correlated with age, although the relationship is ultimately curvilinear, since there is a negative effect for the squared value of age which is also usually significant. Taking as a reference the absolute sizes of coefficients, we find that the effect of age on the probability of switching from paid employment to business ownership becomes negative for individuals who are around 50 years old (which is in line with the results found by Evans and Jovanovic, 1989). The maximum age for which there is an overall positive effect on the probability of switching from paid employment to entrepreneurship is about six years higher for people who switch with a non-employment spell in-between (indirect transitions) than for people who switch directly. Differences between starters and acquirers are less important.

The results for age confirm that, while older people are more likely to recognize opportunities and raise the required capital to set up the business, the positive effect of age fades as age increases. However, it must be noted that the individuals' age is measured in our sample at the time of entry into the labour market (that is, in the database), since the age at which the individual switches occupations is an endogenous decision. This means that for our data the effect of age on the decision to become an entrepreneur after being a paid employee is always positive, as all individuals observed are under 50 years old.

Higher (tertiary) education has no significant effect on the probability of switching from paid labour to entrepreneurship, while there is a positive effect associated with secondary education. Above all, this reflects the composition of the Portuguese labour force (and therefore of our data sample), since people with tertiary education are a small minority. Since the returns to education are likely to be very high in paid employment for this minority, relative to the remaining labour force, the opportunity cost of switching to entrepreneurship should be very high. This effect will likely offset the expected positive effect that would result from the fact that more educated individuals should be more capable of recognizing opportunities and implementing businesses to exploit those opportunities.

Table 2.4   Binomial Logit Results: Probabilities of Transitions into Entrepreneurship/Business Ownership

Variables	Direct Transitions			Indirect Transitions		
	All	Acquirers	Starters	All	Acquirers	Starters
GENDER	-0.550 ***	-0.388 ***	-0.950 ***	-0.597 ***	-0.420 ***	-0.934 ***
	0.077	0.102	0.138	0.044	0.059	0.074
AGE	1.332 ***	0.985 **	1.935 **	0.836 ***	0.672 **	0.942 **
	0.339	0.449	0.619	0.191	0.255	0.323
AGE^2	-0.027 **	-0.019 *	-0.041 **	-0.015 **	-0.012 **	-0.017 **
	0.008	0.010	0.014	0.004	0.006	0.008
EDUCATION (SECONDARY)	0.566 ***	0.468 ***	0.738 ***	0.273 ***	0.141 **	0.381 ***
	0.075	0.100	0.138	0.043	0.057	0.074
EDUCATION (TERTIARY)	0.545	0.561	0.547	0.000	-0.029	0.058
	0.457	0.613	0.896	0.189	0.243	0.337
QUALIFICATION (HIGH-LEVEL)	2.484 **	2.035	2.122 **	0.813 **	0.579	1.010 **
	1.071	1.306	0.998	0.263	0.360	0.482
EXPERIENCE	0.467 ***	0.710 **	0.521 **	0.653 ***	0.506 ***	0.687 ***
	0.121	0.211	0.087	0.061	0.083	0.099
EXPERIENCE^2	-0.074 **	-0.116 **	-0.045 **	-0.077 ***	-0.062 ***	-0.087 ***
	0.021	0.041	0.026	0.010	0.014	0.016
MODE OF EXIT	0.105	0.052	0.238	-0.085 *	0.062	0.252 *
	0.098	0.130	0.173	0.050	0.073	0.179

Table 2.4   Binomial Logit Results: Probabilities of Transitions into Entrepreneurship/Business Ownership (cont'd)

Variables	Direct Transitions			Indirect Transitions		
	All	Acquirers	Variables	All	Acquirers	Variables
TECH SERVICE	-0.014	-0.023	-0.033	0.870*	1.663*	-0.412
	0.220	0.229	0.323	0.493	0.901	1.041
TECH INDUSTRY	0.080	0.072	0.090	-0.011	0.037	-0.219
	0.177	0.242	0.165	0.102	0.129	0.185
LOGSIZE	-0.203***	-0.226***	-0.145***	-0.269***	-0.199***	-0.331***
	0.021	0.029	0.037	0.012	0.016	0.022
LOGWAGE	0.011***	0.014**	0.009***	0.003	0.004	0.001
	0.000	0.000	0.000	0.003	0.003	0.000
CONSTANT	-17.184	-13.834	-22.362	-12.120	-10.648	-12.462
	3.619	4.786	6.610	2.044	2.725	3.443
LOG LIKELIHOOD	-2322	-1395	-686	-7607	-4613	-2432
NR OBS	4179	3037	1135	17605	13307	4298
lr CHI2	460	213	176	1469	483	824
Prob>chi2	0.000	0.000	0.000	0.000	0.000	0.000

Notes:
Standard errors in brackets
*** Coefficient significant at 1%
** Coefficient significant at 5%
* Coefficient significant at 10%

The negative relationship between high levels of education and entry into entrepreneurship found in this study is compatible with the findings of, for instance, Evans and Leighton (1989) and De Wit and van Winden (1989).

Given the structure of the sample, the significantly positive effect for the secondary education variable, which results mostly from comparison with primary or no school attendance, can be argued to represent the aforementioned positive effect of education on the ability for opportunity recognition and implementation. This is at least partially supported by the fact that coefficients for the secondary education dummy variable are of a larger magnitude for the probability of direct transitions from paid employment to entrepreneurship than for the probability of indirect transitions (that is, of entering entrepreneurship after a non-employment spell). While this may not always be the case, direct transitions from paid employment to entrepreneurship are more likely to entail an opportunity cost (corresponding to the income the individual gives up in order to become a business owner) and are therefore more likely to occur due to the recognition of a viable opportunity and a perceived ability to exploit it. For the same reason, indirect transitions to entrepreneurship, which entail a low (or insignificant) opportunity cost, are more likely to be associated with the lack of viable alternatives than with opportunity recognition.

Individuals who are highly qualified workers or top managers, and individuals who have accumulated several years of experience as paid employees before switching firms or occupations, are more likely to become entrepreneurs. However, the effect of the qualification variable is only significant for people who start their own businesses. Moreover, the coefficients for this variable are of considerably higher magnitude for direct transitions between occupations than for indirect ones. As for the age variable, the relationship between the number of years of experience accumulated in paid employment and the probability of switching to entrepreneurship is ultimately curvilinear, since there is a negative effect for the squared value of this variable which is also significant. Taking as a reference the absolute sizes of coefficients, we find that the effect of experience in paid employment on the probability of switching from paid employment to business ownership becomes negative after about six years in paid employment for direct transitions and about eight years for indirect transitions.

As a whole, these results show that people with more experience and higher professional qualifications are more likely to be able to recognize and implement better business opportunities, changing directly from paid employment to self-employment. It can also be suggested that there is a sort of 'locus-of control' effect at work here which increases the willingness to become an entrepreneur (Van Praag and Van Ophem 1995), since these individuals are more likely to leave their current employment to become business owners even though the opportunity cost (a manager, highly qualified or experienced worker's salary) is likely to be higher than average.

It can be argued that the fact that positive effects of professional qualification on the probability of becoming an entrepreneur are only significant for starters reinforces the perceptions suggested above: more qualified and (up to a point) experienced workers are more likely to recognize more innovative opportunities and have the required knowledge and willingness to set up a new firm to exploit those opportunities, instead of choosing to enter business ownership by acquiring or inheriting an existing business. These workers are also more likely to find the required financing to set up a new, innovative firm.

When exit from paid employment occurs simultaneously with the extinction of the firm where the individual was employed, it is more likely that the transition between occupations being observed was not desired by the individual and therefore that the choice of occupation was more strongly influenced by necessity than by opportunity recognition. However, the dummy variable assigned to these cases has no significant effects on the probability of direct transitions to entrepreneurship, while effects for indirect transitions are weakly significant and contradictory, so no meaningful conclusions can be drawn.

Having worked in a technology-intensive sector (whether services or industry) seems to have no significant effect on the decision to become an entrepreneur. Results concerning the effect of the size of the first firm on the probability of becoming an entrepreneur are consistent and very significant: the smaller the firm in which the individual worked as a paid employee, the greater the chance that the individual will become a business owner, either directly or indirectly. On the one hand, this suggests that working in a small firm, possibly in or close to management, tends to increase individuals' willingness to become entrepreneurs, and possibly also their ability to recognize and take advantage of opportunities; on the other hand, since small firms have been shown to pay lower wages than large firms (Evans and Leighton 1989), pecuniary factors may also play a role here.

The higher the wage earned in his or her paid employment position, the more likely an individual is to switch directly to entrepreneurship when leaving that position. This result verifies the positive effects on the probability of transition to entrepreneurship found for professional qualification and employment experience. After controlling for education, individuals earning higher wages (that is, more qualified and experienced) will be more likely to recognize opportunities and to be willing to exploit them. They are also less likely to suffer from liquidity constraints, unlike those who, even having earned higher wages as paid employees, experience a spell in non-employment after exiting paid employment, thus explaining the non-significant effect of this variable on the probability of indirect transitions to entrepreneurship.

CONCLUDING REMARKS

Entrepreneurship is vital for the advancement of innovation, market re-structuring, competitiveness and employment growth. In this chapter we have examined the factors influencing the probability of entering entrepreneurship or business ownership or self-employment after being a paid employee, making use of a detailed matched employer–employee database, allowing us to take into account, amongst other issues, the mode of entry into entrepreneurship (that is, start-up versus acquisition) and the type of transition (that is, directly from paid employment to business ownership, or with a non-employment period in-between).

A model of the determinants of occupational choice for individuals leaving paid employment was assembled and estimated in order to assess the effects of a wide array of individual- and organizational-level variables on the probability of an individual who leaves paid employment becoming a business owner. Results seem to suggest that while the ability to discover and implement valuable business opportunities is an important factor in generating transitions from paid employment to entrepreneurship, elements associated with personal willingness to become an entrepreneur and bear the opportunity costs of leaving a paid employment position corresponding to an above-average income also play an important role in this process.

Particularly with regard to direct transitions from paid employment to entrepreneurship, older and more experienced individuals (up to a point, since these effects are curvilinear) are more likely to switch over to business ownership instead of seeking another position as a paid employee. The same applies for individuals with higher professional qualifications and for individuals who work in smaller firms, thus suggesting that factors contributing to 'locus-of-control' play an important role in increasing the probability of transitions from paid employment to entrepreneurship. While higher levels of education seem to discourage transitions to entrepreneurship, likely because of opportunity costs associated with high wages in paid employment, highly educated individuals represent a very small percentage of those leaving paid employment. If only secondary education is considered versus primary or no education, the effect of a higher level of educational attainment on the probability of entering business ownership after leaving paid employment also becomes significant and positive, thus reinforcing these conclusions.

The findings of this study therefore suggest that the factors that influence positively the ability to recognize and implement new venture opportunities may also have a positive effect on the willingness to become an entrepreneur. The association of these two elements seems to be strong enough to offset the opportunity costs associated with the wages an experienced and highly qualified worker may obtain by taking up a new paid employment position upon leaving his or her first paid employment post. However, highly educated workers represent a very small proportion of those leaving paid employment, that is, those who are liable to enter entrepreneurship. This suggests that once in paid employment the opportunity costs for highly educated people to switch occupations (whether to become a paid employee in another firm or to become a business owner) are very significant. This may reduce the pool of potentially successful entrepreneurs who may become so after being paid employees.

NOTES

* The authors wish to thank the Portuguese Ministry for Social Security and Labour (MSST) and CIRIUS-ISEG for allowing us to use the Quadros de Pessoal data for this study. We also thank attendees of the 2006 IECER (Interdisciplinary European Conference on Entrepreneurship Research) in Regensburg for comments and suggestions. Support from the Portuguese Foundation for Science and Technology is gratefully acknowledged.

1. The self-employed are those individuals who earn no wage or salary, but who derive their income from exercising their profession or business on their own account and at their own risk (Parker 2004).

2. Note that this second category does not include sole traders. A few studies of occupational choice have explored two additional categories: 'members of producers' co-operatives' and 'unpaid family workers'. These categories will not be a subject of this study since they are of reduced importance in Portugal, as in most OECD countries.

3. When the economy is growing, there are more paid employment opportunities available, thus the risk of taking up self-employment is lower because if the business fails, there are many alternative employment opportunities available in the market.

4. Le (1999) and Parker (2004) provide comprehensive surveys of the empirical literature on the diverse variables used to explore transitions to self-employment.

5. Evans and Leighton (1989) find that better-educated and more stable workers can be found more frequently in larger firms. It can then be suggested that transitions to entrepreneurship from paid employment for pecuniary reasons are more likely to occur for individuals working in small firms.

6. For a complete description of the database, see: Mata and Portugal (1994) and Escária and Madruga (2003).

7. For people who do not switch firms or occupations during the period under analysis, it is impossible to distinguish a 'before' moment from an 'after' moment and therefore no variables regarding people's backgrounds can be accounted for. People who switch from paid employees to business owners in the same firm are also excluded, since this type of phenomenon may be determined by other variables (associated, for instance, with family businesses).

8. This variable was built based on the professional qualification (that is, employee level of responsibility, or hierarchical position attained) reported by the firms for each individual. A high-level qualification corresponds to the 'Highly Qualified' and 'Top Manager' positions.

These variables may be used as a proxy for internal locus of control, as highly qualified or positioned employees usually believe that they have some control over their future occupational choices.
9. These classifications draw on the OECD typology. In order to use this classification, industry-level data was broken down to the three-digit level.

REFERENCES

Acs, Z.J., D.B. Audretsch and D.S. Evans (1994), 'Why does the self-employment rate vary across countries and over time?' Discussion Paper 871, London: Centre for Economic Policy Research, CEPR.

Alba-Ramirez, A. (1994), 'Self-employment in the midst of unemployment: the case of Spain and the United States', *Applied Economics*, **26** (3), March, 189–204.

Blanchflower, D.G. (2000), 'Self-employment in OECD countries', *Labour Economics*, **7** (5), 471–505.

Blanchflower, D.G. and B. Meyer (1992), 'A Longitudinal Analysis of Young Entrepreneurs in Australia and the United States', in R.G. Gregory and T. Karmel (eds), *Youth in the Eighties*, Papers from the Australian Longitudinal Survey Research Project, Canberra: DEET and Centre for Economic Policy Research, Australian National University, pp. 63–96.

Blanchflower, D. and A. Oswald (1991), 'Self-employment and Mrs Thatcher's enterprise', CEP Discussion Papers 30, Centre for Economic Performance, LSE.

Blanchflower, D.G. and A.J. Oswald (1998), 'What makes an entrepreneur?' *Journal of Labour Economics*, **16** (1), 26–60.

Blanchflower, D.G., A. Oswald and A. Stutzer (2001), 'Latent entrepreneurship across nations', *European Economic Review*, **45** (4–6), 680–91.

Borjas, G.J. (1986), 'The self-employment experience of immigrants', NBER Working Papers 1942, National Bureau of Economic Research, Inc.

Brock, William A. and David S. Evans (1989), 'Small business economics', *Small Business Economics*, **1** (1), 7–20.

Burke, E.E., F.R. Fitzroy and M.A. Nolan (2002), 'Self-employment wealth and job creation: the roles of gender, non-pecuniary motivation and entrepreneurial ability', *Small Business Economics*, **19** (3), 255–70.

Calvo, G.A. and S. Wellisz (1980), 'Technology, entrepreneurs and firm size', *Quarterly Journal of Economics*, **95**, 663–77.

Carrasco, R. (1999), 'Transitions to and from self-employment in Spain: an empirical analysis', *Oxford Bulletin of Economics and Statistics*, **61** (3), 315–41.

Chell, E., J. Haworth and S. Brearly (1991), *The Entrepreneurial Personality: Concepts, Cases and Categories*, London: Routledge.

Cowling, M. (2000), 'Are entrepreneurs different across countries?' *Applied Economic Letters*, **7** (12), December, 785–9.

Destré, G. and V. Henrard (2004), 'The determinants of occupational choice in Colombia: an empirical analysis', Cahiers de la Maison des Sciences Economiques bla04065, Maison des Sciences Economiques, Université Paris 1 Panthéon-Sorbonne.

DeWit, G. (1993), 'Models of self-employment in a competitive market', *Journal of Economic Surveys*, **7**, 367–97.

DeWit, G. and F.A. Van Winden (1989), 'An empirical analysis of self-employment in the Netherlands', *Small Business Economics*, **1**, 263–72.

Escária, V. and P. Madruga (2003), 'The Construction of a Longitudinal Matched Employer-Employee Microdata Data Set', mimeo, CIRIUS, ISEG, Technical University of Lisbon.

Evans, D.S. and B. Jovanovic (1989), 'An estimated model of entrepreneurial choice under liquidity constraints', *Journal of Political Economy*, **97** (4), 808–27.

Evans, D.S. and L.S. Leighton (1989), 'Some empirical aspects of entrepreneurship', *American Economic Review*, **79** (3), 519–35.

Evans, D.S. and L.S. Leighton (1990), 'Small business formation by unemployed and employed workers', *Small Business Economics*, **2** (4), 319–30.

Hamilton, B.H. (2000), 'Does entrepreneurship pay? An empirical analysis of the returns to self-employment', *Journal of Political Economy*, **108** (3), 604–31.

Hisrich, R. and C. Brush (1984), 'The women entrepreneur: management skills and business problems', *Journal of Small Business Management*, **22** (1), 30-37.

Jovanovic, B. (1982), 'Selection and the evolution of industry', *Econometrica*, **50** (3), 649–70.

Lazear, E.P. (2005), 'Entrepreneurship', *Journal of Labor Economics*, **23** (4), October, 649.

Lazear, E.P. (2004), 'Balanced skills and entrepreneurship', *American Economic Review*, **94** (2), 208–11.

Lazear, E.P. and R.L. Moore (1984), 'Incentives, productivity, and labour contracts', *Quarterly Journal of Economics*, **99** (2), 275–96.

Le, A.T. (1999), 'Empirical studies of self-employment', *Journal of Economic Surveys*, **13** (4), 381–416.

Lee-Gosselin, H. and J. Grise (1990), 'Are women owner managers challenging our definitions of entrepreneurship? An in-depth survey', *Journal of Business Ethics*, **9** (2), 423–33.

Lucas, R.E. (1978), 'On the size distribution of business firms', *Bell Journal of Economics*, **9**, 508–23.

Mata, J. and P. Portugal (1994), 'Life duration of new firms', *Journal of Industrial Economics*, **42**, 227–46.

McCelland, D.C. (1961), *The Achieving Society*, Princeton, NJ: Van Nostrand.

Miller, R. (1984), 'Job matching and occupational choice', *Journal of Political Economy*, **92**, 1086–1120.

Moore, C.S. and R.W. Mueller (2002), 'The transition from paid to self-employment in Canada: the importance of push factors', *Applied Economics*, **34**, 791–801.

OECD (2000), 'The Partial Renaissance of Self-Employment', in *OECD Employment Outlook*, Organisation for Economic Co-operation and Development, Paris.

Parker, S. (2004), *The Economics of Self-Employment and Entrepreneurship*, Cambridge: Cambridge University Press.

Rees, H. and A. Shah (1986), 'An empirical analysis of self-employment in the UK', *Journal of Applied Econometrics*, **1**, 101–8.

Reynolds, P.D., W.D. Bygrave, E. Autio, L.W. Cox and M. Hay (2002), *Global Entrepreneurship Monitor: 2002 Executive Report*, Ewing Marion Kauffman Foundation.

Scase, R. and R. Goffee (1982), *The Entrepreneurial Middle Class*, London: Croom Helm.

Taylor, M.P. (1996), 'Earnings, independence or unemployment: why become self-employed?' *Oxford Bulletin of Economics and Statistics*, **58** (2), May, 253–66.

Taylor, M.P. (1999), 'Survival of the fittest? An analysis of self-employment duration in Britain', *Economic Journal*, **109** (454), C140–C155.

Van Gelderen, M.W., A.R. Thurik and N. Bosma (2005), 'Success and risk factors in

the pre-startup phase', *Small Business Economics*, **24** (4), 365–80.
Van Praag, C.M. and H. Van Ophem (1995), 'Determinants of willingness and opportunity to start as an entrepreneur', *Kyklos*, **48** (4), 513–40.
Wagner, J. (2005), 'Nascent and infant entrepreneurs in Germany: evidence from the Regional Entrepreneurship Monitor (REM)', IZA Discussion Papers 1522, Institute for the Study of Labor (IZA).

3. Accurate Portrayal or Lazy Stereotype? The Changing Nature of the Asian Business Sector in the UK

Spinder Dhaliwal and Andy Adcroft

INTRODUCTION

Traditionally, ethnic minority enterprises are perceived as being concentrated in low entry threshold industries with low value-added activity and limited opportunity for market expansion. However, the continued success of Asian entrepreneurs in the UK testifies to the sustainability of the Asian business community, which appears to combine the dynamism of the free market with the dynamic, risk-taking heroism of the entrepreneur. Accordingly, Asian enterprises have attracted the attention of academics, policy makers and practitioners and are increasingly enjoying a higher profile in the media. When charting the success of the Asian entrepreneur, such studies have tended to focus on the transformation from 'rags to riches' and on the characteristics of the owner, the start-up and the barriers to accessing finance. This study analyses the longer-established, more successful enterprises of the Asian business community and seeks to draw out trends within this increasingly important sector of the economy and consider their economic sustainability. The primary objective of this chapter is to consider and explain how the Asian business sector in the UK sustains and maintains its economic performance and, in doing this, the chapter raises a number of important ancillary issues such as the extent to which the dominant stereotypes of the Asian enterprise and Asian entrepreneur maintain their validity and currency.

Since the 1980s, a recurring theme in the commentary on the performance and characteristics of the UK economy has been its top-heavy nature; national levels of output, turnover, profitability, research and development expenditure and so on are determined by the larger organizations (see, for example, Williams 2001). These assumptions have resulted in two streams of policy initiative and suggestion. The first suggests that improved economic performance can be achieved only by accepting the reality of this situation and so policy attention should be directed to the behaviour of these big economic corporations. The second, and more relevant for the purposes of this chapter, suggests that long-term economic prosperity can only be attained through the reversal of this trend and the development of a thriving small and medium-sized enterprise (SME) sector.

The UK's record as far as the creation of new businesses and SMEs is concerned has, over the past two and a half decades, not been overly successful. For example, since the early 1990s the Bank of England's data suggest that the stock of small businesses has fallen by roughly 50 000 (Bank of England 2002). For the economy as a whole the key issue in this respect is the difference between the number of start-ups and the number of closures. The Department of Trade and Industry reports the overall negative outcome of this equation with, for example, over 1.5 million jobs lost in British SMEs over the past few years (www.sbs.gov.uk). At the broad macro level this has resulted in an economy where wealth creation is focused on large firms; by 2002, whilst SMEs accounted for over 99 per cent of all enterprises, they accounted for just 52 per cent of total turnover and roughly 55 per cent of all employment (DTI 2002). These macro figures also reflect a number of international weaknesses; the proportion of the UK's population engaged in business start-ups or new business growth is, for example, just half of that of the United States and only just comparable with mainland European economies like Germany and Italy (Flash Eurobarometer 2002). If the overall results are disappointing, it is inevitable that they serve to mask a number of successful sectors such as the UK's Asian business sector (ABS); historically, from just 8 per cent of the UK's population this sector accounts for over 10 per cent of all new start-ups (Barrett et al. 1996) and self-employment rates in the UK's Asian communities are over 25 per cent higher than in the white community (Small Business Service 2003)

In considering the nature of the ABS in the UK, most academic research offers a rich analysis of the entrepreneurial events, activities and personalities which underpin this thriving business sector. However, much of this analysis lacks a hard empirical economic foundation. The aims of this chapter are to examine a number of much-neglected issues within this important area of entrepreneurial research.

THE ECONOMIC SIGNIFICANCE AND STEREOTYPING OF ASIAN ENTREPRENEURS

A significant proportion of the literature on ethnic minority businesses in the UK either explicitly or implicitly uses stereotypes as a central point of analysis. For example, first generation businesses are usually seen as embodying a home and work environment where traditions and values are maintained in order to deliver comfort and security. This approach survived as the culture was heavily interwoven with religious beliefs and the view that there was no need to integrate with the wider host population. Long hours and mentally and physically demanding work often led to the Asian entrepreneur developing emotional ties with the business where the entrepreneur spends more time at work than with the family (Janjuha and Dickson 1998). Brought up in the West and exposed to influences from their schools, the media and peer groups, the next generation of Asian entrepreneurs are stereotyped with the characteristic of increasing independence. Faced with this challenge, the typical response was that the first generation closed ranks to outsiders and became increasingly reliant on advice from the community or co-ethnic professionals (Dhaliwal 2002).

The push–pull factor explanation of the development of the ABS is also prevalent in the stereotyping literature. Push factors are reactive to negative circumstances such as discrimination in the workplace as a motive for turning to self-employment, whereas pull factors can be considered as much more proactive motivations, such as a desire for rewards and independence. For example, Chavan and Agarwal (2000) argue that the first generation moved into business due to push factors whereas second and third generations placed a greater significance on the pull factors. For first generation entrants into the ABS, many businesses were set up as a cohesive family strategy which kept the family members together and in employment (Ram and Jones 1998 and Dhaliwal 2000). Furthermore, the status of being business people was enjoyed as it carried weight in the local community (Dhaliwal 1998 and 2000). This was particularly the case with East African Asians trying to recapture the self-esteem they lost as they were forced to leave their businesses behind in Africa to become an unwelcome minority in the UK where the businesses compensated, to some degree, for the lack of respect from the wider community (Gidoomal 1997).

Cultural stereotypes of success for the first generation entrepreneur include thrift, hard work and reliance on family labour (Werbner 1990 and Waldinger et al. 1990) which, according to Soar (1991), give Asian entrepreneurs a competitive edge on other businesses. However, the stereotype also suggests that cultural factors may restrict growth by creating excessive reliance on the local ethnic community market, informal sources of finance and family-controlled businesses (Jones et al. 1992, Metcalf et al. 1996, Ram 1994 and Basu and Goswami 1999). The result of this is the stereotypical Asian business which is perceived to be concentrated in low entry threshold industries with low value-added activities and limited opportunities for market expansion through the development of non-local sales.

A significant body of research (for example, Ram 1996, Ram and Jones 1998) suggests that this performance of the ABS has occurred against a backdrop characterized by a lack of support; the growth in the sector would seem to have happened despite, rather than because of, the support mechanisms in place. For example, Ram and Jones (1998) have identified government initiatives in the support for minority ethnic businesses which lack both continuity and consistency. Although the business support sector has evolved significantly, research suggests that these support structures have not proved popular with many EMBs (Curran and Blackburn 1993). For example, African-Caribbean entrepreneurs were significantly more likely to use the support of an agency than either White- or Asian-owned businesses (Ram and Deakins 1995). Whilst equal opportunity agendas and quotas suggest that there is a wide-scale recognition of this poor take-up of support services by EMBs, there is, as yet, no national co-ordinated policy to address this issue. Activity tends to occur at the local level through support organizations exploring different avenues as to how to increase the take-up of their services by EMBs or to customize their services to meet the specific needs of EMBs. However, Ram and Carter (2003) suggest that this approach tends to focus on myopic target-setting, such as a focus on a specific ethnic minority group each year, rather than the development of a cohesive long-term strategy. More recently Smallbone et al. (2003) conducted a large-scale survey into the accessing of finance which showed variation between ethnic minority groups. This shows that support needs to target the specific group rather than treat minority businesses as homogenous.

The macro picture reinforces this view as take-up rates for these support services are universally very low; typically only 4–5 per cent of all new start-ups access the various support networks (Storey 1994 and Barratt et al. 1996) and, within the EMB community, take-up rates are even lower (Bank of England 2002). Fadahunsi et al. (2000) suggest that the two main causes of this are problems of cultural reluctance and wider issues of trust. This conclusion is further supported by Dhaliwal (2003) amongst others, who argues that the main sources of business advice and support for the ABS are professional accountants followed by family and friends. Ram and Carter (2003) note the diversification into professions and explore the case of ethnic minority accountants operating as entrepreneurs. The most recent evidence (Bank of England 2002) suggests that little has changed and suggests that official support agencies are not sufficiently tailored to the specific needs and demands of EMBs in general and the ABS in particular. The government's Small Business Service is keen to address this issue and has made it a part of its seven key policy themes.

Despite all of these shortcomings in support structures and the resultant low take-up rates, ethnic minorities in the UK have, nevertheless, generally higher self-employment rates than the rest of the population (Barrett et al. 1996). Although there is some disparity between the different groups, this move towards business start-ups can be accounted for by both push and pull factors (Ram 1996, Ram and Jones 1998). The push factors which force individuals into entrepreneurship as a personal economic choice include prejudice found in employment and frustration at being overlooked for promotion. Pull factors include cohesive family structures and strategies, the desire for a greater degree of independence and keeping the rewards of your own efforts (Ram and Jones 1998, Dhaliwal 2003).

Having considered the growth in the EMB sector and the ABS in the context of a relatively unsupportive environment, the chapter now turns to consider how this sector has been treated once it has been established. In dealing with the phenomena of EMBs and the ABS, this study would argue that much of the literature makes use of stereotyping and the result of this is that, rather than deal with the sector on a case-by-case basis, it is treated as an homogenous group. These stereotypes take a number of different forms. For example, Asians tend to be risk averse, relying first on personal savings and then family money followed by community support, before finally considering bank finance (Dhaliwal 2003). The ABS is characterized as being more easily frustrated with bureaucracy, thus preferring informal relationships and minimum paperwork. A common problem faced by new entrants into the ABS is overambitious and poorly written business plans which, given the banks' reluctance to talk to potential business customers until they have produced viable business plans, serves to deter many serious business propositions.

There is a paradox at the heart of much of the literature on Asian entrepreneurship. On the one hand are the quantitative studies that suggest a thriving and flourishing sector, and on the other is the deeper evidence, often qualitative in nature, which suggests a largely unsupportive environment and a business sector characterized by uniformity, homogeneity and a whole series of different stereotypes. This has implications for both economic and social sustainability.

The chapter finally turns to the issue of purpose and an explanation of what may come out of the analysis which follows. The chapter does not intend to draw specific conclusions and recommendations from this data. In questioning the value of the dominant stereotype, for instance, the aim is not to close one debate but rather to open new debates and potential avenues of investigation. Thus, the intention is to examine broad trends and, in so doing, attention will be drawn to the consistency within the results of the analysis both in terms of the data itself and in terms of other studies carried out in the general area.

METHODOLOGY AND DATA

The data on which much of this chapter relies are drawn directly from the annual wealth index produced by *Eastern Eye* magazine in the UK. This source, edited by the lead author of this chapter, provides a respected guide to Asian wealth in the UK. In this case, 'Asian' is defined more specifically as South Asian, and so the index is drawn, in the main, from those of Indian, Pakistani, Bangladeshi or East African origin. Whilst this is therefore an unusual and possibly underutilized resource, we would argue that its value and usefulness is supported by a number of factors. In particular we draw attention to the consistency in compiling the index across the seven years of its publication where the methodology has remained constant throughout. First, stakes in public companies are valued on their rating at the end of each year as published in the *Financial Times*; second, whilst the valuation of privately owned companies is dealt with on a case-by-case basis, it is inevitable that in some cases sectoral price–earnings ratios or equivalent companies will be used as a proxy; third, assumptions sometimes have to be made about the value of, for example, holding companies located in tax havens; and, finally, individual wealth is often aggregated into family wealth. Thus the data collection and presentation process used in each of the seven years for which figures are available is consistent and follows the same guidelines. For example, to appear in the wealth index, individuals must generate their wealth from primarily UK-based activities.

In attaching weight and significance to any conclusions that are drawn or recommendations that are made in a study of this nature it would be impossible to draw specific conclusions about, for example, generalizability, or to make a series of bold recommendations. Here we would make a further point about the quality of the data and also point out the intentions behind this chapter. In drawing conclusions about both the traditional stereotype of Asian entrepreneurs and the economic significance of the top end of the ABS, the constituents of the wealth index are an important consideration. Practically all of the wealth which appears in the index is generated from business activities; less than 1 per cent of the total over the seven-year period is generated from non-business activities (which are mainly lottery wins and inheritance). Using, for example, the DTI definition of an SME, the inference is drawn that most of the wealth is generated from this sector.

BUCKING THE TREND: THE NUMBERS BEHIND ASIAN WEALTH CREATION

This section of the chapter considers two key issues: first, how does this sector of the economy perform in terms of the creation of wealth and, second, what are the main drivers behind that wealth creation? The analysis of Asian wealth creation which follows rests on the a priori assumption that wealth must be created; it is not, for example, simply harvested. This is neither a new nor an original idea. For example, as far back as the 1930s, Schumpeter (1934, 1939) argued for the central role of the entrepreneur in wealth creation and economic development and, more recently, Chaharbaghi and Newman (1997) have discussed a 'crisis of wealth creation' which again places the entrepreneur in a central role. At the broader, macroeconomic level, writers like Hutton (1996) discuss this issue of wealth creation in a wider economic context and draw attention to two central weaknesses in the UK economy. The first weakness is the inability of the economy to deliver sustained economic growth over the long term due to a lack of competitiveness. Whilst measures of international competitiveness are riddled with difficulty, when measured by simple comparative economic performance, the UK's record against its cross-Channel and transatlantic competitors is poor over the long term.

The second structural weakness of the UK economy is its top-heavy nature, which means that when growth does occur it tends to be concentrated in a few giant firms. In terms of overall wealth creation in the UK, the 600 biggest companies account for something in the region of 70 per cent of total wealth (Williams 2001). The study, therefore, makes the general point that the performance of Asian wealth creators must be analysed in the context of a top heavy and sluggish economy with an ever widening gap between top and bottom.

Table 3.1 offers some basic data on the top 200 Asian wealth creators in the UK along with some broader economic data for the purposes of comparison. Over the past seven years, the UK economy has demonstrated sustained growth which can be characterized as more steady than spectacular. This is in marked contrast to the sector of the economy on which this chapter focuses: Asian wealth creation has happened at almost three times the level of the economy as a whole.

This part of the Asian sector has grown, on average, at just over 8 per cent per annum compared to just over 3 per cent for the economy as a whole. Just as growth rates are significantly different, so too are the constituents of this growth. Table 3.2 suggests that, unlike the UK economy, the Asian wealth-creating sector is not overly reliant on just a few stellar performers. For example, since 1998, the top 10 per cent of Asian wealth creators have

accounted for a diminishing proportion of total wealth generated; whilst
almost two-thirds of Asian wealth was generated by the top 20 performers in
1998, by 2004 this proportion had fallen to under a half.

Table 3.1 Index of Real Asian Wealth Generation and GDP 1998–2004

Year	Nominal Asian Wealth Creation	Real Asian Wealth Creation	Real GDP
1998	100.0	100.0	100.0
1999	117.9	116.1	104.4
2000	145.4	139.1	106.4
2001	160.6	150.9	110.1
2002	165.7	153.2	113.2
2003	159.5	145.7	117.5
2004	175.0	156.6	120.9

Source: *Eastern Eye* (1998–2004), www.oecd.org.

Table 3.2 Components of Asian Wealth Generation 1998–2004

Year	Asian Wealth Generated (£ mill.)	High Value (£ mill.)	Low Value (£ mill.)	Share Taken by Top 10% of Wealth Generators (%)
1998	4437.4	500	2.0	60.5
1999	5232.3	450	5.0	54.9
2000	6453.6	325	6.0	48.9
2001	7124.9	300	6.0	45.6
2002	7354.7	450	8.8	43.4
2003	7078.4	460	4.0	44.8
2004	7767.5	500	4.0	45.8

Source: *Eastern Eye* (1998–2004).

Despite the proportionate fall in the contribution of these elite wealth
creators, the point should not be lost that in 2004 the top 10 per cent
accounted for almost £900 million more wealth than seven years previously.
This suggests that the general British economic problem of slow growth is not
one seen in this element of the ABS, and this conclusion is reinforced through
further examination of key components of this wealth creation.

Over the period of analysis there have been some significant changes in the
composition of wealth creation. For example, there has been a shift in

activities away from traditional manufacturing companies towards newer, higher-tech, higher-value companies in industries like pharmaceuticals. However, despite these changes in activity, there are relatively few changes in the value of individual wealth at the top end of the scale. Between 1998 and 2004, the average value of those entrepreneurs at the top of the scale was usually between £400 and £500 million. Given the falling proportion of wealth accounted for by the top 10 per cent of wealth creators, changes in the composition of wealth creation elsewhere would not necessarily be expected. At the bottom of the scale, for example, the entry-level criterion for joining the elite wealth creators has increased dramatically from an initial £2 million in 1998 through to a high of almost £9 million in 2002 before stabilizing at £4 million in 2004. Stability at the top coupled with the changes towards the bottom of the league table have resulted in a dramatic growth in average wealth across the sample; in the period average wealth has grown by over two-thirds. Our general conclusion on this issue is that growth in this area of the ABS is characterized by economic push from the middle and bottom rather than economic pull from the top.

This chapter now turns away from the issue of absolute wealth creation and considers the main drivers behind that wealth creation. The data and commentary suggest that this sector of the economy has behaved in a significantly different manner from the UK economy as a whole in two important respects. First of all, as we have already seen, growth and success in this sector is not driven solely by the large firms at the top but has a significant bottom-up element to it. Second, the industries which are driving the growth are now significantly different from the traditional Asian businesses of the past; this is a sector of the economy which would appear to be making a successful transition from old to new economy activities. Williams (2001), for example, in discussing the UK economy as a whole, draws attention to its increasingly 'hollowed out' nature as a result of unsuccessful transition where more and more firms are retreating into areas of low technology, sheltered competition, low-wage locations and inorganic growth. In the Asian business sector, however, whilst traditional businesses do remain important, the highest wealth-creating sector was the pharmaceuticals industry and, whilst this is not reflected in a simple league table, other industries like fashion and IT have grown strongly (Table 3.3).

One of the main causes of this shift in ranking is the variable growth rates across the different sectors under discussion. In real terms the fastest growth has been seen in the pharmaceuticals sector, which has grown almost fiftyfold in the time period, and the big loser has been the basic textiles sector, which has contracted by just over 5 per cent in real terms. Given that the time series is for just seven years, it is probably too early to conclude that these represent structural shifts in wealth creation, but the changes that have taken place are notable nonetheless.

Table 3.3   Ranking of Sectors by Contribution of Asian Entrepreneurs to Total Wealth Creation 1998 and 2004

Ranking	1998	2004
1	Manufacturing	Pharmaceuticals
2	Retailing and Wholesaling	Manufacturing
3	Fashion and Textiles	Fashion and Textiles
4	IT/Media/Internet	Retailing and Wholesaling
5	Food and Drink	Hotels/Property
6	Hotels/Property	IT/Media/Internet
7	Pharmaceuticals	Food and Drink

Source: Eastern Eye (1998–2004).

For example, one of the main criticisms of the UK economic performance over the past quarter of a century has been its apparent inability to make the shift from an industrial to a post-industrial base but, as Table 3.4 demonstrates, the Asian sector would seem capable of making that shift: whilst the increase in wealth creation from the manufacturing sector has been relatively small, between them, the pharmaceutical, fashion and new economy sectors have seen wealth creation increase by more than £2.2 billion.

Table 3.4   Asian Wealth Creation by Sector 1998–2004 (£ million)

	1998	1999	2000	2001	2002	2003	2004
Food and Drink	386.0	569.0	724.8	697.8	548.8	582.5	760.0
Hotels/Property	321.2	509.4	634.7	730.0	1212.8	1113.8	900.5
IT/Media/Internet	489.6	496.0	390.5	568.5	704.1	725.6	770.0
Manufacturing	853.2	847.0	1236.5	1154.5	1068.5	989.8	1147.0
Pharmaceuticals	31.0	295.4	448.0	943.0	1222.4	1264.5	1517.0
Retailing and Wholesaling	647.9	650.0	953.2	901.7	1019.6	1080.7	1024.0
Fashion and Textiles	632.5	700.0	499.4	631.6	831.0	837.3	1068.0
Other	1076.0	1165.5	1566.5	1497.8	747.5	484.2	581.0

Source: Eastern Eye (1998–2004).

These shifts in make-up are also influenced as much by the growth in some sectors as by the decline in others. The crowding-out explanation of British deindustrialization may be paralleled in the Asian sector as new entrants tend to come from growing rather than mature industries. For instance in the broad Asian 'rag trade' sector (comprising fashion and textiles) there is a major shift from basic, low-value activities such as subcontracting towards more specialized high-value fashion houses such as The Legendary Joe Bloggs. Whilst there is certainly a cyclical element to these changes, the overall picture in Table 3.5 perhaps suggests something more structural.

Table 3.5   Composition of the Asian 'Rag Trade' 1998–2004 (% share)

	1998	1999	2000	2001	2002	2003	2004
Fashion	48	58	76	69	63	63	66
Textiles	52	42	24	31	37	37	34

Source: Eastern Eye (1998–2004).

The final element of this sectoral analysis is comparative in nature and looks at the performance of the Asian sectors against performance in the UK sectors as a whole (Table 3.6). In this case a comparison is made between the performance of the two fastest-growing Asian sectors, pharmaceuticals and hotels and property, and two of the poorer performing sectors, manufacturing and fashion and textiles.

Table 3.6   Comparative Sectoral Performance 1998–2004

		1998	1999	2000	2001	2002	2003	2004
Pharmaceuticals	Asian		100	152	319	414	428	514
	UK		100	124	108	77	83	90
Hotels/Property	Asian	100	159	198	227	378	347	280
	UK	100	97	90	89	72	80	81
Manufacturing	Asian	100	99	145	135	125	116	134
	UK	100	122	100	91	62	67	67
Fashion and	Asian	100	111	79	100	131	132	169
textiles	UK	100	140	130	123	120	155	164

Source: Eastern Eye (1998–2004), www.oecd.org, www.comdirect.co.uk, www.londonstockexchange.com

Whilst the individual cases have their own peculiarities, the general conclusion drawn is that this Asian sector has outperformed the wider UK economy. The quadrupling of value in the pharmaceuticals sector has happened at the same time as relative stagnation in the UK sector as a whole and, given continuing uncertainty in the tourism and property industries, the growth in the Asian sector has been more pronounced than the general trend despite a significant downturn in the past two years. In terms of the poorer-performing sectors, the Asian manufacturing sector has more than sustained its position against further hollowing in the UK and, in the fashion and textiles sector over the period, growth has been roughly the same as the national sector as a whole.

CONCLUSION

The aim of this chapter was to consider how and why the Asian business sector is able to sustain and improve its economic performance. Given the data and analysis presented, three key interpretations are offered:

- First, the capacity for wealth creation in the upper reaches of the ABS would appear to be much higher than in the UK economy as a whole and across many sectors.
- Second, in this part of the ABS, overall growth is pushed by the lower and middle section of the sector. More specifically, the Asian business sector behaves differently from the UK economy as a whole, where growth is dependent on a few large companies at the top.
- Third, there is a change in the composition of the sector with important shifts away from the traditional Asian business sectors like retailing, textiles and manufacturing towards higher-tech and higher-value activities with higher levels of economic sustainability.

This raises a number of key issues for academic researchers in the area and policy makers; in particular it raises some key questions about the extent to which the traditional stereotyping and characterization of the ABS maintains its value and currency. Traditional stereotypes tend to focus on the Asian business as a traditional and 'old' economy set of activities whereas this research suggests, for this part of the ABS at least, something very different; the upper echelons of the ABS are subject to constant and reasonably dynamic change which has had a major impact on its ability to grow and sustain itself. The implications of all this for ethnic minority theory is to appreciate the changing dynamics of this sector and to challenge existing stereotypes.

The chapter also raises related issues for policy makers. Over the past two and half decades the promotion of SMEs in the UK has tended to focus on the promotion of specific industries and certain economic activities and, as the chapter has argued, this has led to limited success. For policy makers, therefore, consideration of alternative methods of promotion and support, perhaps through ethnic or socio-cultural characteristics, may be a priority.

This study is not without its limitations and the conclusions that we draw are both tentative and equivocal; we would suggest that the value of the chapter may lie in the new avenues for investigation opened. In particular we would suggest two areas for future research. First, further testing of the push–pull thesis is required through, for example, more qualitative-based research in order to widen understanding of the motivations behind this dynamic economic sector. Second, further investigation is required concerning the more traditional and old economy activities within the Asian business sector. For example, future research could focus on the next tier of Asian businesses below that examined in this chapter where industries such as textiles may well still be thriving. The next challenge for ourselves and others, therefore, is to move the debate forward through the addition of both depth and breadth to the analysis in order that we can more fully understand the dynamics of this economic sector.

REFERENCES

Bank of England (2002), *Finance for Small Firms: A Ninth Report*, London: Bank of England.

Barrett, G., T. Jones and D. McEvoy (1996), 'Ethnic minority business: theoretical discourse in Britain and North America', *Urban Studies*, 4 (5), 783–809.

Basu, A. and A. Goswami (1999), 'South Asian entrepreneurship in Great Britain: factors influencing growth', *International Journal of Entrepreneurial Behaviour and Research*, 5 (5), 251–75.

Chaharbaghi, K. and V. Newman (1997), 'The crisis of wealth creation', *Management Decision*, 35 (4), 527–40.

Chavan, M. and R. Agarwal (2000), 'Characteristics of ethnic women entrepreneurs', Conference Proceedings, 12th Annual Australian Council of Small Businesses, Singapore, June.

Curran, J. and R.A. Blackburn (1993), 'Ethnic enterprise and the high street bank: a survey of ethnic businesses in two localities', Small Business Research Centre, Kingston University.

Department of Trade and Industry (DTI) (2002), *SME Statistics for the UK*, London: HMSO.

Dhaliwal, S. (1998), 'Silent contributors – Asian female entrepreneurs and women in Business', Roehampton Institute, London: Centre for Asian Entrepreneurial Research (CAER).

Dhaliwal, S. (2000), 'Assessing the support needs of ethnic minority businesses', paper presented at the 23rd ISBA National Small Firms Policy and Research

Conference.

Dhaliwal, S. (2002), 'Are banks giving us fair deal?' *Eastern Eye*, **11**, 6.

Dhaliwal, S. (2003), 'Engaging with the black and minority ethnic business community', paper presented at ICSB Conference, Belfast.

Eastern Eye (1998–2004), 'Britain's 200 Richest Asians'.

Fadahunsi, A., D. Smallbone and S. Supri (2000), 'Networking and ethnic minority enterprise development: Insights from a North London study', *Journal of Small Business and Enterprise Development*, **7** (3), 228–40.

Flash Eurobarometer (2002), *Attitudes to Entrepreneurship in Europe and the United States*, Paris: European Commission.

Gidoomal, R. (1997), *The UK Maharajas*, London: Nicholas Brealey Publishing.

Hutton, W. (1996), *The State We're In*, London: Vintage.

Janjuha, S. and K. Dickson (1998), 'The ties that bind: an exploration of succession within South Asian family firms in Britain', paper presented at the 21st ISBA National Small Firms Conference, Durham.

Jones, T., D. McEvoy and G. Barrett (1992), *Small Business Initiative: The Ethnic Minority Business Component*, Swindon: ESRC.

Metcalf, H., T. Modood and S. Virdee (1996), *Asian Self-Employment: The Interaction of Culture and Economics in England*, London: Policy Studies Institute.

Ram, M. (1994), *Managing to Survive: Working Lives in Small Firms*, Oxford: Blackwell.

Ram, M. (1996), 'Supporting ethnic minority enterprise: views from the providers', paper presented to the 19th ISBA National Firms Policy and Research Conference, Birmingham.

Ram, M. and S. Carter (2003), 'Paving professional futures: ethnic minority accountants in the United Kingdom', *International Small Business Journal*, **21** (1), 55–72.

Ram, M. and B. Deakins (1995), 'African-Caribbean entrepreneurship in Britain', *University of Central England Occasional Papers on Business*, **10**.

Ram, M. and T. Jones (1998), *Ethnic Minorities in Business*, Milton Keynes: Small Business Research Trust Report, HMSO.

Schumpeter, J. (1934), *The Theory of Economic Development*, Cambridge, MA: Harvard University Press.

Schumpeter, J. (1939), *Business Cycles*, Maidenhead: McGraw-Hill.

Small Business Service (2003), *SME Statistics for the UK*, London: HMSO.

Smallbone, D, M. Ram, D. Deakins and R. Baldock (2003), 'Access to finance by ethnic minority businesses in the UK', *International Small Business Journal*, **21** (3), 291–313.

Soar, S. (1991), 'Business development strategies in TECs and ethnic minorities', Conference Report, presented at the conference Developing Businesses in TECs, Home Office Ethnic Minority Business Initiative, Warwick University, May.

Storey, D. (1994), *Understanding the Small Business Sector*, London: Routledge.

Waldinger, R., H. Aldrich and R. Ward (eds) (1990), *Ethnic Entrepreneurs*, London: Sage.

Werbner, P. (1990), 'Renewing an industrial past: British Pakistani entrepreneurship', *Manchester in Migration*, **8**, 7–41.

Williams, K. (2001) 'Business as Usual', *Economy and Society*, 30 (4) 399-411.

4. Personal and Organizational Success Factors of Women SMEs[1] in Russia

Tatiana Iakovleva and Jill Kickul

INTRODUCTION

The growth in the number of women-led businesses has contributed to the global economy and to the surrounding communities that they serve. The presence of women around the world driving small and entrepreneurial organizations has had a tremendous impact on employment and on business environments worldwide. Plenty of studies identifying women SME (small and medium-sized enterprise) success factors have been carried out in advanced countries (Chaganti and Parasuraman 1997, Lerner and Almor 2002). Economic research on entrepreneurship in transition economies is less developed and only a few studies have used a rigorous scientific approach (Tkachev and Kolvereid 1999). The lack of knowledge on female entrepreneurs is especially apparent. According to Ylinenpää and Chechurina (2000), Russian women have only limited options to achieve a leading position in industry, politics or other spheres of social production. Those difficulties serve as 'push' factors for women to enter the entrepreneurial sector, where starting new smaller firms serves the double purpose of generating an additional family income and creating an arena for self-fulfilment. It is important to clarify what factors contribute to the superior performance and growth of women-owned businesses. The purpose of this study is to add new theoretical and empirical insights into the success factors of small firms owned and run by women and currently operating within the turbulent Russian economy.

Our research presents a conceptual framework exploring personal and organizational factors that are linked to four key elements that facilitate firm success, including: (1) individual factors; (2) organizational factors; (3) external environment; and (4) the entrepreneurial orientation (EO) of the firm. Based on a review of the literature and our model, hypotheses were developed and tested.

CONTEXT OF STUDY

The history of modern entrepreneurship in Russia began just over ten years ago, when in 1987 entrepreneurship was legally allowed. Until then, private enterprises were prohibited in the Soviet Union. By the end of Gorbachev's presidency of the Soviet Union in 1991 most forms of private business had become legal (Tkachev and Kolvereid 1999). As early as 2000, over 891 000 small entrepreneurs were operating in Russia (Russian SME Resource Centre). Over 25 per cent of the population of Russia is employed in SMEs today, which accounts for 12–15 per cent of the gross domestic product (GDP) of the country.

During the first years of development towards the market economy the emerging entrepreneurial sector in Russia in general may be characterized by what Ageev et al. (1995) labelled as 'speculative' or even 'predatory' entrepreneurship. The dominant mode of entrepreneurship was focusing on creating value and making profit from trade and financial operations, exploiting weaknesses in the state legislation and taxation system, and even utilizing illegal or unethical measures (Bezgodov 1999). However, over the passing decade the situation has changed and modern entrepreneurship in Russia is oriented towards longitudinal value and job creation (Ylinenpää and Chechurina 2000).

Little is known about entrepreneurship in Russia. Based on the previous research in this area in Russia it is possible to draw a 'portrait' of the typical entrepreneur. The average age of Russian entrepreneurs is between 30 and 50 years old with a one-third share of young people (Turen 1993). Usually about 70–80 per cent of entrepreneurs from the samples have a high educational level (Babaeva 1998). It should be in kept in mind that almost all research on entrepreneurs previously done in Russia was taken from a sociological point of view and data were gathered from urban areas. The share of women entrepreneurs is between 10 per cent (Turen 1993) and 30 per cent, which is the lowest share of women among all social groups of the population except for the military (Bezgodov 1999). The characteristics of entrepreneurs working in small trade marketplaces are different. They are mostly women (70 per cent), and the large majority of them are either pensioners or students (Babaeva 1998). This social group is actually not investigated at all. Some of these marketplace workers are registered as sole proprietors, while others are not. In this study over 90 per cent of respondents are registered as sole proprietors, which allow us to open a 'black box' concerning this phenomenon.

Based on previous research it is possible to conclude that most entrepreneurs perceive the external environment as highly unfriendly. High taxes, an inconsistent legislation system, high dependence of economic life upon political turbulence, and inflation were mentioned as factors influencing business in Russia (Iakovleva 2001, Ylinenpää and Chechurina 2000). Lack of start-up capital and the prevailing business laws and tax system affect the entrepreneurial behaviour of women in Russia especially. Other barriers mentioned by Russian female entrepreneurs in Ylinenpää and Chachurina's study as influencing entrepreneurship development in Russia include: high taxes (90 per cent of respondents), legal inconsistencies (81 per cent), lack of availability of capital (67 per cent), bank instability (66 per cent), inflation (66 per cent), corruption (55 per cent) and criminality (39 per cent). This is quite different from the problems of American women entrepreneurs, who more concerned about the functional sides of business – profitability, management and growth, and innovation (Babaeva 1998). The motivation to start a business varies, but in comparison with Western studies Russian women have more tangible motives such as the search for income or striving for financial rewards. In Ylinenpää and Chachurina's study, this is explained by the problematic economic situation in Russia, where the ambition to secure an acceptable standard of living is a high-priority issue.

While the profile of Russian entrepreneurs as well as their motivation to start a business has been explored in some studies during the last decade, there is an absence of studies looking at the combination of different factors to explain the performance of those Russian SMEs driven by women. This study addresses this research gap by testing a model explaining the performance of women SMEs in Russia.

THEORY

As Aldrich and Martinez (2001) argue: 'understanding how and why some entrepreneurs succeed remains a major challenge for the entrepreneurship research community. In entrepreneurship, as in the biblical story, many are called but few are chosen' (2001, p. 41). While the performance of new ventures has been studied widely (see, for example, Cooper and Gascon 1992, Wiklund 1998), there is no consensus regarding the basic constructs that affect a new venture performance. This can be explained by the presence of different theoretical imperatives, which concern firm or entrepreneur performance from different viewpoints. Many variables are used to produce predictive models for survival and growth, but results from prior studies are heterogeneous and findings are often contradictory. Most authors classify success factors in three categories: the entrepreneur, the firm and the socio-economic environment. The last decade has shown a tendency to combine these constructs in one model (Wiklund 1999). The problem with these models is the relatively low explanatory power. One possible reason for this is the mediation and moderation effects that are not taken into consideration when explaining results. In this study we will try to address this research gap. Applying structural equation modelling (SEM) allows us to explore interrelationships between the dependent variables as well as their direct and indirect effects on the firm's success.

The Entrepreneur's Personality and Competencies

The personality of the entrepreneur is often perceived by practitioners as one of the most fascinating topics in the field of entrepreneurship (Delmar and Davidsson 2000). The psychological perspective in entrepreneurship research has, until recently, concentrated on discovering stable individual characteristics such as personality traits, including risk-taking propensity, need for achievement and locus of control (Brockhaus 1982). However, studies focusing on entrepreneurs' personalities, backgrounds, early experience and traits have been widely criticized and have generally produced disappointing findings (Gartner 1990). Recently there has been a shift from studying the personality of the entrepreneur towards the behavioural aspects of entrepreneurs (Gartner et al. 1992, Lumpkin and Dess 1996). Two groups of models can be defined: 'attitude-based' models and 'motivation-based' models.

Attitude models explain how attitudes to entrepreneurship shape people's behaviour. Attitudes are considered to be important determinants of behaviour if certain conditions are met (Bagozzi et al. 1992). Entrepreneurial intensity represents the founder's attitude towards early business performance or the founder's degree of commitment to the business. While commitment to the entrepreneurial endeavour can be described as the passion required for the success of the enterprise, the degree of commitment exhibited by the entrepreneur is identified here as entrepreneurial intensity. It is characterized in this study as a single-minded focus to work towards the growth of the venture, often at the expense of other worthy goals. The difference between general personality traits and indicators of entrepreneurial intensity were highlighted by Baum (1995), whose study indicated that while measures of general traits and personality were a poor indicator of venture growth, more specific applications of these traits such as 'growth specific motivation' showed far stronger relationships with growth performance (Pistrui et al. 1999, Welsch and Pistrui 1993).

The second group are the cognitive motivation models. The cognitive motivation models explain both highly complex behaviour and differences in choices and performance through entrepreneur competencies. Self-assessed competencies are the core of individuals' beliefs about their personal 'capabilities to mobilize the motivation, cognitive resources, and courses of action needed to exercise control over events in their lives' (Wood and Bandura 1989, p. 364; Chandler and Hanks 1994a). One of the core entrepreneurial competencies is opportunity competence – the ability to recognize and develop market opportunities through various means.

We begin our examination with the fundamental hypothesis that people with strong entrepreneurial characteristics, including opportunity competence and entrepreneurial intensity, are more likely to have successful and higher-performance ventures than are entrepreneurs who do not have these characteristics (Covin and Miles 1999, Stewart et al. 1998). Therefore:

Hypothesis 1a: There will be a positive relationship between opportunity competence and firm performance.

Hypothesis 1b: There will be a positive relationship between entrepreneurial intensity and firm performance.

The Entrepreneurial Firm's Resources

Internal firm resources are seen as the basic input into the production process. Firm-specific resources include items of capital equipment, skills of individual employees, patents, brand names, finance and social capital (Barney 1991). The resource-based view (RBV) suggests that differences in performance among firms may be best explained through differences in firm resources and their accumulation and usage (Barney 1991, Grant 1991). A wider range of both resources and resource-based capabilities are assumed to contribute to the higher performance of a firm (Chandler and Hanks 1998). Lumpkin and Dess (2001) argue that the type of resources available will influence the type of strategic processes firms employ to gain advantage. Some resources can be exploited primarily through cost advantages and thus are more likely to be employed within a competitive aggressiveness approach. Other firms might lack the unique and valuable resources needed for low-cost leadership, but have developed elements of valuable structural capital (Stewart 1997), such as structures and processes that enable them to create new resources more quickly and cheaply than their rivals. A wider range of resource capabilities enhances firms' strategies, as firms should select their strategies based upon resource capabilities (Castrogiovanni 1991). Empirical studies show the existence of a relationship between organizational resources and performance, including resources such as availability of financial capital (Cooper and Gascon 1992, Wiklund 1999) and social capital – organizational or individual networks (Donckels and Lambrecht 1995, Hansen 1995). Financial capital provides a buffer against unforeseen difficulties that may arise due to a variety of different reasons (Castrogiovanni 1991). By using social relationships, entrepreneurs 'cash in' on the patterns of expectations, norms, governance structures and social resources built into these previous interactions. The costs and the risks of start-ups can be reduced by using social assets such as friendship, trust, gratitude and obligation (Starr and MacMillan 1990). Thus:

Hypothesis 2a: There will be a positive relationship between financial capital and firm performance.
Hypothesis 2b: There will be a positive relationship between social capital and firm performance.

The Environmental Context

The environment undoubtedly impacts upon venture survival and growth as well as the likelihood of additional start-ups in that environment (Covin and Slevin 1989). It has been found that resource availability, including venture capital, technical labour force, loans, support services and a favourable entrepreneurial subculture also have a major influence on performance (Bamford et al. 1997, Kolvereid 1992). This can be broadly named 'environmental munificence'. Environmental munificence is the scarcity or abundance of critical resources needed by one or more firms operating within an environment (Castrogiovanni 1991). Thus:

Hypothesis 3: There will be a positive relationship between environmental munificence and firm performance.

The Entrepreneurial Strategy of the Firm

A significant stream of research has examined the concept of entrepreneurial orientation (EO). EO is a term that addresses the mindset of firms engaged in the pursuit of new ventures and provides a useful framework for researching entrepreneurial activity. Such activities include planning, analysis, decision making, and many aspects of an organization's culture, value system and mission (Hart 1992). Thus, an entrepreneurial orientation may be viewed as a firm-level strategy-making process that firms use to enact their organizational purpose, sustain their vision and create competitive advantage(s) (Rauch et al. 2004). The EO of the firm is assumed to influence positively the firm growth and performance (Lumpkin and Dess 2001, Wiklund 1998). The salient dimensions of EO have been derived from a review and integration of the strategy-making process and the entrepreneurship literature (for example Covin and Slevin 1991, Miller and Friesen 1982). Based on Miller and Friesen's (1982) conceptualization, three dimensions of EO have been identified and used consistently in the literature: innovativeness, risk-taking, and proactiveness. Innovativeness reflects a firm's tendency to engage in and support new ideas, novelty, experimentation and creative processes that may result in new products, services or technological processes (Lumpkin and Dess 1996). Risk-taking involves taking bold actions by venturing into the unknown, borrowing heavily and/or committing significant resources to ventures in uncertain environments. Proactiveness suggests a forward-looking perspective characteristic of a marketplace leader that has the foresight to act in anticipation of future demand and shape the environment (Lumpkin and Dess 2001). Proactive forms can introduce new goods and services ahead of their competitors. A first-mover can control access to the market by dominating distribution channels. By introducing new products and services firms can establish industry standards. All this can positively influence the performance of the firm, and some empirical findings support this proposition (Zahra and Covin 1995). Recent studies have shown the contingency effect that EO has on firm knowledge-based resources and performance (Wiklund and Shepherd 2003). Following the call by Wiklund and Shepherd (2003) for further research on the moderating effect of EO and internal firm resources, as well as entrepreneurial competencies towards firm performance, these effects will be investigated in this study. Thus:

Hypothesis 4a: There will be a positive relationship between entrepreneurial orientation and firm performance.

Hypothesis 4b: The relationship between entrepreneurial competence and firm performance will be mediated by entrepreneurial orientation.

Hypothesis 4c: The relationship between entrepreneurial intensity and firm performance will be mediated by entrepreneurial orientation.

Hypothesis 4d: The relationship between entrepreneurial firm resources and firm performance will be mediated by entrepreneurial orientation.

Hypothesis 4e: The relationship between environmental munificence and firm performance will be mediated by entrepreneurial orientation.

Summarizing, we propose following the model illustrated in Figure 4.1.

METHODOLOGY

Overview and Participants

To test the hypotheses a sample of Russian women-led SMEs was used. The objective of the survey was to collect data from women entrepreneurs in

Russia. Data were obtained from the Russian Women's Microfinancial Network (RWMN).

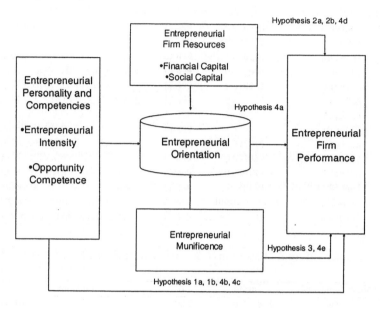

Figure 4.1   Conceptual Model Explaining Firm Performance

The mission of the RWMN is to support the development of sustainable, women-focused, locally managed microfinance institutions (MFIs) throughout Russia by creating an effective financial and technical structure that provides high-quality services to partner MFIs over the long term. With assistance from Women's World Banking (WWB), which has been active in Russia since 1994, several women-led organizations and local micro-lending institutions formed RWMN, which was registered as a local non-profit organization in October 1998. Today RWMN operates in six regions in Russia: Kostroma, Tver, Kaluga, Belgorod, Vidnoe and Tula, with the head office in Moscow. Each division is an independent local organization that provides micro loans for clients, with no less than 51 per cent of clients being women.

After the questionnaire was compiled and pre-tested with the help of seven Russian women entrepreneurs who commented on each question, it was sent in electronic form to Moscow. RWMN was responsible for printing it out, and distributing it to its divisions. Data were collected by the workers of local divisions during face-to-face interviews with respondents. As a result we received 601 completed questionnaires. Five of them were discounted due to lack of data, and the sample was then filtered according to two controls – only women should be left (five male responses were found) and we only considered decision makers (positive answer to the question: 'Are you the responsible for the main decisions taken in the enterprise?'). That resulted in the 555 questionnaires. Some descriptive statistics are presented in Table 4.1.

Table 4.1 Sample Characteristics

Variables	Number	%
Respondents		
Respondent status		
Founders or (and) owners (shareholders)	525	95
Directors or (and) managers (just employees)	30	5
Average respondent age	40 years	
Higher education		
Yes	252	49
No	271	51
Entrepreneurial experience of relatives		
Yes	76	14
No	469	86
Enterprises		
Subsidiary of another business		
Yes	24	5
No	525	95
Family business		
Yes	310	56
No	242	44
Average firm age	8	
Average number of employees	4	
Legal form		
Limited liability companies	33	6
Closed joint-stock companies	3	0.5
Open joint-stock companies	2	0.4
Sole proprietorships	514	93
Industry		
Manufacturing	28	5
Trade and catering consumption	442	80
Service	81	15

The sample mainly consists of sole proprietorships with 94 per cent of businesses having no more than ten employees (and 60 per cent having just two employees), being woman-led and woman-owned (95 per cent), operating mainly in the service industry (80 per cent), with 56 per cent of the enterprises being family businesses. One more interesting finding is that only 49 per cent of the respondents had a higher education, in comparison to 80 per cent from previous findings. As expected, this profile differs from the typical Russian SME profile with regard to industry structure, legal form, number of employees and family business issues (see, for example, Iakovleva 2005, Bezgodov 1999).

While the sample is not representative as a general profile of Russian entrepreneurs, its particular value is in providing a portrait of women-led small enterprises. While governmental efforts are focused on stimulating entrepreneurial growth in the country and especially women-led enterprises, it is important to understand the specific issues concerned with such enterprises.

Dependent Variable: Firm Performance

Performance is a multidimensional concept. There is little consistency in what is meant by the term 'performance' in different studies. Three different measures are most often associated with the concept of performance: survival of the firm, firm growth and firm profitability (Delmar 2000). It is advised that studies should include the multiple dimensions of performance and use multiple measures of those dimensions (Murphy et al. 1996). In this study only existing firms are considered, and questions related to both growth and profitability are applied. Establishing a measurement of performance is extremely complex for young and small firms. Such traditional financial measures as return on investments or net profits are problematic when studying new ventures, since even successful start-ups often do not reach profitability for a considerable period of time (Weiss 1981). Traditional financial measures are especially unreliable in the Russian context. Due to heavy taxation rates, small enterprises seldom report true economic results in their accounts. The other specific reason for not applying such direct measures in the Russian context is that Russian statutory accounting norms and practices differ greatly from international accounting norms and practices. Researchers interested in the performance of emerging businesses must acquire data that meet the criteria of relevance, availability, reliability and validity when the only attainable source of data is a self-administered evaluative questionnaire (Chandler and Hanks 1993).

Performance is measured with the help of questions about importance and satisfaction concerning certain points (please refer to Table 4.2). Respondents were asked to indicate the degree of importance their enterprise has attached to the following items over the past three years: sales level, sales growth, turnover, profitability, net profit, gross profit and the ability to fund enterprise growth from profits. Then they were asked how satisfied they had been with the same indicators over the past three years.

Table 4.2   PCA for Composite Performance

Variables	Factor Loadings	Communality
Composite Performance		
Sales level satisfaction*importance	0.87	0.76
Sales growth satisfaction*importance	0.89	0.80
Turnover satisfaction*importance	0.87	0.75
Profitability satisfaction*importance	0.90	0.81
Net profit satisfaction*importance	0.88	0.78
Gross profit satisfaction*importance	0.88	0.78
Ability to fund business from the profit satisfaction*importance	0.80	0.64
Eigenvalue	5.31	
Per cent variance explained	75.85	
Cronbach's alpha	0.95	

Notes:
Factor loadings 0.3 or smaller are suppressed
KMO = 0.925, Bartletts's test of Sphericity App. Chi-Sq 3392.079
df = 21, Sig. 000
* indicates multiplied

A slightly modified version of questions used by Iakovleva (2005) was applied. Originally questions were taken partly from Chandler and Hanks (1993) and partly from Westhead et al. (2005) and transformed after the consultation with Russian entrepreneurs. The questionnaire we used for this study was pre-tested with seven Russian women business owners, and some questions were subsequently reformulated. Based on these 14 questions, the composite performance index was constructed following the principle used in expectancy theory and later in the theory of planned behaviour (Ajzen 1991). First, questions about importance were rescaled from a seven-point Likert scale (1 to 7) to a -3 to 3 scale and then satisfaction and importance scores were multiplied. A principal component analysis was then done, which resulted in one factor which we called 'performance' ($\alpha = 0.95$).

Independent Variables

The environmental context
In order to concentrate on narrowly defined parts of the environment rather than on overall industry parameters, the perceived environments should be chosen (Miller and Tolouse 1988). Evaluating task environment by implementing subjective measures allows us to gain necessary insights and expertise.

The perceived external environment was operationalized with the help of the munificence item. Respondents were asked to rate disagreement/ agreement with statements using a seven-point Likert scale (1 = strongly disagree, 5 = strongly agree). Three items are taken from Brown and Kirchhoff (1997): the business's industry may be characterized by high growth; banks and other suppliers of loan capital are generally very interested in financing businesses like mine; investors are generally very interested in financing businesses like mine. One item was taken from Isaksen and Kolvereid (2005): investors would generally understand the technology used in my business quite easily. Cronbach's alpha for this component is 0.64.

The entrepreneurial firm resources
Firm resources were operationalized with the help of two components – financial capital and social capital. Several studies show that access to financial capital influences the performance and growth of the small firm (Cooper and Gascon 1992, Wiklund 1999). Financial capital was operationalized with the help of four questions. The first three questions are taken from Shane and Kolvereid (1995): availability of bank loans; availability of capital from suppliers; availability of capital from family and friends. The last item is taken from Borch et al. (1999): availability of financial resources relative to competitors. Cronbach's alpha for this component is 0.77.

Social capital was operationalized with the help of four questions: employee's network as an informational source, firm network as an instrument to influence the environment; network as the way to broader opportunities; and manager's network as an important firm resource. Questions are taken from Borch et al. (1999). Cronbach's alpha for this component is 0.88.

Entrepreneurial orientation

EO was measured with the help of nine items. Three items are taken from Chandler and Hanks (1994): we strive to be the first to have new products available; we stress new product development; we engage in novel and innovative marketing techniques. Three items are taken from Covin and Slevin (1989): we emphasize a policy of growth primarily through external financing (borrowing, capital issues, and so on); in dealing with competitors we typically initiate actions which competitors then respond to; we are very often the first business to introduce new products or services, administrative techniques, operating technologies. Two items are taken from Miller and Friesen (1982); they were rescaled to a seven-point one-side Likert scale so that they would be in the same format as the other questions: owing to the nature of the environment bold, wide-ranging acts are viewed as useful and common practice; we have a strong proclivity for profitable, but risky projects. One item is taken from Lumpkin and Dess (2001): we have a strong tendency to be ahead of other competitors in introducing new products or ideas. Cronbach's alpha for this component is 0.87.

The entrepreneurial intensity

Respondents were asked to rate disagreement/agreement with eight statements using a seven-point Likert scale (1 = strongly disagree, 5 = strongly agree). Seven items are taken from Gundry and Welsch (2001): I would rather own my own business than earn a higher salary employed by someone else; I would rather own my own business than pursue another promising career; I am willing to make significant personal sacrifices in order to stay in business; I would work somewhere else only long enough to make another attempt to establish my business; my business is the most important activity in my life; I would do whatever it takes to make my business a success; there is no limit to how long I would make the maximum effort to establish my business. One item is taken from Isaksen and Kolvereid (2005): I am willing to work more for the same salary in my own business than as an employee in an organization. Cronbach's alpha for this component is 0.89.

The entrepreneur competencies

Entrepreneurial competencies were operationalized with the help of opportunity competence. Items were measured according to recommendations by Bandura (2001) and Betz and Hackett (1998). The respondents were asked to indicate their degree of confidence in performing the tasks successfully. The scale ranged from 0 = no confidence at all, to 5 = some confidence and 10 = complete confidence. Six items were taken from De Noble et al. (1999): ability to see new market opportunities for new products; ability to discover new ways to improve existing products; ability to design products that solve

current problems; ability to create products that fulfil customers' unmet
needs; ability to identify new areas for potential growth; ability to bring a
product concept to market in a timely manner. Cronbach's alpha for this
component is 0.89.

Control Variables

Firm age, firm legal form, industry, respondent age, education, respondent
status and external firm environment are suggested as control variables. Firm
age was measured on a metric scale as the number of years an enterprise has
existed from the moment of establishment (official registration). It was
recommended that age of the business be used as a control variable in
business performance studies (Murphy et al. 1996). For example, it is
reasonable to expect that new firms will have a lower performance than older
firms. Industry differences is a widely used variable in performance studies
(Cooper et al. 1994, Wiklund and Shepherd 2003). Industry was taken into
consideration by entering two dummy variables for three possible industries:
manufacturing, service, and sales and distribution. Manufacturing was used as
a reference category. Respondent age was entered into regression to check the
hypotheses where individual-level independent variables were used. Age was
measured as a metric variable.

The respondent's education level can be related to the enterprise outcome.
Education was entered as a dummy variable (1 = with higher education, 0 =
without higher education). Moreover, an important control variable is
whether a respondent is an owner or founder of the business as opposed to an
employee (director or key manager).

In our subsequent structural model analyses, we included all measures
(including control variables). Although some relationships were not proposed
directly in our hypotheses, we included all measures to assess the overall
model fit and to examine the unique contribution of each of our proposed
relationships.

ANALYTIC APPROACH

We tested our hypotheses using SEM since it effectively estimates parameters
of our model. A covariance matrix was used as input for estimation of the
structural models. Lisrel VIII (Joreskog and Sorbom 1993) was utilized to
analyse the structural relationships. Aggregation was conducted for each
common construct in order to have unidimensional composite scales for the
structural models (Anderson and Gerbing 1988). In order to adjust for

measurement error in the scale scores, the path from the latent variable to its indicator was set equal to the product of the square root of the scale's internal reliability. The error variance was set equal to the variance of the scale score multiplied by 1 minus the reliability. This approach has been explained by Williams and Hazer (1986) and Joreskog and Sorbom (1993) and has been demonstrated as a reasonable approximation in determining error variance (Netemeyer et al. 1990).

RESULTS

The zero-order correlations between all potential dependent, independent and control variables are presented in the Appendix.

In order to determine the structural relationships proposed in our model (see Figure 4.1), a series of models was evaluated by comparing the change in chi-square associated with the restriction of certain paths to zero (Bentler and Bonett 1980). The proposed structural model, which contains all potential paths to entrepreneurial intentions (a fully saturated model as shown in Figure 4.1), was first evaluated. This first model assessed the direct relationships that were proposed in Hypotheses 1–4a. With the exception of the relationship between social capital and firm performance, all direct relationships were significant at the 0.05 level. Thus, Hypotheses 1a, 1b, 2a, 3 and 4a were supported (see Table 4.3).

From the initial individual relationship findings from this saturated model, four nested models were evaluated to test the mediational hypotheses of entrepreneurial orientation (Hypotheses 4b, 4c, 4d, 4e). For each of the relationships and hypotheses, we restricted the paths from the direct relationship to firm performance (for example for Hypothesis 4b we restricted the relationship between entrepreneurial competence and firm performance; for Hypothesis 4c we restricted the relationship between entrepreneurial intensity and firm performance, and so on).

Table 4.4 summarizes the description of these models. Significant changes in the chi-square of these models from the saturated model (first model tested) indicate support for the reinstatement of the restricted paths and therefore support for the direct influence of the variables on firm performance (that is, not full mediation of entrepreneurial orientation). As shown in Table 4.4, to test Hypothesis 4b we restricted the path from entrepreneurial competence to firm performance and found that by deleting this path/relationship, the chi-square difference between this model and the saturated model was significant. Thus, the path/relationship between entrepreneurial competence and firm performance should not be omitted (Hypothesis 4a was not supported).

Table 4.3   Summary of Hypotheses, SEM and Lisrel Estimates

Overall Model Analyses (Figure 4.1)	Fit Indices = Chi-Square = 6.05, p>0.05 RMSEA = 0.029 CFI = 0.99 NNFI = 0.98		
Hypothesis	Description	Standard-ized Lisrel Estimate	Hypothesis Conclusion
Hypothesis 1a: There will be a positive relationship between opportunity competence and firm performance	Entrepreneurial Competence→ Firm Performance	0.21*	Supported
Hypothesis 1b: There will be a positive relationship between entrepreneurial intensity and firm performance	Entrepreneurial Intensity→ Firm Performance	0.08*	Supported
Hypothesis 2a: There will be a positive relationship between financial capital and firm performance	Financial Capital→ Firm Performance	0.10*	Supported
Hypothesis 2b: There will be a positive relationship between social capital and firm performance	Social Capital→ Firm Performance	-0.05	Not Supported
Hypothesis 3: There will be a positive relationship between environmental munificence and firm performance	Environmental Munificence→ Firm Performance	0.22*	Supported
Hypothesis 4a: There will be a positive relationship between entrepreneurial orientation and firm performance	Entrepreneurial Orientation→ Firm Performance	0.12*	Supported

Notes: $*p < 0.05$

Similar results were found for Hypotheses 4c and 4e (that is, the relationships between entrepreneurial intensity and firm performance, and environmental munificence and firm performance – as mediated by entrepreneurial orientation – were not supported).

Table 4.4   Summary of Hypotheses, SEM and Lisrel Estimates

Tests for Mediation			
Hypothesis 4b: The relationship between entrepreneurial competence and firm performance will be mediated by entrepreneurial orientation	Restriction of path from Entrepreneurial Competence→ Firm Performance	Fit Indices = Chi-Square = 28.25, p < 0.05 RMSEA = 0.089	Chi-Square Difference (Difference from Figure 4.1) = 2.20, p < 0.05
		CFI = 0.98	Partial Mediation
		NNFI = 0.86	Not Supported
Hypothesis 4c: The relationship between entrepreneurial intensity and firm performance will be mediated by entrepreneurial orientation	Restriction of path from Entrepreneurial Intensity→ Firm Performance	Fit Indices = Chi-Square = 10.31, p > 0.05 RMSEA = 0.042	Chi-Square Difference (Difference from Figure 4.1) = 4.26 p < 0.05
		CFI = 0.99	Partial Mediation
		NNFI = 0.97	Not Supported
Hypothesis 4d: The relationship between entrepreneurial firm resources and firm performance will be mediated by entrepreneurial orientation	Restriction of path from Entrepreneurial Firm Resources→ Firm Performance	Fit Indices = Chi-Square = 11.66, p > 0.05 RMSEA = 0.040	Chi-Square Difference (Difference from Figure 4.1) = 5.61, p > 0.05
		CFI = 0.99	Partial Mediation
		NNFI = 0.97	Supported
Hypothesis 4e: The relationship between environmental munificence and firm performance will be mediated by entrepreneurial orientation	Restriction of path from Environmental Munificence→ Firm Performance	Fit Indices = Chi-Square = 28.76, p < 0.05 RMSEA = 0.090	Chi-Square Difference (Difference from Figure 4.1) = 22.71 p < 0.05
		CFI = 0.98	Partial Mediation
		NNFI = 0.85	Not Supported

However, for Hypothesis 4d we found mediational support. That is, when we restricted the paths/relationships between firm resources (financial and social capital), we found that the relationship between these resources and firm performance were mediated by entrepreneurial orientation. (As shown in Table 4.4, the chi-square difference was not significant at 2 degrees of freedom.)

DISCUSSION AND CONCLUSIONS

While the process by which women-led entrepreneurial firms plan and achieve continual growth often reflects a complex set of resources and motivators, our findings take an important initial step towards identifying the factors that support this strategic path. Identifying constructs facilitating firm performance and growth has added value for practitioners, scholars and policy makers as they formulate and implement new strategies and programmes that support women entrepreneurs as they continue to identify market opportunities, confront industry and environmental changes and seek new innovations for their businesses.

In conducting this research, a unified framework for new firm performance was proposed and tested, giving scholars and policy decision makers a better understanding of the critical resources, inputs and external environmental conditions that influence the growth and performance of women-owned firms. Based on our findings it is possible to conclude that the ability of female entrepreneurs to identify opportunities, the richness of growth opportunities in the environment, the entrepreneurial behaviour of the firm as well as the availability of financial resources and personal commitment to keeping the business going are crucial factors associated with superior firm performance. In our analysis we also found support for the mediation effect of EO on the firm's resources. Studying the mediating effect of EO complements those studies that have found a contingent relationship between EO and knowledge-based resources (Wiklund and Shepherd 2003) and EO and external environment (Covin and Slevin 1989, Zahra and Covin 1995). This finding has important theoretical implications, as it partly explains the problem with relatively low explanatory power in combined models where this mediation effect was ignored. Through our analyses examining the mediation effect of EO towards firm growth, we have added new insights and perspectives that explain the key drivers as well as the complex interplay of several of our factors in explaining the firm's success.

One more contribution of this study is that data were collected in a novel context and new, reliable measures were constructed. Results point to the conclusion that the performance of Russian female enterprises can be explained with the help of Western theories. Finding a positive main effect only between firm resources and firm performance as well as between firm EO and firm performance confirms this. These findings open the way for researchers in former Soviet-based economies, facilitating the research on phenomena like entrepreneurship; phenomena which are so important for the development of any economy.

The emergence and growth of women-owned businesses have contributed to the global economy and to their surrounding communities. The presence of women around the world driving small and entrepreneurial organizations has had a tremendous impact on employment and on business environments worldwide. Scholars of strategic management have noted that firm and organizational resources (including the competency and intensity of the owner) are key elements in highly successful firms. However, little work has been done concerning the impact of structural components in the context of entrepreneurial ventures. Given the significant differences between large, established firms and entrepreneurial ventures, uncovering which resources and capabilities are necessary takes on added importance in facilitating the performance of smaller women-led organizations. As in many entrepreneurial firms, accumulating valuable resources is not enough to support a sustainable strategic and competitive advantage (Teece et al. 1997). The ever-changing competitive environments render a seemingly sustainable strategic advantage obsolete. Instead, competitive advantages arise from a firm's capability constantly to redeploy, reconfigure and rejuvenate its capabilities and to innovate in response to the changing environmental conditions. In utilizing a very large sample of women entrepreneurs in Russia, this research contributes to our understanding of how the strategic advantage, based on entrepreneurial orientation, acts as a critical link between different types of individual- and firm-level resources to influence firm performance. It is these collective activities as well as the process that may give women-led ventures the increased capacity and foundation for continual growth, renewal and sustainability of their firms, their markets and the broader communities they serve.

DIRECTIONS FOR FUTURE RESEARCH

The differences between high-growth enterprises and low-growth enterprises have been attributed to factors such as the previous experience of the founder, and the ability to establish goals for staff and effectively handle conflict (Brush and Hisrich 1988). Research has also focused on the entrepreneur's willingness to grow, and on strategic activities. The presence of good working relationships with customers, financiers and other constituents to the business has also been reportedly related to effective growth strategies (Kamau et al. 1999). While motivations to undertake business ownership have become more generally understood through research, more work is needed to examine the factors that contribute to sustained entrepreneurship, especially in the stages beyond start-up (Bhave 1994).

Cliff (1998) proposed that women entrepreneurs prefer a managed approach to business growth as opposed to following more risky growth strategies. Growth orientation has been found to relate significantly to actual firm performance. More research on strategies for managing and sustaining growth in women-owned businesses would increase our understanding of how growth needs differ across different stages of the firm's life cycle (Gundry et al. 2002).

A challenge for many business owners lies in obtaining the appropriate assistance and information needed to take the business to the next level of growth (Gundry et al. 2002). Additional research should examine how women entrepreneurs across cultures utilize these resources and leverage the importance of these activities, including information seeking and training and education, to develop and grow their businesses further.

NOTES

1. Russian legislation and state statistics deal with two categories of economic entities, including (1) small entrepreneurship entities; and (2) medium-sized and large enterprises. Small entrepreneurship entities are defined as including individual entrepreneurs (IEs) (referred to in this chapter as sole proprietorships), farm enterprises (FEs) and small enterprises registered as legal entities (SEs).

REFERENCES

Ageev, A., M. Gratchev and R. Hisrich (1995), 'Entrepreneurship in the Soviet Union and post-socialist Russia', *Small Business Economics*, 7, 365–7.
Ajzen, I. (1991), 'The theory of planned behaviour', *Organizational Behaviour and Human Decision Processes* 50, 179–211.
Aldrich, H.E. and M.A. Martinez (2001), 'Many are called, but few are chosen: an evolutionary perspective for the study of entrepreneurship', *Entrepreneurship Theory and Practice*, 25 (4), 41–56.
Anderson, J.C. and D.W. Gerbing (1988), 'Structural equation modeling in practice: A review and recommended two-step approach', *Psychological Bulletin*, 103, 411–23.
Babaeva, L. (1998), 'Russian and American female entrepreneurs' (Российские м Американские женщины-предприниматели), *Sociological Review* (Социологические исследования), 8, 134–5.
Bagozzi, R.P., F.D. Davis and P.R. Warshaw (1992), 'Development and test of a

theory of technological learning and usage' *Human Relations*, **45** (7), 660–86.

Bamford, C.E., T.J. Dean and P.P. McDougall (1997), 'Initial strategies and new venture growth: an examination of the effectiveness of broad versus narrow breadth strategies', *Frontiers of Entrepreneurship Research*, www.babson.edu/entrep/fer/papers97/bamford/bam.htm, 20 December 2006.

Bandura, A. (2001), 'Guide for constructing self-efficacy scales (revised)', available from Frank Pajares, Emory University.

Barney, J. (1991), 'Firm resources and sustained competitive advantage', *Journal of Management*, **17**, 99–120.

Baum, J. (1995), 'The relation of traits, competencies, motivation, strategy and structure to venture growth', *Frontiers of Entrepreneurship Research*, www.babson.edu/entrep/fer/papers95/baum.htm, 20 December 2006.

Bentler, P.M. and D.G. Bonett (1980), 'Significance tests and goodness of fit in the analysis of covariance structures', *Psychological Bulletin*, **88**, 588–606.

Betz, N.E. and G. Hackett (1998), 'Manual for the occupational self-efficacy scale', http://seamonkey.ed.asu.edu/gail/occse1.htm, accessed 31 October 2001.

Bezgodov, A. (1999), *Entrepreneurship Sociology* (очерки социологии предпринимательства), St. Petersburg: Petropolis (СПБ: «Петрополис»).

Bhave, M. (1994), 'A process model of entrepreneurial venture creation', *Journal of Business Venturing*, **8**, 223–42.

Borch, O.J., H. Morten and K. Senneseth (1999), 'Resource configuration, competitive strategies, and corporate entrepreneurship: an empirical examination of small firms', *Entrepreneurship Theory and Practice*, **42** (1), 49–71.

Brockhaus, R. (1982), 'The psychology of the entrepreneur', in C.A. Kent, D.L. Sexton and K.H. Vesper (eds), *Encyclopedia of Entrepreneurship*, Englewood Cliffs, NJ: PrenticeHall, pp. 39–71.

Brown, T.E. and B.A. Kirchhoff (1997), 'The effects of resource availability and entrepreneurial orientation on firm growth', *Frontiers of Entrepreneurship Research*, www.babson.edu/entrep/fer/papers97/kirtchoff/kir1.htm, 20 December 2006.

Brush, C. and R. Hisrich (1988), 'Women entrepreneurs: strategic origins impact on growth', in B.A. Kirchhoff, W.A. Long, W.E. McMullan, K.H. Vesper and W.E. Wetzel (eds), *Frontiers of Entrepreneurship Research*, Wellesley, MA: Babson College, pp. 612–25.

Castrogiovanni, G.J. (1991), 'Environmental munificence: a theoretical assessment', *Academy of Management Review*, **16** (3), 542–65.

Chaganti, R. and S. Parasuraman (1997), 'A study of the impacts of gender on business performance and management patterns in small businesses', *Entrepreneurship Theory and Practice*, **21** (2), 73–6.

Chandler, G.N. and S.H. Hanks (1993), 'Measuring the performance of emerging businesses: a validation study', *Journal of Small Business Management*, **8**, 391–408.

Chandler, G.N. and S.H. Hanks (1994), 'Founder competence, the environment, and venture performance', *Entrepreneurship Theory and Practice*, **18** (3), 223–37.

Chandler, G.N. and S.H. Hanks (1998), 'An examination of the sustainability of founders' human and financial capital in emerging business ventures', *Journal of Business Venturing*, **13** (5), 353–69.

Cliff, J.E. (1998), 'Does one size fit all? Exploring the relationship between attitudes towards growth, gender, and business size', *Journal of Business Venturing*, **13** (6), 523–42.

Cooper, A. and F. Gascon (1992), 'Entrepreneurs, processes of founding, and new-firm performance', in D. Sexton and J. Kasarda (eds), *The State of the Art of Entrepreneurship*, Boston, MA: PWS-Kent, pp. 301–40.

Cooper, A., F.J. Gimeno-Gascon and C. Woo (1994), 'Initial human and financial capital as predictors of new venture performance', *Journal of Business Venturing*, **9**, 371–95.

Covin, J. and M. Miles (1999), 'Corporate entrepreneurship and the pursuit of competitive advantage', *Entrepreneurship Theory and Practice*, **23** (3), 47–64.

Covin, J. and D. Slevin (1989), 'Strategic management of small firms in hostile and benign environments', *Strategic Management Journal*, **10** (1), 75–87.

Delmar, F. (2000), 'Entrepreneurship, growth, and innovation', in B. Green et al. (eds), *Risk Behaviour and Risk Management in Business Life*, Dordrecht, The Netherlands: Kluwer Academic Publishers, pp. 197–200.

Delmar, F. and P. Davidsson (2000), 'Where do they come from? Prevalence and characteristics of nascent entrepreneurs', *Entrepreneurship and Regional Development*, **12**, 1–23.

De Noble, A.F., D. Jung and S.B. Ehrlich (1999), 'Entrepreneurial self-efficacy: the development of a measure and its relation to entrepreneurial action', *Frontiers of Entrepreneurship Research*, www.babson.edu/entrep/fer/papers99/I/I_C/IC.html, 20 December 2006.

Donckels, R. and J. Lambrecht (1995), 'Networks and small business growth: an explanatory model', *Small Business Economics*, **7** (3), 273–89.

Gartner, W.B. (1990), 'What are we talking about when we talk about entrepreneurship?' *Journal of Business Venturing*, **5** (1), 15–28.

Gartner, W., B. Bird and J. Starr (1992), 'Acting as if: differentiating entrepreneurial from organizational behaviour', *Entrepreneurship Theory and Practice*, **16** (3), 13–31.

Grant, R.M. (1991), 'The resource based theory of competitive advantage: Implications for strategy formulation', *California Management Review*, **33** (3), 114–35.

Gundry, L.K., M. Ben-Yoseph and M. Posig (2002), 'The status of women's entrepreneurship: pathways to future entrepreneurship development and education', *New England Journal of Entrepreneurship*, **5** (1), 39–50.

Gundry, L.K. and H.P. Welsch (2001), 'The ambitious entrepreneur: high-growth strategies of women-owned enterprises', *Journal of Business Venturing*, **16** (5), 453–70.

Hansen, B.E. (1995) 'Rethinking the univariate approach to unit root testing', *Econometric Theory*, **11**, 1148–71.

Hart, S.L. (1992), 'An integrative framework for strategymaking processes', *Academy of Management Review*, **17** (2), 327–51.

Iakovleva, T. (2001), *Entrepreneurship Framework Conditions in Russia and in Norway: Implications for the Entrepreneurs in the Agrarian Sector*, Hovedfagsoppgaven, Norway: Bode Graduate School of Business.

Iakovleva, T. (2005), 'Entrepreneurial orientation of Russian SMEs', in G.T. Vinig and R.C.W. Van der Voort (eds), *The Emergence of Entrepreneurial Economics*, Amsterdam and Boston, MA: Elsevier, pp. 83–98.

Isaksen, E. and L. Kolvereid (2005), 'Growth objectives in Norwegian start-up businesses', *International Journal of Entrepreneurship and Small Business*, **2** (1), 17–26.

Jöreskog, K.G. and D. Sörbom (1993), *LISREL VIII: A Guide to the Program and Applications*, Chicago, IL: SPSS.

Kamau, D.G., G.N. McLean and A. Ardishvili (1999), 'Perceptions of business growth by women entrepreneurs', *Frontiers of Entrepreneurship Research*, www.babson.edu/entrep/fer/papers99/IV/IV_C/IVC.html, 20 December 2006.

Kolvereid, L. (1992), 'Growth aspirations among Norwegian entrepreneurs', *Journal of Business Venturing*, **12**, 213–25.

Lerner, M. and T. Almor (2002), 'Relationships among strategic capabilities and the performance of women-owned small ventures', *Journal of Small Business Management*, **40** (2), 109–25.

Lumpkin, G.T. and G.G. Dess (1996), 'Clarifying the entrepreneurial orientation construct and linking it to performance', *Academy of Management Review*, **21** (1), 135–72.

Lumpkin, G.T. and G. Dess (2001), 'Linking two dimensions of entrepreneurial orientation to firm performance: the moderating role of environment and industry life cycle', *Journal of Business Venturing*, **16**, 429–51.

Miller, S. and P. Friesen (1982), 'Innovation in conservative and entrepreneurial firms: two models of strategic momentum', *Strategic Management Journal*, **3**, 1–25.

Miller, R.W. and J.-M. Tolouse (1988), 'Strategy, structure, CEO personality and performance in small firms', *American Journal of Small Business*, Winter, 1988, 47–61.

Murphy, G.B., J.W. Trailer and R.C. Hill (1996), 'Measuring performance in entrepreneurship research', *Journal of Business Research*, **36** (1), 15–24.

Netemeyer, R., M. Johnston and S. Burton (1990), 'Analysis of role conflict and role ambiguity in a structural equations framework', *Journal of Applied Psychology*, **75**, 148–57.

Pistrui, D., J. Liao and H. Welsch (1999), 'A factor-analytic framework for operationalizing expansion plans', paper presented at the US Association for Small Business and Entrepreneurship, Clearwater, FL, 14-17 January.

Rauch, A., J. Wiklund, M. Frese and G. Lumpkin (2004), 'Entepreneurial orientation and business performance: cumulative empirical evidence', *Frontiers of Entrepreneurship Research*, www.babson.edu/entrep/fer/FER_2004/web-content/ Section%20VI/P1/VI-P1.html, 20 December 2006.

Russian SME Resource Centre, http://www.rcsme.ru.

Shane, S. and L. Kolvereid (1995), 'National environment, strategy and new venture performance: a three country study', *Journal of Small Business Management*, April, 37–50.

Starr, J. and I. MacMillan (1990), 'Resource cooptation via social contracting: Resource acquisition strategies for new ventures', *Strategic Management Journal*, **11** (5), 79–93.

Stewart, T. (1997), *Intellectual Capital*, New York: Doubleday Press.

Stewart, W., W. Watson, J. Carland and J. Carland (1998), 'A proclivity for entrepreneurship: a comparison of entrepreneurs, small business owners, and corporate managers', *Journal of Business Venturing*, **14**, 189–214.

Teece, D., G. Pisano and A. Shuen (1997), 'Dynamic capabilities and strategic management', *Strategic Management Journal*, **18** (7), 509–33.

Tkachev, A. and L. Kolvereid (1999), 'Self-employment intentions among Russian students', *Entrepreneurship and Regional Development*, **11** (3), 269–80.

Turen, A. (ed.) (1993), *Russian Entrepreneurship: Experience of Sociological Analysis*, Moscow: Moscow.

Weiss, L.A. (1981), 'Start-up businesses: a comparison of performance', *Sloan Management Review*, **23** (1), 37–53.

Welsch, H. and D. Pistrui (1993), 'Entrepreneurship commitment and initiative in

Romania', paper presented at Research in Entrepreneurship (Rent VII), Budapest, Hungary.

Westhead, P., D. Ucbasaran and M. Wright (2005), 'Decisions, actions and performance: do novice, serial and portfolio entrepreneurs differ?' *Journal of Small Business Management*, **43** (4), 393–417.

Wiklund, J. (1998), 'Small firm growth and performance', Doctoral dissertation, Jonkoping International Business School, Jonkoping University.

Wiklund, J. (1999), 'The sustainability of the entrepreneurial orientation – performance relationship', *Entrepreneurship Theory and Practice*, **24**, 37–48.

Wiklund, J. and D. Shepherd (2003), 'Knowledge-based resources, entrepreneurial orientation, and the performance of small and medium-sized businesses', *Strategic Management Journal*, **24**, 1307–14.

Williams, L.J. and J.T. Hazer (1986), 'Antecedents and consequences of satisfaction and commitment in turnover models: a reanalysis using latent variable structural equation methods', *Journal of Applied Psychology*, **71**, 219–31.

Wood, R. and A. Bandura (1989), 'Social cognitive theory of organizational management', *Academy of Management Review*, **14** (3), 361–84.

Ylinenpää, H. and M. Chechurina (2000), 'Perceptions of female entrepreneurs in Russia', Conference Proceedings, 30th European Small Business Seminar, Gent, Belgium.

Zahra, S. and J. Covin (1995), 'Contextual influences on the corporate entrepreneurship-performance relationship: a longitudinal analysis', *Journal of Business Venturing*, **10** (1), 43–59.

Table 4A.1 Means, Standard Deviations and Correlations (1–6)

Variables (n = 457)	Mean	SD	1	2	3	4	5	6
1 Firm age	6.7	3.42	1.0					
2 Legal status	3.8	0.74	-0.042	1.0				
3 Industry	2.1	0.44	-0.115*	0.065	1.0			
4 Respondent age	39.6	8.4	0.376**	-0.035	-0.115*	1.0		
5 Education	0.49	0.5	0.022	-0.153**	0.087	0.012	1.0	
6 Owner-manager	0.94	0.23	0.029	0.263**	0.012	-0.100*	-0.047	1.0
7 Munificence	0.0128	1.01	0.062	-0.162**	-0.144**	0.102*	0.059	-0.026
8 Entrepreneurial intensity	0.0086	0.98	0.045	0.011	0.018	0.048	0.103*	0.043
9 Opportunity competence	0.0091	0.99	0.041	-0.054	-0.029	0.100*	0.085	-0.031
10 Financial capital	0.0581	0.99	0.177**	-0.067	-0.150**	0.124**	0.008	-0.015
11 Social capital	0.0192	0.97	0.036	-0.158**	-0.002	0.049	0.144**	-0.038
12 EO	0.0332	0.98	0.135**	-0.074	-0.167**	0.062	0.103*	-0.017
13 Performance	0.0393	0.98	-0.001	0.012	-0.109*	-0.047	0.043	0.023

Notes:
* Correlation significant at the 0.05 level (2-tailed)
** Correlation significant at the 0.01 level (2-tailed)

Table 4A.1 Means, Standard Deviations and Correlations (cont'd) (7–13)

Variables (n = 457)	Mean	SD	7	8	9	10	11	12	13
1 Firm age	6.7	3.42							
2 Legal status	3.8	0.74							
3 Industry	2.1	0.44							
4 Respondent age	39.6	8.4							
5 Education	0.49	0.5							
6 Owner-manager	0.94	0.23							
7 Munificence	0.0128	1.01	1.0						
8 Entrepreneurial intensity	0.0086	0.98	0.190**	1.0					
9 Opportunity competence	0.0091	0.99	0.351**	0.314**	1.0				
10 Financial capital	0.0581	0.99	0.475**	0.229**	0.384**	1.0			
11 Social capital	0.0192	0.97	0.346**	0.252**	0.438**	0.420**	1.0		
12 EO	0.0332	0.98	0.408**	0.271**	0.466**	0.521**	0.474**	1.0	
13 Performance	0.0393	0.98	0.353**	0.249**	0.349**	0.321**	0.228**	0.343**	1.0

Notes: ** Correlation significant at the 0.01 level (2-tailed)

5.   Entrepreneurship: Only a Few are Chosen but Some are Even Chosen Twice

Pamela Mueller and Michael Niese

INTRODUCTION

Entrepreneurship and self-employment are important economic phenomena. Nearly 10 per cent of the labour force in Germany is self-employed.[1] Nevertheless, the self-employed group is rather heterogeneous. Some are very successful and continue to be self-employed throughout their entire career. Others sell or close down their businesses and enter paid employment or unemployment, and some of them once again re-enter self-employment. These individuals are called serial entrepreneurs (Westhead and Wright 1998). According to Sternberg (2000), 30 per cent of the working population views bankruptcy of a start-up company as a personal defeat of the founder, thus indicating that failure has a negative stigma in Germany. Therefore, it is rather surprising that Wagner (2003) reports that about 18 per cent of business owners in Germany are restarters who have previously gained self-employment experience.

The fact that the same individual enters and exits self-employment repeatedly is observed in other countries as well. At least three studies provide evidence that there are a significant number of restarters. First, Westhead and Wright (1998) identified 25 per cent of principal owner-managers of independent businesses as serial entrepreneurs in Great Britain. Second, about 19 per cent of the businesses in Scotland are operated by serial entrepreneurs (Westhead et al. 2005). Additionally, a third study reveals that in Finland nearly 30 per cent of those employees who transit to self-employment are serial entrepreneurs (Hyytinen and Ilmakunnas 2006).

Governments have turned to entrepreneurship and have established programmes which encourage individuals who are willing to start a business. The motivation of these public programmes is usually to generate additional employment. The success of these programmes is questionable and has hardly been evaluated (Parker 2004). First of all, new and small businesses are shrouded with uncertainty. Most of them are imitating existing firms, thereby competing on the fringe. The net employment impact of those start-ups seems to be very small or even non-existent because the majority of the start-ups can only survive when they force other young and small firms to exit the market. However, some start-ups operate in markets that are ignored by large corporations or have not even existed before. This kind of market entry is recognized as an important factor which intensifies competition and increases economic efficiency. Some start-ups enter the market with innovative products and processes and create new markets; others are very successful and become tomorrow's large corporations.

During the time period after market entry, the entrepreneur can learn about his entrepreneurial abilities and talent. Jovanovic (1982) developed a model in which firms of able and lucky entrepreneurs will grow and succeed. On the other hand, firms with less talent and with unlucky entrepreneurs will shrink and be forced to exit the market. Various firm selection models interpret market exit as an expression of failure and conclude that these individuals do not possess the skills and talent necessary for running a business (Jovanovic 1982, Pakes and Ericson 1998, Kihlstrom and Laffont 1979). According to Frank (1988), firm performance depends on the founder's work effort, luck and entrepreneurial talent. Consistent with other models, the entrant does not truly know his own talent for running a firm prior to market entry. Nevertheless, entrants learn at different speeds about their entrepreneurial abilities, which are dependent on the effort they expend. As a consequence, market exit signals that these individuals were not able to prove their entrepreneurial talent and are not suited to run a business. Therefore, the phenomenon of serial entrepreneurship contradicts the models of firm entry, market selection and exit. The implication of Jovanovic's model is that entrepreneurs who exit never re-enter the market because the entrepreneur does not change his belief about his abilities.

Nevertheless, new firm survival not only depends on entrepreneurial talent and luck but also on financial resources, market barriers and technological conditions (Agarwal and Audretsch 2001, Brüderl et al. 1992). Especially, market barriers such as large requirements for financial capital and possible sunken investments hamper market entry and exit in manufacturing industries. Even in cases where market entry is observed against the odds of high market barriers, only a small proportion of entrants survive and grow. Those markets can be characterized by a revolving door. This raises the question why some of the unsuccessful entrepreneurs are taking a second chance.

This study discerns non-entrepreneurs (individuals that have never started a firm), novice entrepreneurs and serial entrepreneurs. Since the characteristics of the self-employed are well known (see Parker 2004 for an overview) this study focuses on the differences between novice and serial entrepreneurs. Various questions motivated this study: Do serial entrepreneurs have a different attitude to risk? Are serial entrepreneurs forced into self-employment due to necessity or are they motivated by opportunities of advancement? This chapter is structured as follows: the section on 'The Motivation of Entrepreneurs to Re-enter Self-Employment' reviews the literature regarding novice and serial entrepreneurship. The employed data set and definitional issues are presented in the 'Data and Descriptive Statistics' section. In 'Empirical Results', statistical differences between novice and serial entrepreneurs are reported. A conclusion is offered in the final section.

THE MOTIVATION OF ENTREPRENEURS TO RE-ENTER SELF-EMPLOYMENT

In accordance with the literature on firm entry and exit, serial entrepreneurship seems to be inefficient. One implication of the Jovanovic model (1982) is that entrepreneurs who exit never return because they do not possess the capability to run a business. These entrepreneurs know that the output price cannot rise above the level at which they left, and they will never obtain more information to change their beliefs about their entrepreneurial ability. Prior to market entry, self-employed individuals are uncertain about their true entrepreneurial talent. These abilities can only be tested by entering the market. The founder's entrepreneurial talent has a positive impact on the survival and growth of the new venture (Lucas 1978, Frank 1988). New firms of founders who do not possess the skills and talent necessary for running a business will experience poor performance, shrink and have to exit the market (Jovanovic 1982). Frank (1988) concludes that the decision to close the start-up depends on the balance of financial returns and work effort. If the entrepreneurial talent and ability is low, financial returns will be low or non-existent even though the individual's effort is high. In this case, the logical consequence is the closure of the firm and the unskilled entrepreneur transits to paid employment. These models do not take into account that failed entrepreneurs have gained valuable information from their failure and may choose to re-enter self-employment (see Parker 2004, p. 213, Stam et al. 2006).

However, entrepreneurial talent is not the only determinant for a successful start-up process. Baldwin and Rafiquzzaman (1995) found significant differences between successful and unsuccessful start-ups with regard to the initial endowment and development. In comparison to failed start-ups, successful newcomers are larger, are more productive and attain higher profit margins during the first three years after entry. Active learning might also be a crucial determinant for survival. As soon as entrants realize that their productivity is too low, they try to compensate for this shortcoming with investments in research and development (Pakes and Ericson 1998).

It seems reasonable to differentiate between two types of serial entrepreneurs because various reasons might have caused the market exit. The exit of some self-employed individuals can be induced by low productivity or profitability. Others might have decided to close their firm voluntarily and change to paid employment because of higher returns due to a better job offer, for instance. Kangasharju and Pekkala (2002) found that the well-educated self-employed in Finland are more likely to switch to paid employment in boom years. The first type of serial entrepreneur had to exit the market previously because of their low performance and insufficient competitiveness. In particular, these entrepreneurs are not expected to re-enter self-employment because they could not prove their entrepreneurial talent. This raises the question of why they try again; their motivation is rather unclear. This type of serial entrepreneur might be convinced that they could have survived if their financial resources had been larger, they had chosen a different industry, their trial period for proving their entrepreneurial talent had been longer, or general business conditions had been better. Last but not least they may be convinced that they will be luckier next time around. In addition, they might also be pushed into self-employment due to the lack of alternatives. This type of serial entrepreneur may be especially vulnerable to systematic overoptimism (Camerer and Lovallo 1999). It is questionable whether they could augment their entrepreneurial capabilities and return successfully to self-employment (Stam et al. 2006). The other type of serial entrepreneur voluntarily gave up self-employment earlier and then returned to it. Although the business was viable, he decided to sell it and transit to paid employment (see also Kangasharju and Pekkala 2002). This decision might have been driven by higher income prospects in paid employment. For some reason, the person who was formerly self-employed chooses to re-enter self-employment. A positive attitude to risk, the parents of the self-employed person and strong entrepreneurial aspirations may motivate them to found a firm once again. Some of the re-starters may benefit from financial resources accruing from the cash-out of their former business. These entrepreneurs – called portfolio entrepreneurs – experience higher growth rates in both employees and profit (Westhead et al. 2005).

Does market exit really prove the founder's inability to run a firm? The economic paradox of serial entrepreneurship leads to the question of what makes serial entrepreneurs unique. What can we learn about their motivation to do it again? Is it a special attitude to life? Does the serial entrepreneur grasp every entrepreneurial opportunity he can? Are they mostly necessity entrepreneurs? Possible characteristics and determinants of serial entrepreneurs are discussed in the following section.

It is generally agreed that well-educated individuals are better informed about profitable opportunities, are more likely to possess the necessary skills and are more likely to have the financial resources required for starting a business (Davidsson and Honig 2003, Kim et al. 2006, Wagner 2004). Nevertheless, the relationship between education and serial entrepreneurship might also be ambiguous – depending on the type of serial entrepreneurship. First, serial entrepreneurs with a high level of education could be expected to have a greater likelihood of restarting a firm than people without such an education because they are better informed about existing opportunities. Second, if necessity rather than opportunity is the driver behind serial entrepreneurship, these people might be less educated; thus, they choose self-employment due to the lack of other employment opportunities. Finally, formal qualifications might not necessarily be required for entrepreneurship (Parker 2004, p. 73; Casson 2003, p. 208). A positive or negative relationship cannot be detected empirically. Wagner (2003) does not find any statistically significant relationship between higher education and the propensity to restart a business. Since human capital generally increases the survival chances of newly founded businesses (Brüderl et al. 1992), it might be that novice entrepreneurs with greater human capital are less forced to think about restarting because their first attempt has already been successful.

Family members, friends, and colleagues provide both social networks and the potential resources necessary for self-employment (for example Davidsson and Honig 2003). According to a great number of studies, the children of self-employed parents have a greater propensity to become entrepreneurs (for example Dunn and Holtz-Eakin 2000). This phenomenon may be explained by the fact that self-employed parents can offer an informal introduction to business methods, transfer valuable work experience and provide access to capital and equipment, business networks, consultancy and reputation (Parker 2004, p. 85; Dunn and Holtz-Eakin 2000). Additionally, growing up in a family where one or both parents are self-employed may lead to a pro-business attitude, desire for independence, autonomy and wealth creation, and reduce the age at which an individual enters self-employment (Parker 2004, p. 85; Dunn and Holtz-Eakin 2000).

Davidsson and Honig (2003) and Mueller (2006) found that having self-employed parents significantly increases the prospects of an employee being a nascent entrepreneur. In addition to parents, the spouse or a close friend may also provide valuable social capital. Serial entrepreneurs can benefit from their knowledge, entrepreneurial experience and business networks, which may result in easier access to capital and equipment. Furthermore, if they are satisfied with being self-employed, they may encourage others to restart a business. Wagner (2003) showed that the personal contact with a young entrepreneur increases the likelihood of an entrepreneurial restart.

Financial assets may facilitate the transition to entrepreneurship because individuals possessing wealth do not necessarily need to request money from banks and can finance the start-up process themselves. Furthermore, financial assets are valuable during the time period when revenues or profits have not yet been made. Nevertheless, individuals with vast amounts of wealth probably choose other careers, might prefer to be 'angel' investors, and are less likely to start their own business (see also Kim et al. 2006). In contrast, individuals who hardly possess any personal wealth may also have only a few career options and choose entrepreneurship out of necessity. Therefore, it is rather unclear whether financial assets determine an entrepreneurial restart.

Unemployment may be a push factor into self-employment. In particular, individuals with no other job prospects might have to choose self-employment as an alternative to paid employment. British studies found that between 20 and 50 per cent of new entrants to self-employment were previously unemployed (either directly or recently) (Meager 1992). According to Evans and Leighton (1989), unemployed individuals were about twice as likely to become self-employed as employees. As mentioned above, some serial entrepreneurs may alternate between unemployment and self-employment. They do not choose to run a firm because of opportunity, but due to lack of alternatives. This would be consistent with the findings of Evans and Leighton (1989), who found that especially those unemployed individuals with an unstable work history have a higher likelihood of being and becoming self-employed.

Risk aversion is most likely to reduce the probability that an individual would choose to become an entrepreneur (Kihlstrom and Laffont 1979). Therefore, individuals with a pro-risk attitude are more inclined to become self-employed. Especially serial entrepreneurs might be less risk averse since they turn to self-employment repeatedly, knowing the risk and uncertainty attached to the start-up process. Wagner (2003) used the term 'fear of failure' as an indicator of risk aversion. His results clearly show that individuals who are less afraid of failure are more likely to make an entrepreneurial restart.

Certain (psychological) traits may also represent a predisposition for some individuals to enter self-employment (for an overview, see Parker 2004, pp. 76–83). The need for achievement rather than the desire for money might be one unique factor linking self-employed individuals. The importance of self-realization might be one characteristic of entrepreneurs. On the other hand, employees might be characterized by the need for success at their workplace because becoming a manager of a large corporation promises to be more attractive than starting a new business. Therefore, serial entrepreneurs might be less interested in success at work and rather want to achieve something in their life such as independence.

DATA AND DESCRIPTIVE STATISTICS

Data on entrepreneurs are taken from the German Socio-Economic Panel Study (SOEP) conducted by the German Institute for Economic Research (DIW). The SOEP is a representative longitudinal panel study of private households in Germany which began in 1984 and is carried out annually. Households in East Germany were included in the survey beginning in 1990. The SOEP survey contains demographic characteristics such as gender, age, education, data on the respondent's employment status, work experience and some basic characteristics of the workplace. The SOEP database has been used several times to analyse the issue of self-employment.[2]

In 2004, data were collected from 22 019 individuals throughout Germany of whom 17 811 ranged between the ages of 18 and 65. About 43 per cent of the respondents (9388) are blue- or white-collar workers and less than 5 per cent (953) are civil servants. The self-employed respondents comprise 10.5 per cent of the working population. About 5000 respondents (23 per cent) are retired as of 2004. The unemployment rate of the employable respondents (under 65 years old) is about 8 per cent. The analysis was restricted to those respondents who could be observed each year between 2002 and 2004, which led to 17 547 respondents. In 2003 and 2004, 330 respondents switched to self-employment either from paid employment, unemployment, retirement or schooling. Only 15 founders (4 per cent) became self-employed in the agricultural sector. About 30 per cent of the founders started their venture, for instance, as medical practitioners, attorneys, architects, journalists, interpreters or tax accountants. More than 20 per cent of those who turned to self-employment previously had a business and could be characterized as serial entrepreneurs (Table 5.1).

Those respondents entering self-employment significantly differ from the group of individuals who abstain from self-employment. With regard to human capital, founders are more likely to have graduated from a university and gained work experience in a small company. While about 30 per cent of novice entrepreneurs stem from small companies, roughly 70 per cent worked in a large company or were unemployed before turning to self-employment.

Otherwise, 50 per cent of the serial entrepreneurs gained work experience in a small firm. Interestingly, about 20 per cent of the founders were unemployed, compared to 8 per cent of the control group.

Empirical Entrepreneurship in Europe

Table 5.1   Characteristics of Novice and Serial Entrepreneurs

	Non-Entre-preneurs	Novice and Serial Entre-preneurs	Mean Comp. Test	Novice	Serial	Mean Comp. Test
Previously self-employed [1 = yes]	3.24% 0.18	23.03% 0.42	0.000	0%	100%	—
University degree [1 = yes]	19.95% 0.40	36.36 0.48	0.000	36.65% 0.48	36.84% 0.49	0.922
Work experience in a small firm (< 20 empl.) [1 = yes]	16.12% 0.37	31.82 0.47	0.000	29.53% 0.46	39.47% 0.49	0.103
Job tenure	5.96 9.09	4.74 8.67	0.016	4.81 8.49	4.52 9.32	0.795
Unemployed [1 = yes]	9.27% 0.29	23.03% 0.42	0.000	27.95% 0.45	6.58% 0.25	0.000
Retired [1 = yes]	23.26 0.42	7.88% 0.27	0.000	5.11% 0.22	17.11% 0.38	0.001
Parents are/were self-employed [1 = yes]	11.51% 0.32	15.15% 0.36	0.040	14.17% 0.35	18.42% 0.39	0.366
Risk attitude [0, 10]	4.31 2.35	5.68 2.37	0.000	5.73 2.35	5.54 2.46	0.544
Financial assets (4 out of 6) [1 = yes]	21.40% 0.41	31.21% 0.46	0.000	32.68% 0.47	26.32% 0.44	0.295
Importance of success at work [1, 4]	2.17 0.88	1.74 0.69	0.000	1.71 0.68	1.86 0.80	0.123
Importance of self-fulfilment [1, 4]	2.18 0.75	1.91 0.75	0.000	1.86 0.75	2.08 0.74	0.024
Female [1 = yes]	53.24% 0.50	38.18% 0.49	0.000	38.19 0.49	38.16% 0.49	0.996
Age	47.91 16.81	43.56 13.43	0.000	41.66 12.29	49.92 15.11	0.000
Observations	17 217 (98.12%)	330 (1.88)	—	254 (76.97%)	76 (23.03%)	—

Only 7 per cent of the serial entrepreneurs were unemployed, therefore, in particular novice entrepreneurs might have been pushed into self-employment out of necessity. Some founders were previously retired (8 per cent), which might suggest that some founders enter self-employment in order to supplement their pension. Since the self-employed are solely responsible for their pension, this might be a characteristic of serial entrepreneurs who are forced into another venture. This is confirmed since 14 per cent of the serial entrepreneurs were previously retired in contrast to only 5 per cent of the novice entrepreneurs. Employees are most likely to have higher opportunity costs entering self-employment for the first time as they approach the age of retirement.

Social capital measured by self-employed parents is more distinct for the group of founders than for non-entrepreneurs and is largely based on serial entrepreneurs. More than 20 per cent of the serial entrepreneurs had parents who were or currently are self-employed. Entrepreneurs are more likely to possess financial assets than the control group. However, the descriptive statistics show that the novice can count on financial assets more than serial entrepreneurs. This might indicate that financial assets are important to actually start a venture; however, serial entrepreneurs might have already invested part of their financial assets.

The importance of achieving success at work and achieving self-fulfilment do not motivate individuals to start a business. Respondents who do not turn to self-employment rank more highly in both categories. Starting a venture is accompanied by risk and uncertainty, high workload, problems and challenges, which might deter some people from turning to self-employment. Nevertheless, serial entrepreneurs rank the importance of self-fulfilment higher than novice entrepreneurs.

EMPIRICAL RESULTS

The empirical evidence shows a significant amount of serial entrepreneurship in different European countries (Westhead and Wright 1998, Wagner 2003, Hyytinen and Ilmakunnas 2006). This observation contradicts the models of firm dynamics and firm selection. They suggest that it is inefficient to give an unsuccessful founder a second chance because the market exit proves the founder's inability to run a firm. Nevertheless, several founders turn to self-employment more than once. Serial entrepreneurs seem to have a strong overall commitment to self-employment: they can be characterized as a tumbler bouncing back to self-employment.

In our empirical analysis we try to answer the question of why individuals turn to self-employment when they have already been self-employed in the past. We use logistic regression estimates to explore this question. First, we analyse the likelihood of becoming self-employed while controlling the fact that the founder was previously self-employed. Second, we try to discern why someone chooses to become self-employed at least twice.

The motivation and determinants to set up a business are quite clear and well known (Casson 2003, Evans and Leighton 1989). Human capital increases the propensity to turn to self-employment (Table 5.2, Model I). Obviously, individuals with greater human capital are better informed about profitable opportunities to start a firm. Most founders gained the necessary skills to run a firm in a small company where they were employed before they made the transition to self-employment. Work experience gained in small and young firms enables employees to learn first-hand information about running a business as well as possible constraints, problems and solutions during the start-up process (Wagner 2004). Unemployment is also an important source of entrepreneurship. Keeping in mind that business founders did not stay in their previous jobs as long as those who abstain from self-employment, it can be concluded that several start-ups are merely driven by necessity and less by opportunity.

However, what makes an entrepreneur is not only necessity but also certain kinds of personal characteristics. Business founders are relatively young and less risk averse. In addition, disproportionately few women turn to self-employment. The propensity to set up one's own business increases with the fact that the parents are or were self-employed. Self-employed parents may provide both social networks and potential resources. They may function as role models, indicating that self-employment is a viable and profitable career option.

Furthermore, they can offer an informal introduction to business methods, transfer valuable work experience, and provide access to capital and equipment, business networks, consultancy and reputation (Parker 2004, p. 85; Dunn and Holtz-Eakin 2000). Interestingly, self-employment is not a vehicle for achieving self-fulfilment and success at work. For entrepreneurs it is more important to follow their own path than to achieve greater financial rewards. Nevertheless, financial assets facilitate the transition to self-employment.

The second model (II) in Table 5.2 controls for previous self-employment experience. The main result is that compared to Model I no major changes occur. This suggests that novice and serial entrepreneurs are motivated or hampered by the same characteristics and circumstances. They vary greatly in comparison to non-entrepreneurs, but they differ only slightly between each other.

Table 5.2 Propensity to Turn to Self-Employment

	Propensity to Turn to Self-Employment	
	(Model I)	(Model II)
Previously self-employed	—	1.924**
		(0.000)
University degree	0.689**	0.664**
	(0.000)	(0.000)
Work experience in a small firm	0.810**	0.720**
(<20 employees)	(0.000)	(0.000)
Job tenure at last employer	−0.041**	−0.026**
	(0.000)	(0.005)
Parents are/were self-employed	0.388*	0.353*
	(0.016)	(0.031)
Unemployed	0.889**	0.942**
	(0.000)	(0.000)
Retired	−0.701*	−0.633
	(0.031)	(0.052)
Risk attitude [0, 10]	0.187**	0.173**
	(0.000)	(0.000)
Financial assets (4 out of 6)	0.428**	0.454**
	(0.001)	(0.000)
Importance of self-fulfilment [1, 4]	−0.175	−0.172
	(0.061)	(0.068)
Importance of success at work [1, 4]	−0.440**	−0.444**
	(0.000)	(0.000)
Female	−0.441**	−0.2389**
	(0.000)	(0.001)
Age	0.070*	0.039
	(0.011)	(0.151)
Age square	−0.001	−0.000
	(0.054)	(0.251)
Constant	−5.629**	−5.030**
	(0.000)	(0.000)
Pseudo R^2	11.93	14.83
Observations	17 547	17 547

Notes:
P-value in parentheses
** Significant at the 1% level
* Significant at the 5% level

The second model reveals some differences in respect to gender. Women have a smaller propensity to return to entrepreneurship than men, but with a smaller distinction than in the case of the novice entrepreneurs.

Table 5.3 investigates the differences between non-entrepreneurs, novice entrepreneurs and serial entrepreneurs in more depth. The first model analyses the propensity for novice entrepreneurs to turn to self-employment. The results are very similar to those for all entrepreneurs. This is consistent with the fact that novice entrepreneurs account for 75 per cent of all entrepreneurs. A university degree and work experience in small firms increase the likelihood of becoming self-employed for the first time. The longer someone works for a certain company the less likely he is to start his own firm. People with long job tenure are more likely to remain in paid employment. Obviously, they incur high opportunity costs in starting a venture. Correspondingly, unemployment is a major driver for setting up a business. These kinds of necessity start-ups are financially supported by the German government (for example IchAG). Between 2001 and 2004, the number of unemployed business founders more than tripled (KfW 2005).

Males, less risk averse and with large financial assets, have a higher propensity to become novice entrepreneurs. Others, especially those who focus on success at work, stay employed. Holding human capital, financial assets and so on indicates that predominantly for skilled labour in large corporations, paid employment promises higher rewards on average. Interestingly, the importance of self-fulfilment reduces the propensity to turn to entrepreneurship for the first time. In many cases, self-fulfilment is not associated with work, suggesting a negative relation with novice entrepreneurship.

Serial entrepreneurs have gained rich experience in running a business before (Model II) and they decide to re-enter self-employment. The results indicate that serial entrepreneurs are not driven by the importance of success at work and that they are not mainly motivated by money. Rather, they prefer to be their own boss. Work experience in small firms especially increases the propensity to start a business more than once. In contrast to novice entrepreneurs, financial assets do not increase the likelihood of re-entering self-employment. This implies that serial entrepreneurs have already used part of their financial assets at an earlier market entry. Employees are obligated to contribute to state-owned pension funds. Therefore, most former employees do not have to become self-employed in order to supplement their pension. Short job tenures with prior employers and a pro-risk attitude are good signals for identifying potential re-starters.

The direct comparison of novice and serial entrepreneurs reveals only small differences (Model III). Serial entrepreneurs do not normally turn from unemployment to self-employment. Necessity entrepreneurship is more typical for novice founders. The results for job tenure suggest that serial entrepreneurs have a rather unstable employment path.

Table 5.3   Differences between Novice and Serial Entrepreneurs

	Propensity to Turn to Self-Employment		
	Novice versus Non-Entreprs.	Serial versus Non-Entreprs.	Serial (1) versus Novice (0) Entreprs.
	(Model I)	(Model II)	(Model III)
University degree	0.729**	0.583*	−0.408
	(0.000)	(0.021)	(0.189)
Work experience in a small firm	0.681**	1.251**	0.573
(< 20 employees)	(0.000)	(0.000)	(0.069)
Job tenure at last employer	−0.030**	−0.073**	−0.052*
	(0.005)	(0.000)	(0.012)
Parents are/were self-employed	0.347	0.515	0.125
	(0.063)	(0.089)	(0.758)
Unemployed	1.213**	−0.756	−1.642**
	(0.000)	(0.118)	(0.002)
Retired	−0.402	−1.356*	−0.358
	(0.329)	(0.012)	(0.611)
Risk attitude [0, 10]	0.185**	0.198**	−0.018
	(0.000)	(0.000)	(0.769)
Financial assets (4 out of 6)	0.502**	0.0226	−0.468
	(0.000)	(0.402)	(0.150)
Importance of self-fulfilment [1, 4]	−0.246*	0.044	0.215
	(0.023)	(0.806)	(0.293)
Importance of success at work [1, 4]	−0.434**	−0.466**	−0.140
	(0.000)	(0.007)	(0.531)
Female	−0.425**	−0.536*	0.070
	(0.002)	(0.031)	(0.830)
Age	0.105*	0.082	0.014
	(0.003)	(0.087)	(0.846)
Age square	−0.001**	−0.000	0.000
	(0.004)	(0.555)	(0.547)
Constant	−6.260**	−8.463**	−2.335
	(0.000)	(0.000)	(0.177)
Pseudo R^2	12.07	9.99	13.95
Observations	17471	17293	330

Notes:
P-value in parentheses
** Significant at the 1% level
* Significant at the 5% level

They not only switch more often between self-employment and paid employment, but they also do not remain at one place of employment for a significant length of time. Concerning paid employment, novice entrepreneurs pursue a more stable employment path. Before turning to self-employment, they work for one employer for a significant amount of time. This indicates that serial entrepreneurs in particular are driven by opportunity and not by necessity (Westhead and Wright 1998).

CONCLUSION

Serial entrepreneurship represents a significant share of entrepreneurial activity in Germany: some 23 per cent of those who started a venture between 2002 and 2004 were previously self-employed. Although bankruptcy carries a stigma, failure does not discourage serial entrepreneurs. Certainly, market exit does not have to be forced by poor performance. Some entrepreneurs might exit voluntarily and then re-enter at a later point in time.

Market selection models imply that re-entry does not exist because the former entrepreneur cannot change his belief about his abilities and skills in operating a firm. He knows that he cannot be more profitable the second time around. However, the former entrepreneur could be confident that he will be luckier on his second attempt. Furthermore, serial entrepreneurs might augment their entrepreneurial abilities and skills through their former self-employment experience (Stam et al. 2006).

This study shows that serial entrepreneurs hardly differ from novice entrepreneurs. Nevertheless, serial entrepreneurs have an unstable work history, which cannot be characterized by unemployment but rather by a greater number of job changes – serial entrepreneurs not only switch between paid employment and self-employment but also more often between different employers. Serial entrepreneurship seems to be an attitude to life rather than driven by necessity or profitable opportunities. Another explanation for the similarities between novice and serial entrepreneurs might be that a novice entrepreneur can become a serial entrepreneur.

NOTES

1. As a consequence of the socialist system in the Eastern part of Germany, the self-employment rate in East Germany was only about 5 per cent in 1991. However, the East Germans were able to make up the leeway, and the self-employment rate in 2004 finally also constituted 10 per cent.

2. A list of recent publications based on the SOEP database is available on DIW's website (www.diw.de).

REFERENCES

Agarwal, Rajshree and David B. Audretsch (2001), 'Does entry size matter? The impact of the life cycle and technology on firm survival', *Journal of Industrial Economics*, **49**, 21–43.

Baldwin, John R. and Mohammed Rafiquzzaman (1995), 'Selection versus evolutionary adaption: learning and post-entry performance', *International Journal of Industrial Organization*, **13**, 501–22.

Brüderl, J., P. Preisendörfer and R. Ziegler (1992), 'Survival chances of newly founded business organizations', *American Sociological Review*, **57**, 224–42.

Camerer, C. and D. Lovallo (1999), 'Overconfidence and excess entry: an experimental approach', *American Economic Review*, **89**, 306–18.

Casson, Mark (2003), *The Entrepreneur: An Economic Theory*, Cheltenham, UK and Northampton, MA, USA: Edward Elgar.

Davidsson, Per and Benson Honig (2003), 'The role of social and human capital among nascent entrepreneurs', *Journal of Business Venturing*, **18**, 301–31.

Dunn, Thomas and Douglas Holtz-Eakin (2000), 'Financial capital, human capital and the transition to self-employment: evidence from intergenerational links', *Journal of Labor Economics*, **18**, 282–305.

Evans, David S. and Linda S. Leighton (1989), 'Some empirical aspects of entrepreneurship', *American Economic Review*, **79**, 519–35.

Frank, Murray Z. (1988), 'An intertemporal model of industrial exit', *Quarterly Journal of Economics*, **103**, 333–44.

Hyytinen, Ari and Pekka Ilmakunnas (2006), 'What distinguishes a serial entrepreneur?', paper presented at the workshop on Firm Exit and Serial Entrepreneurship, 13–14 January, Max Planck Institute of Economics, Jena, Germany.

Jovanovic, Boyan (1982), 'Selection and the evolution of industry', *Econometrica*, **50**, 649–70.

Kangasharju, A. and S. Pekkala (2002), 'The role of education in self-employment success in Finland', *Growth and Change*, **33**, 216–37.

KfW (2005), *MittelstandsMonitor 2005*, Frankfurt a.M.: Kreditanstalt für Wiederaufbau (KfW).

Kihlstrom, Richard E. and Jean-Jacques Laffont (1979), 'A general equilibrium entrepreneurial theory of firm formation based on risk aversion', *Journal of Political Economy*, **87**, 719–48.

Kim, Phillip H., Howard E. Aldrich and Lisa A. Keister (2006), 'Access (not) denied: The impact of financial, human, and cultural capital on entrepreneurial entry in the United States', *Small Business Economics*, **27**, 5–22.

Lucas, Robert E. (1978), 'On the size distribution of business firms', *Bell Journal of Economics*, **9**, 508–23.

Meager, N. (1992), 'Does unemployment lead to self-employment?' *Small Business Economics*, **4**, 87–103.

Mueller, Pamela (2006), 'Entrepreneurship in the region: breeding ground for nascent entrepreneurs?', *Small Business Economics*, **27**, 41–58.

Pakes, Ariel and Richard Ericson (1998), 'Empirical implications of alternative models of firm dynamics', *Journal of Economic Theory*, **79**, 1–45.

Parker, Simon C. (2004), *The Economics of Self-Employment and Entrepreneurship*, Cambridge: Cambridge University Press.

Stam, Erik, David Audretsch and Joris Meijaard (2006), 'Renascent men or entrepreneurship as a one-night stand. Entrepreneurial preferences subsequent to firm exit', paper presented at the workshop on Firm Exit and Serial Entrepreneurship, 13–14 January, Max Planck Institute of Economics, Jena, Germany.

Sternberg, Rolf (2000), *Entrepreneurship in Deutschland, Das Gründungsgeschehen im internationalen Vergleich, Länderbericht Deutschland 1999 zum Global Entrepreneurship Monitor*, Berlin: edition sigma.

Wagner, Joachim (2003), 'Taking a second chance: entrepreneurial restarters in Germany', *Applied Economics Quarterly*, **49**, 255–72.

Wagner, Joachim (2004), 'Are young and small firms hothouses for nascent entrepreneurship? Evidence from German micro data', *Applied Economics Quarterly*, **50**, 379–91.

Westhead, Paul, Deniz Ucbasaran, Mike Wright and Martin Binks (2005), 'Novice, serial and portfolio entrepreneur behaviour and contributions', *Small Business Economics*, **25**, 109–32.

Westhead, Paul and Mike Wright (1998), 'Novice, portfolio, and serial founders: Are they different?' *Journal of Business Venturing*, **13**, 173–204.

6. Productive, Unproductive and Destructive Entrepreneurship in an Advanced Transition Setting: The Example of Latvian Small Enterprises[*]

Arnis Sauka and Friederike Welter

INTRODUCTION

According to the entrepreneurship literature the nature and extent of entrepreneurial value creation affects not only the sustainability and success of the venture, but also influences its wider contribution to the development of the economy. At the society or economy level entrepreneurship and small and medium-sized companies (SMEs)[1] are generally viewed as contributing positively to economic growth (Kirzner 1973, Foss and Foss 2002). Although there are also diverse arguments (Brown et al. 1990, Davidsson and Delmar 2000, Dunne et al. 1996) from a macroeconomic perspective; several authors highlight the innovativeness and the potential for generating new jobs as a main role and particular strength of SMEs (Birch 1979, Storey 1994, for example). At the venture and individual levels, the value creation of the SME sector is commonly reflected by the expansion and growth of an enterprise, which involves both a monetary dimension such as the generation of profits, and a variety of sources of satisfaction, including non-pecuniary ones. Research also confirms SME activity and entrepreneurship as a driving force for economic growth in transition economies (Smallbone and Welter 2001).

Entrepreneurship, however, can take various forms, and not everything labelled as 'entrepreneurial' is actually desirable (Baumol 1990, 1993; Dallago 1997). On the one hand, it is often emphasized that the main engine of entrepreneurial activity is profit as well as various forms of self-fulfilment. On the other hand, Baumol (1993) points out that if we define entrepreneurs simply as people who are innovative when it comes to generating profits or adding to their power and prestige, it cannot be expected that they will be concerned with how much or little the activities employed to achieve these goals will contribute to the net economic output. In this context, a key question concerns the activities entrepreneurs pursue in order to create value, pointing to the necessity of distinguishing between 'positive' and 'negative' activities and their outcomes or, as Baumol argues (1990, 1993), productive, unproductive and destructive entrepreneurship.

Several authors (Baumol 1990, 1993; Dallago 1997, 2000; Foss and Foss 2002) have contributed to these concepts. Rent-seeking, in the form of litigation, lobbying, takeovers, tax evasion and avoidance efforts as well as the 'use of the legal system'; illegal and shadow activities, including drug dealing, prostitution, racketeering and blackmailing; and various forms of corruption are often mentioned with regard to unproductive or destructive entrepreneurship activities. Job generation and innovativeness, if not used for rent-seeking purposes, are mainly associated with a 'productive value' at society and economy levels (Baumol 1990, 1993; Foss and Foss 2002, Dallago 2000, for example). In general it can be argued that at a firm level unproductive entrepreneurship may constrain the more long-term growth prospects of enterprises in situations where the development of new markets is dependent on increased legal compliance and legitimacy (Welter and Smallbone 2004). At the economy level unproductive entrepreneurship may hamper the contribution of entrepreneurship to economic development. Davidsson and Henrekson (2002, p. 1) emphasize that productive entrepreneurship is an 'essential factor of the economic performance of a country'. Little work, however, has been done to assess the value creation of small firms from this perspective, either in transition or in more advanced economy contexts.

Against this background, we set out to explore different forms of entrepreneurship in an advanced transition setting, that is, a country which has recently joined the European Union. We use a novel approach to develop a conceptual framework for the analysis of SME value creation. Empirically the chapter draws on a survey of SMEs in Latvia, which was conducted in early summer 2005. The chapter is structured as follows: In the section 'Productive, Unproductive, Destructive Entrepreneurship and Value Creation: A Conceptual Review' we review the literature on these three types of entrepreneurship and on the link to performance and value creation in order to develop our conceptual framework. In 'Sample and Methodology' we operationalize these concepts and introduce the data. The subsequent section presents the main results and the final section provides conclusions and implications for further research.

PRODUCTIVE, UNPRODUCTIVE, DESTRUCTIVE ENTREPRENEURSHIP AND VALUE CREATION: A CONCEPTUAL REVIEW

The Concept of Productive, Unproductive and Destructive Entrepreneurship

Analysing the determinants which influence the allocation of entrepreneurial inputs and the flow of entrepreneurial talent, and drawing on examples from economic history, Baumol (1990, 1993) distinguishes between productive, unproductive and destructive entrepreneurship activities. Productive entrepreneurship 'refers, simply, to any activity that contributes directly or indirectly to net output of the economy or to the capacity to produce additional output' (Baumol 1993, p. 30). Innovation can be perceived as a productive contribution of entrepreneurs, for example, as can those financial activities which facilitate production, or any activities which contribute to producing goods and services (Baumol 1993). Foss and Foss (2002) add to this by introducing the element of new discovery, referring to 'productive entrepreneurship' as the discovery of new attributes, opportunities, procedures and the like, where the discovery leads to an increase in joint surplus.

Research demonstrates that in a transition context productive entrepreneurship cannot be taken for granted (for example, Aidis 2006, Kuznetsov et al. 2000, Manolova and Yan 2002, Peng 2000, Smallbone and Welter 2001, Van de Mortel 2002, Yan and Manolova 1998). Aidis (2006), for example, distinguishes between two main levels influencing decision making: environmental factors (such as micro and macro environment and the role of government) and personal factors (such as norms, values and individual characteristics and skills). All factors together influence an individual's decision making and awareness regarding the selection between productive or unproductive entrepreneurship. Dallago (2000) emphasizes the importance of social capital in order to produce a social basis for trust, reputation and relational contracts, pointing out that this does not suffice to explain the allocation of these factors to productive use, but that this is essential in order to have a proper economic system.

A key idea in defining unproductive and destructive entrepreneurship is that not all that is entrepreneurial is necessarily desirable. Often, an entrepreneur makes no productive contribution to the real output of an economy, and in some cases even plays a destructive role (Baumol 1990). This happens when the structure of pay-offs in an economy is such as to render unproductive activities like rent-seeking more profitable than productive activities (Baumol 1993). In this light, Baumol argues that the allocation of resources to either productive or unproductive usage varies according to the society. Weak and unstable formal institutions (Baumol 1990), and norms and societal values (Welter and Smallbone 2004) might foster unproductive entrepreneurship.

Unproductive and destructive entrepreneurship can take many forms (Baumol, 1990, 1993; Dallago, 1997, 2000). These include, but are not limited to, rent-seeking, illegal activities and shadow activities, different forms of corruption, and others. Rent-seeking mainly refers to activities whose objective is the 'acquisition of some of the monopoly profit or the economic rents currently generated or potentially available in the economy' (Dallago 1997, p. 104). Baumol (1993, p. 51) emphasizes rent-seeking as the 'expenditure of resources in (deliberate) pursuit of economic rents by means that do not (automatically) contravene the accepted rules of society'. Examples include the granting of exclusive licences, or the enactment of laws by which the productive process is affected directly or through litigation. Various forms and types of rent-seeking can be distinguished, such as litigation, takeovers, tax evasion and avoidance efforts or acquiring a monopoly, as well as different uses of the legal system; and rent-seeking seems to constitute the prime threat to productive entrepreneurship (Baumol 1993). Rent-seeking activity can be innovative (Dallago 1997, 2000; Baumol 1990, 1993), such as the discovery of a previously unused legal gambit that is effective in diverting rents to those who are first exploring it, or 'smart' speculative financial transactions, for example. Such an activity, however, does not contribute much, if any, value to the productive capacity of an economy (Baumol 1990).

Illegal entrepreneurial activities are mostly associated with activities such as production and distribution of illegal drugs, racketeering and blackmail. Although likely to be profitable, this type of entrepreneurial behaviour is seen as unproductive because little, if any, value is added to the economy and society (Baumol, 1993). Moreover, these activities contravene the legal and normative framework of a society. This type of activity will have a destructive effect on the economy, especially if it attracts followers.

In relation to a transition context, several empirical studies show that legal and illegal or grey activities coexist and most new and small firms are actually involved both in productive and rent-seeking activities at the same time (for example, Glinkina 2003, Los 1992, Rehn and Taalas 2004, Scase 2003, Smallbone and Welter 2001). In early transition conditions where the legislation and rules are not yet in place, deviant activities such as tax avoidance can well be necessary to ensure the survival and growth of the enterprise, thus making a substantial or at least some contribution to economic development (Smallbone and Welter 2006).

Performance, Outcomes and Value Creation

There appears to be no lack of suggestions but also no consensus concerning the question of which activities can actually be regarded as unproductive, productive or destructive. The key challenge here is that in practice there are only few genuine 'unproductive entrepreneurship activities' (Davidsson and Wiklund 2001, Davidsson 2004). As argued by Baumol himself (1993), activities tainted by rent-seeking, for example, cannot be regarded as unproductive in every case. Referring to the link between economic growth and the volatility of new venture creation, Davidsson and Wiklund (2001, p. 91) suggest that some rent-seeking efforts may also have a significant positive impact on the growth of both the firm and the economy. They argue, for example, that 'legal, yet redistributive' and 'illegal, yet societal beneficial' entrepreneurial activities are both possible and should not be disregarded as marginal phenomena.

In this context, the authors draw attention to the outcomes of these activities, distinguishing between outcomes on the individual (venture) and societal levels, which result in four types of enterprise (Davidsson and Wiklund 2001, Davidsson 2004): 'hero' or 'success enterprises', 'robber' or 're-distributive enterprises', 'catalyst' and 'failed enterprises' (Figure 6.1).

Individual (Venture)-Level Outcome

	+	-
+ Societal-Level Outcome	Quadrant I Hero or success enterprises	Quadrant II Catalyst enterprises
-	Quadrant III Robber or redistributive enterprises	Quadrant IV Failed enterprises

Source: Davidsson and Wiklund (2001, p. 91) and Davidsson (2004, p. 13)

Figure 6.1   New Enterprise Outcomes on Different Levels

They conclude that most existing studies tend to portray new enterprises as belonging to either the 'hero' or the 'failed' type. However, as they argue further, 'there are reasons to believe that neither robber nor catalyst enterprises are marginal phenomena that could be disregarded' (Davidsson and Wiklund 2001, p. 91), suggesting that catalyst enterprises, for example, may have a significant impact on the economy.

According to Davidsson and Wiklund (2001), hero enterprises (Quadrant I, Figure 6.1) are those creating value for society through the introduction of new combinations while simultaneously creating personal wealth. This type of entrepreneur benefits both from making profits and/or achieving personal goals as well as adding value to society. In the context of Baumol's concept, they are 'analytically unproblematic' and basically form the bulk of productive entrepreneurship (Davidsson 2004).

The robber enterprise (Quadrant III, Figure 6.1) creates personal wealth but little if any value for society. That means that a company makes profits and/or owners (or managers) achieve their personal goals, but that this type of enterprise does not add anything to economic growth, because it is mainly involved in illegal and rent-seeking activities.

Failed enterprises (Quadrant IV, Figure 6.1) represent genuine failures, in other words, enterprise attempts that never take off, therefore lacking any positive spillover effect on other actors (Davidsson and Wiklund 2001). One could argue that this type of business activity can be disregarded from the point of view of value creation. In an early-stage transition context, however, such an activity can bring value to society in the long run, as it allows entrepreneurs to learn by doing and to accumulate management experience.

Catalyst enterprises (Quadrant II, Figure 6.1) represent cases where, albeit unsuccessful at the firm level, companies do add something to society and the economy. Baumol (1993) and Dallago (1997), for example, state that all that is necessary for entrepreneurship to be productive is for an activity to yield a positive marginal product. In this context situations can arise where ideas and methods developed by one enterprise are imitated or sometimes stolen and successfully exploited by others (Davidsson and Wiklund 2001). In such a situation the initial inventor of the product or service does not make any profit, but might still contribute to society by having driven the process of discovery and creative destruction. Another case of this type of entrepreneurship would be when the potential threat of the new enterprise leads competitors to make innovative responses that benefit society while keeping the new enterprise out of the market (Davidsson and Wiklund 2001).

Developing a Conceptual Framework

As can be seen from the literature review, most of the previous work refers to productive, unproductive and destructive entrepreneurship in terms of activities. There is no agreement in the literature concerning SME value creation (see, for example, Baumol 1990, 1993; Dallago 1997, 2000; Foss and Foss 2002) as to whether productive or unproductive entrepreneurship refers to activities only, or to outcomes, or to both. As argued by entrepreneurship scholars (Davidsson and Wiklund 2001, Davidsson, 2004), 'unproductive entrepreneurship activities' can also bring some positive outputs both on the venture level and the economy level. On the other hand, 'productive entrepreneurship activity' on the firm level will not necessarily lead to a successful company performance or a contribution to society. This mix of two different dimensions – behaviour and outcome – in combination with a blurred and often inappropriate use of terminology, could be a key to the problems which arise in the further development of this concept and in its empirical assessment. We therefore suggest that there is a need to distinguish between activities and output in order to assess productive and unproductive entrepreneurship and value creation empirically (Figure 6.2).

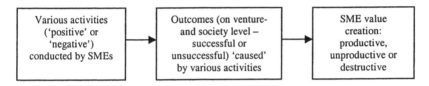

Source: Authors

Figure 6.2   Assessment of SME Value Creation: Productive, Unproductive or Destructive Entrepreneurship

In the context of this discussion, activities as such cannot be productive, unproductive or destructive as argued by Baumol (1990, 1993), but need to be assessed together with their outcomes. These include any of the entrepreneurs' efforts aimed at profit making or personal satisfaction. Referring to the notion that the generation of profits and 'achievement satisfaction' are the main driving forces behind entrepreneurship behaviour,[2] we argue that activities usually occur on the venture level. Drawing on an institutionalist perspective, we can distinguish between 'conforming' and 'deviant' activities (Warren 2003, Welter and Smallbone 2003). 'Conforming' entrepreneurship activities involve, for example, paying taxes, honest competition and so on. 'Deviant' entrepreneurship activities include rent-seeking and corruption as well as different kinds of illegal, shadow and unethical behaviours.

Our classification of deviant activities within a transition context is given in Table 6.1. It should be noted, however, that several activities could fall into more than one category. Tax evasion and other rent-seeking activities as well as 'order self-generation', for example, can also take illegal forms.

Rather than offering clear cut-offs, our classification should be understood as a first approximation of the type of conforming and deviant activities conducted by SMEs in a transition context.

Table 6.1   Examples of 'Deviant' Activities within a Transition Context

'Rent-seeking' activity	Unethical behaviour	Illegal activity
Litigation	Nomenclature business	Racketeering
Lobbying	*Blat*	Prostitution
Takeover	Order self-generation activity	Illegal drug dealing
Different forms of tax evasion and avoiding efforts	Squeezing out of market	Different forms and kinds of unofficial payments
Acquiring monopoly profit		

Source: Authors, based on Baumol (1990, 1993).

Both conforming and deviant activities could result in 'positive' and 'negative' value creation on both venture and society levels. An activity would have a positive outcome if it contributed successfully to the development of a venture or an economy, and vice versa. It is therefore outcomes on different levels, 'created' by different activities of SMEs, which result in productive, unproductive or destructive entrepreneurship from the point of view of value creation. In this context, both short-term and long-term effects should be considered, as some deviant activities may have a positive, but short-term impact either on company performance or on the company's contribution to the growth of the economy, while in the long term the same activities might lead to a harmful outcome.

Considering the difficulties of providing a clear-cut distinction between different entrepreneurial activities and in line with Dallago (1997, p. 104), who suggested that the entrepreneur's social role can be productive in the sense that he contributes directly or indirectly to the net output of the economy or to the capacity to produce additional output, we suggest supplementing the existing concept (see Figure 6.1) with two additional categories, namely 'directly productive' and 'indirectly productive' entrepreneurship.

Our approach is presented in Figure 6.3. Quadrant I represents directly productive entrepreneurship, where SMEs perform successfully on both venture and society levels, thus creating value on both the economy and firm levels. 'Indirectly productive entrepreneurship' can be represented either by Quadrant II or Quadrant IV. In the former case, although SMEs are not successful on the venture level, they can still bring some 'indirect' value to society, as discussed above with regard to followers. Learning by doing from an unsuccessful previous business experience can be one example of an indirectly productive contribution of companies as represented by Quadrant IV. Unproductive entrepreneurship in Quadrant II is mostly associated with a lack of managerial ability to implement innovative ideas, products or services or to exploit opportunities. Finally, Quadrant III represents either unproductive or destructive value creation.

In this context, the key question of our empirical analysis in the following sections is which activities entrepreneurs pursue in order for their business to expand and grow and also to gain personal satisfaction, and how the nature and extent of these activities influence the value a company creates in terms of productive, unproductive or destructive entrepreneurship.

Individual Level

	Quadrant I	Quadrant II
+	Directly productive entrepreneurship	Unproductive or indirectly productive entrepreneurship
-	Quadrant III	Quadrant IV
	Unproductive or destructive entrepreneurship	Unproductive, indirectly productive

Society Level

Source: Authors, based on Davidsson and Wiklund (2001, p. 91), Davidsson (2004, p. 13)

Figure 6.3   Directly and Indirectly Productive, Unproductive and Destructive SME Entrepreneurship

SAMPLE AND METHODOLOGY

Sample

A total of 133 face-to-face interviews were conducted in Riga, Latvia during May and June 2005. The interviewees were randomly sampled. The sampling frame was defined to include owners and owner-managers of SMEs (less than 250 employees, including sole proprietorship) who had the right to sign business documents of that particular enterprise, whose firms were registered in Riga and were operational at the time of the survey. Company data were obtained from official statistics of the Latvian Company Register, collected in the Lursoft (www.lursfot.lv) database. Riga, the capital city of Latvia, was chosen as almost one-third of the whole population of Latvia lives there, and nearly 60 per cent of the companies are registered in Riga. Tables 6A.1 and 6A.2 in the Appendix present selected characteristics of entrepreneurs and their firms.

The interviews were carried out in Latvian and Russian, depending on the preferences of each respondent. Although a standardized questionnaire was used, the interviews were carried out in the form of conversations. In order not to lead respondents, most questions were open. On average, interviews lasted 100 minutes, with a minimum of one and a maximum of four hours. Initially, potential interviewees were contacted by phone. Out of 550 contacts, 142 agreed to interview. Four of those did not appear due to time restraints. Another five were excluded as they were obviously neither owners nor owner-managers.

How to Measure Productive and Unproductive Entrepreneurship

In this chapter, we employ an explorative approach to look at productive, unproductive and destructive entrepreneurship. We analyse what kind of 'conforming' and 'deviant' activities are conducted by Latvian SMEs. We then have a look at outcomes, attempting to classify these and assessing which activities create which type of outcome on the venture and society levels. In order to achieve this, we classified the questions in the survey instrument according to whether they measured activities or performance, capturing both short- and longer-term perspectives. Tables 6.2 and 6.3 show our classification of activities and outcomes.

Outcomes at the venture and society levels

The venture-level outcome of SMEs is usually captured by indicators representing company expansion and growth. Society- (or economy-) level performance is measured by innovativeness and job generation, as these indicators are considered the main contribution of SMEs to economic development.

Table 6.2   Classification of 'Conforming' and 'Deviant' Activities in the Questionnaire

Rent-seeking versus Conforming Activity	Unofficial Payments Activity versus Conforming Activity	Unethical Behaviour versus Conforming Activity
Under-reporting business income	Unofficial payments in general	Using old networks
Under-reporting number of employees		Order self-generation activity
Concealing actual salary (envelope wages)		Squeezing newcomers out of market
		Picking up business idea

Source: Authors' own survey.

Table 6.3   Classification of Outcomes on Different Levels in the Questionnaire

Venture-Level Performance Indicators	Society-Level Performance Indicators
1. Expansion and growth Short-term generation of profits and turnover Long-term generation of profits and turnover	**1. Innovativeness** Different types of innovative outcomes
2. Satisfaction Personal fulfilment	**2. Employment generation** Short-term employment generation Long-term employment generation
	3. Perceptions about contribution to society

Source: Authors' own survey.

When assessing job generation, it would be good to know what type of jobs we are talking about. Few studies have analysed the quality of jobs provided by SMEs (such as Wagner 1997, for example), and this shortcoming also holds true for our survey. Moreover, at this stage of our data exploration, we set aside the innovation indicator because of problems involved in adequate usage of this indicator to capture the society dimension of entrepreneurial value creation. Instead, we included an indicator to capture the perceptions of SME owners as regards their own contribution at the society level. As exemplified by several empirical studies (Davidsson 1991, for example), perceptions have a strong influence on the behaviour of owners and owner-managers. Table 6.3 gives an overview of the indicators used to measure SME performance on different levels.

EXPLORING PRODUCTIVE, UNPRODUCTIVE AND DESTRUCTIVE ENTREPRENEURSHIP EMPIRICALLY: MAIN RESULTS FROM THE SURVEY

From both short-and longer-term perspectives, the surveyed SMEs show a positive tendency in terms of expansion and company growth. With regard to the short-term perspective, a large share of respondents reported an increase in profits and turnover compared to the year prior to the survey, although only few were able to increase profits and turnover to a considerable extent (more than 40 per cent), obviously reflecting a downturn in the economic situation in 2004 (Table 6.4). Considerable increases are more pronounced in a longer-term perspective both for profits and turnover. Interestingly, respondents scored highly on personal fulfilment, with nearly one-quarter being very satisfied and 50 per cent being satisfied to a great extent.

As regards SMEs' contribution on a society level, almost 60 per cent of the companies surveyed reported stable employment compared to 12 months previously, while in a longer-term perspective a considerable share of companies had contributed to job generation. About 30 per cent of respondents had generated additional employment in the year prior to the survey, with only a small share reporting decreased employment. Companies also show a rather positive attitude regarding their perception of their contribution to society.

We now continue to analyse the activities SMEs pursue in order to achieve these outcomes. It should be noted, however, that the tendencies towards positive outcomes on both the venture and society levels in different time perspectives influence the results and should therefore be considered throughout the further analysis.

Table 6.4   SME Outcomes on Venture and Society Levels

	Venture-Level Outcomes				Society-Level Outcome	
	Short-Term Profits	Short-Term Turnover	Long-Term Profits	Long-Term Turnover	Short-Term Employment	Long-Term Employment
Increased considerably	8.3	9.0	21.1	25.6	6.0	15.0
Increased	42.1	54.9	39.1	45.9	23.3	27.8
Stable	27.1	18.8	15.0	9.0	59.4	39.8
Decreased	18.8	13.5	16.5	10.5	8.3	9.0
Decreased considerably	1.5	1.5	3.0	3.8	0.8	3.0
	Personal Satisfaction				**Perception about Contribution to Society**	
Yes, to a very great extent	24.8				9.0	
Yes, to a great extent	49.6				39.1	
Yes, to some extent	18.0				32.3	
Yes, to a small extent	2.3				15.0	
No	3.8				4.5	

Source: Authors' own calculations.

With regard to rent-seeking activities and outcomes on different levels, our results suggest that at the venture and society levels the most successful companies are those that are less involved in under-reporting their business income or the number of employees. Firms who reported more than 75 per cent of their business income, for example, also showed an increase in short-term profits, although this trend is not consistent, as 40 per cent of those firms with a decrease in profits also had a high level of reporting. Similar results are to be observed for short-term employment growth as a society indicator and for long-term profits and turnover as venture indicators, when explored in the light of under-reporting either business income or the number of employees. Based on these preliminary results, we therefore suggest that companies which are less involved in under-reporting results are more successful at both venture and society levels, regardless of the indicator used to capture their outcomes. More specifically, we can also argue that SMEs that have a lower level of under-reporting results gain more personal satisfaction from business and also have a higher perception of their general contribution to society.

Regarding our indicator 'concealing actual salary (envelope wages)', the above-mentioned tendency is weaker, but still existent. At both the venture and the society levels, those companies which report half of their actual salary perform best. However, here our results also demonstrate that a larger share of under-reported wages also benefits SMEs. In general, it looks as if it were rather profitable for companies to conceal actual salaries. Interestingly, no considerable differences can be observed when comparing short- and longer-term perspectives in this regard.

Concerning unofficial payments, a large share of those companies which stated that they are 'sometimes' involved in unofficial payments in order to get things done were able to increase profits and turnover, and they also stated a high personal fulfilment. Obviously, despite Latvia having joined the EU in 2004, the Latvian business environment is still characterized by elements connected to early transition stages. It should be noted, however, that there appears to be no clear trend with regard to the relationship between venture-level outcomes and deviant activities. A considerable number of those companies which reported an increase in profits and turnover were involved in unofficial payments either 'frequently' (14 out of 133) or 'never' (15 out of 133).

When analysing the indicator 'Using old networks (blat) to get things done', it should be noted that the term '*blat*' is perceived differently in different stages of transition (see Ledeneva 1998 for an overview of what *blat* meant in Soviet times and what it means in transition). In an advanced stage of transition, *blat* refers more to gaining advantages from friends or people with whom entrepreneurs have good personal contact. Those contacts, or 'personal networking', usually occur with government representatives or with representatives from both SMEs and large firms. In the former case, blat resembles 'lobbying', where its main purpose is to influence legislation or to obtain orders. In the case of *blat* between firms, however, such 'personal networks' are mostly employed to increase sales volume by attracting orders or to ensure better conditions for supplies, and so on.

On the other hand, *blat* is also not entirely 'networking' as understood in more advanced economies. As the previous experience of most of the entrepreneurs in the study was during Soviet times (one-third of the entrepreneurs and managers interviewed reported at least 15 years' previous experience in business management, for example, and the same share had been managers of state-owned companies during Soviet times), for them *blat* represents both elements of 'Soviet' networking and the networking to be expected in an advanced market economy. The main point to keep in mind here is that such activities almost always include 'additional payments' and thus are classified as deviant activity. In this context, our data show that performance seems to be better for those companies which often draw on old networks, regardless of whether we explore this issue at a venture or society level, or from a short-term or long-term perspective.

While *blat* appears to be an accepted or at least tolerated kind of activity, thus actually contributing to venture performance and economic development, this changes for the rest of the types of unethical behaviour we studied in the survey. With regard to order self-generation, squeezing newcomers out of the market and picking up business ideas, those companies which reported that they had 'never' been involved in this type of activity performed best. However, here we need to take into account a possible bias in our survey, namely, that entrepreneurs might be hesitant to talk about these activities.

CONCLUSIONS

Our results can be summed up by the following main conclusions. First, although productive, unproductive and destructive entrepreneurship can be rather clearly assessed from a conceptual point of view, it is much more complicated to measure this empirically. Second, those SMEs which are less involved in deviant activities appear to perform better. Third, the same activities which bring value at the venture level also contribute to the society level; and fourth, there is no considerable difference in the contribution of activities to output from either a short-term or long-term perspective. Furthermore, our empirical results also suggest that deviant activities can lead to both successful and unsuccessful outcomes, and the results also confirm previous studies by indicating a mixture of conforming and deviant activities in SMEs.

The most appropriate way to look at productive, unproductive and destructive entrepreneurship is in terms of the value companies create at either the venture or the society level. This, in turn, is a result of either deviant or conforming behaviour of entrepreneurs. In this context, it can be argued that in order to be productive, SMEs first of all have to generate successful outcomes at the venture level. At the same time, however, a company should also contribute positively to the net economy output. An obvious conclusion would be that if one of these elements is missing, although an enterprise can contribute positively at either the venture or the society level, in general entrepreneurial activity would not lead to productive value creation.

Our study is not without its limitations. It should be emphasized that the results presented here only give us a first insight into tendencies regarding the contribution of conforming and deviant activities to SME value creation at different levels. First, our sample is small. Second, in order to gain a more insightful and accurate picture a next step will be to use a multivariate statistical approach.

Nevertheless, we believe that this chapter makes a number of important contributions. First, we operationalize the concept introduced by Baumol (1990) in an attempt to explore the value creation of new and small firms. Second, we make an empirical contribution to the study of entrepreneurship in a transition setting in its own right, by assessing the value creation of small firms in an advanced transition economy. Third, our findings may have important implications for policy makers and actors involved in supporting entrepreneurs and small firms in new European Union (EU) member states.

In terms of implications for future research, apart from the difficulties involved in defining clear-cut points to classify different kinds of conforming and deviant activity, there are of course also limits as to what can be done to assess SME value creation empirically. The main and most challenging limitation of our current approach is the difficulty involved in capturing the 'total outcome' at the society level. In this regard, this study should be perceived as aiming for the 'best possible available solution', rather than as representing 'perfect research'. It would be more appropriate to exploit the issues raised here based on longitudinal data instead of using a retrospective approach. Most of the data necessary for this kind of study are not available in existing databases, however, and would be difficult to acquire through a standardized survey-based approach, as SME entrepreneurs are often reluctant to talk about the 'dark' sides of their entrepreneurial activities.

In terms of implications for policy makers, it is of primary interest to find out what determines the supply of productive entrepreneurship and what means can be used to expand it. According to Baumol (1993, p. 47):

> we do not have to wait patiently for slow cultural change in order to find measures to redirect the flow of entrepreneurial activity toward more productive goals. It may be possible to change economic rules in ways that help to offset undesired institutional influences or supplement other influences to work in beneficial directions.

In the light of our results as presented here we suggest that policy makers in an advanced transition context should be more flexible regarding taxation policies and different administrative regulations, for example. The main challenge for policy makers is to facilitate market entry (and exit) as well as to improve the general environment in order to stimulate expansion and growth of SMEs, without introducing too much bureaucracy.

NOTES

*   Financial support from the TeliaSonera Institute at the Stockholm School of Economics in Riga is gratefully acknowledged. We would like to thank Professor Per Davidsson for valuable comments on earlier versions of the chapter. Any shortcomings are the responsibility of the authors.
1.   There are a number of arguments in the entrepreneurship literature stating that entrepreneurship and SMEs are often 'linked together in a very loose fashion' (Storey and Sykes 1996). One of the main explanations in this regard is that SMEs cannot be viewed as smaller versions of large companies. SMEs handle business in a different way; they have a smaller resource base and less market power than larger enterprises (Burns 2001). On the other hand, although there is no lack of suggestions, there is no commonly accepted definition of what constitutes entrepreneurship. Thus, whether large or small, enterprises could be regarded as one unit of analysis in which entrepreneurship takes place. This chapter explores entrepreneurship at the level of SMEs, considering its importance in terms of innovativeness, employment generation and fostering economic growth in general.
2.   Although referring to Baumol's quote of Veblen (1904) and Hobsbawm (1969), we argue that the main driving force behind entrepreneurship is profit (also in terms of personal fulfilment), we should note that entrepreneurs can also be driven to do business for other reasons, something which has been picked up in the recent discussion on social entrepreneurship. Baumol (1990, p. 10) describes another example, referring to nobles in the context of the Early Middle Ages: 'Many of the turbulent barons enjoyed fighting for its own sake, and success in combat was an important avenue to prestige in their society'. In a different manner, of course, this notion could also apply to today's entrepreneurs.

REFERENCES

Aidis, R. (2006), *Laws and Customs: Entrepreneurship, Institutions and Gender During Transition*, SSEES Occasional Series, University College London, London.

Baumol, W. (1990), 'Entrepreneurship: productive, unproductive and destructive', *Journal of Political Economy*, **98**, 893–921.

Baumol, W. (1993), *Entrepreneurship, Management and the Structure of Payoffs*, London: MIT Press.

Birch, D. (1979), *The Job Generation Process*, Cambridge, MA: MIT Press.

Brown, C., J. Hamilton and J. Medoff (1990), *Employers Large and Small*, Cambridge, MA: Harvard University Press.

Burns, P. (2001), *Entrepreneurship and Small Business*, Basingstoke: Palgrave Macmillan.

Dallago, B. (1997), 'The economic system, transition and opportunities for entrepreneurship', in OECD (ed.), *Entrepreneurship and SMEs in Transition Economies, the Visegrad Conference*, Paris: OECD.

Dallago, B. (2000), 'The organisational and productive impact on the economic system: the case of SMEs', *Small Business Economics*, **15**, 303–19.

Davidsson, P. (1991), 'Continued entrepreneurship: ability, need, and opportunity as determinants of small firm growth', *Journal of Business Venturing*, **6**, 405–29.

Davidsson, P. (2004), *Researching Entrepreneurship*, New York: Springer.

Davidsson, P. and F. Delmar (2000), 'The characteristics of high-growth firms and their job contribution', in B. Green (ed.), *Risk Behaviour and Risk Management in Business Life*, Dordrecht: Kluwer, pp. 204–13.

Davidsson, P. and M. Henrekson (2002), 'Determinants of the prevalence of start-ups and high-growth firms', *Small Business Economics*, **19** (2), 81–104.

Davidsson, P. and J. Wiklund (2001), 'Levels of analysis in entrepreneurship research: current research practice and suggestions for the future', *Entrepreneurship and Theory Practice*, **25** (4), 81–100.

Davidsson, P. and M. Henrekson (2002), 'Determinants of the prevalence of start-ups and high-growth firms', *Small Business Economics*, **19** (2), 81–104.

Dunne, T., M. Roberts and L. Samuelson (1996), 'Patterns of firm entry and exit in US manufacturing industries', in Z.J. Acs (ed.), *Small Firms and Economic Growth*, Vol. 1, Cheltenham, UK and Brookfield, US: Edward Elgar, pp. 278–305.

Foss, K. and K.J. Foss (2002), 'Economic organisation and the trade-offs between productive and destructive entrepreneurship', in N. Foss and P. Klein (eds), *Entrepreneurship and the Firm: Austrian Perspectives on Economic Organisation*, Cheltenham, UK and Northampton, MA, USA: Edward Elgar, pp. 102–27.

Glinkina, S. (2003), 'Small business, survival strategies and the shadow economy', in Robert J. McIntyre and B. Dallago (eds), *Small and Medium Enterprises in Transitional Economies*, New York: Palgrave Macmillan, pp. 51–63.

Hobsbawm, E. (1969), *Industry and Empire from 1750 to the Present Day*, Harmondsworth: Penguin.

Kirzner, I. (1973), *Competition and Entrepreneurship*, Chicago, IL: University of Chicago Press.

Kuznetsov, A., F. McDonald and O. Kuznetsova (2000), 'Entrepreneurial qualities: a case from Russia', *Journal of Small Business Management*, **38** (1), 101–7.

Ledeneva, A.V. (1998), *Russia's Economy of Favours: Blat, Networking and Informal Exchange*, Cambridge: Cambridge University Press.

Los, M. (1992), 'From underground to legitimacy: the normative dilemmas of post-communist marketization', in B. Dallago, G. Ajani and B. Grancelli (eds), *Privatization and Entrepreneurship in Post-Socialist Countries: Economy, Law and Society*, New York: St Martin's Press, pp. 112–42.

Manolova, T. and A. Yan (2002), 'Institutional constraints and entrepreneurial responses in a transforming economy', *International Small Business Journal*, **20**, 163–84.

Peng, M. (2000), *Business Strategies in Transition Economies*, Thousand Oaks, CA, London, New Delhi: Sage.

Rehn, A. and S. Taalas (2004), '"Znakomstva I svyazi" (Acquaintances and connections): Blat, the Soviet Union and mundane entrepreneurship', *Entrepreneurship and Regional Development*, **16**, 235–50.

Scase, R. (2003), 'Entrepreneurship and proprietorship in transition: policy implications for the SME sector', in R. McIntyre and R. Dallago (eds), *Small and Medium Enterprises in Transitional Economies*, London: Palgrave Macmillan, pp. 64–77.

Smallbone, D. and F. Welter (2001), 'The distinctiveness of entrepreneurship in transition economies', *Small Business Economics*, **16**, 249–62.

Smallbone, D. and F. Welter (2006), 'Conceptualising entrepreneurship in a transition context', *International Journal of Entrepreneurship and Small Business*, **3** (2), 190–206.

Storey, D. (1994), *Understanding the Small Business Sector*, London: Routledge.

Storey, D. and N. Sykes (1996), 'Uncertainty, innovation and management', in P. Burns and J. Dewhurst (eds), *Small Business and Entrepreneurship*, 2nd edition, Basingstoke: Macmillan, pp. 73-93.

Van de Mortel, E. (2002), *An Institutional Approach to Transition Processes*,

Aldershot: Ashgate.

Veblen, T. (1904), *The Theory of Business Enterprise*, New York: Scribner.

Wagner, J. (1997), 'Firm size and job quality: a survey of the evidence from Germany', *Small Business Economics*, **9** (5), 411–25.

Warren, E. (2003), 'Constructive and destructive deviance in organizations', *Academy of Management Review*, **28** (4), 622–31.

Welter, F. and D. Smallbone (2003), 'Entrepreneurship and enterprise strategies in transition economies: an institutional perspective', in D. Kirby and A. Watson (eds), *Small Firms and Economic Development in Developed and Transition Economies: A Reader*, Aldershot: Ashgate, pp. 95–114.

Welter, F. and D. Smallbone (2004), 'Comments on entrepreneurship and value creation from an individual and environmental perspective', paper presented at the Rencontre-de-St Gall, Appenzell, Switzerland, September.

Yan, A. and T.S. Manolova (1998), 'New and small players on shaky ground: a multicase study of emerging entrepreneurial firms in a transforming economy', *Journal of Applied Management Studies*, **7** (1), 139–43.

APPENDIX

Table 6A.1   Individual-Level Characteristics

Variable	Measurement scale	Frequency	%
Age	Under 24	2	1.5
	25–34	25	18.8
	35–44	47	35.3
	45–60	44	33.1
	60–75	15	11.3
Gender	Female	45	33.8
	Male	88	66.2
Ethnicity	Latvian	73	54.9
	Russian	45	33.8
	Other	15	11.3
Education	Primary school education	1	0.8
	Professional (non secondary) education	2	1.5
	Secondary-school professional education	26	19.5
	Secondary-school education	24	18.0
	University-level education: undergraduate	66	49.6
	University-level education: graduate (engineer	6	4.5
	University-level education: graduate (master)	7	5.3
	PhD degree	1	0.8
Citizenship	Latvian	108	81.2
	Alien	25	18.8
Civil status	Married	93	69.9
	Unmarried	26	19.5
	Divorced	12	9.0
	Widowed	2	1.5
Years of previous business experience	No previous experience	22	16.5
	Less than 1 year	5	3.8
	1–3 years	15	11.3
	4–7 years	25	18.8
	8–11 years	19	14.3
	12–15 years	6	4.5
	16–19 years	20	15.0
	20 years and more	21	15.8

Table 6A.1 Individual-Level Characteristics (cont'd)

Variable	Measurement Scale	Frequency	%
Type of previous business management experience (answer is Yes)	Worked for state company during USSR times	41	30.8
	Had unsuccessful private business, learned a lesson	17	12.8
	Had private business which still existed	16	12.0
	Worked for private company, same sector	40	30.1
	Worked for state company, same sector	27	30.3
	Worked for private company, different sector	17	12.8
	Worked for state company, different sector	20	15.0
	Worked as a family help for family-owned business	11	8.3
	Got some business experience from abroad	17	12.8
	No previous experience	20	15.0
Previous business training (courses, seminars) before starting current business?	Yes	50	37.6
	No	83	62.4
Additional employment: Other business excluding this one?	Company now owned by respondent	23	17.3
		30	22.6
Main reason for starting business	To provide income to live/ survive	22	16.5
	To increase personal household family income	9	6.8
	As an alternative to unemployment	6	4.5
	To be independent	12	9.0
	Self-fulfilment	8	6.0
	Desire to have own business	21	15.8
	To respond to market opportunities	28	21.1
	Dissatisfaction with previous employment	7	5.3
	Had resources available	8	6.0
	Other	8	6.0

Table 6A.2   Venture-Level Characteristics

Variable	Measurement Scale	Frequency	%
Number of employees	1–9	65	48.9
	10–49	50	37.6
	50–249	18	13.5
Year of foundation (actual start of business operations)	1990–93	32	34.1
	1994–97	39	29.3
	1998–2001	54	40.6
	2002–2005	8	6.0
Legal form of business	Individual merchant	3	2.3
	Limited liability company	124	93.2
	Joined Stock Company	6	4.5
Main activities (first priority)	Manufacture	19	14.3
	Wholesale trade	19	14.3
	Retail trade	30	22.6
	Service	63	47.4
	Construction	2	1.5
Main customers (first priority)	Local private firms	69	51.9
	Foreign private firms	5	3.8
	State enterprises	7	5.3
	Municipal enterprises	1	0.8
	Individuals (non-juridical persons) from Latvia	46	34.6
	Individuals (non-juridical persons) from abroad	5	3.8
Ownership (number of company owners)	1 owner	64	48.1
	2–3 owners	52	39.1
	More than 3 owners	17	12.8
Involvement in business	Full-time	116	87.2
	Part-time	17	12.8
Type of start -up	From scratch	91	68.4
	Using the assets of another company owned or co-owned by you	18	13.5
	Using privatized assets	1	0.8
	From existing state-owned enterprise's assets or facilities	7	5.3
	Took over or bought an existing business	16	12.0

Table 6A.2   Venture-Level Characteristics (cont'd)

Variable	Measurement Scale	Frequency	%
Networking (first priority partners)	No involvement in networking	59	44.4
	Local SMEs	54	40.6
	SMEs from abroad	9	6.8
	Big local private companies	5	3.8
	Big foreign private companies	2	1.5
	Local state companies	1	0.8
	Government	1	0.8
	Other	2	1.5
Type of networking (answer Yes)	New products/service generation	20	15.0
	Improvements in existing products/ services	58	43.6
	To expand within main products market, local	55	41.4
	To expand within main products market, abroad	14	10.5
	Enter new local markets	26	19.5
	Enter new markets abroad	12	9.0
	To create new business	6	4.5
Current performance: profits	No profits	15	11.3
	Less than 5%	29	21.8
	6–15%	51	38.3
	16–30%	29	21.8
	31–45%	4	3.0
	46–60%	1	0.8
Current performance: export volume	No exports	109	82.2
	Less than 5%	12	9
	5–25%	7	5.3
	26–50%	1	0.8
	51–75%	3	2.3
	76–95%	0	0
	More than 95%	1	0.8

Table 6A.3 Conforming versus Deviant Activities

I. Rent-seeking versus Conforming Activities

Variable	Measurement Scale	Frequency	%
Under-reporting business income (net profits)	Report 100% of actual income	19	14.3
	Report more than 75%	45	33.8
	Report 51–75%	29	21.8
	Report 31–50%	20	15.0
	Report 11–30%	14	10.5
	Report less than 10%	5	3.8
Under-reporting number of employment	Report 100% of actual employees	69	51.9
	Report more than 75%	41	30.8
	Report 51–75%	15	11.3
	Report 31–50%	3	2.3
	Report 11–30%	3	2.3
	Report less than 10%	0	0
Hiding actual salary (envelope wages)	1/1 Reported salary is equivalent to 'unofficial'	19	14.3
	1/2	42	31.6
	1/3	33	24.8
	1/4	23	17.3
	1/5	6	4.5

II. Unofficial Payments Activity versus Conforming Activity

Variable	Measurement Scale	Frequency	%
Involvement in unofficial payments	Always	2	1.5
	Frequently	27	20.3
	Sometimes	47	35.3
	Seldom	22	16.5
	Never	34	25.6
	Missing	1	0.8

III. Other Deviant versus Conforming Activity

Variable	Measurement Scale	Frequency	%
Using old	Always	13	9.8
networks	Frequently	52	39.1
	Sometimes	26	19.5
	Seldom	16	12.0
	Never	25	18.8
Order self-	Yes, very often	3	2.3
generation	Yes, often	7	5.3
activity	Yes, but seldom	22	16.5
	Yes, but very rarely	27	20.3
	No, never	73	54.9
Squeezing	Yes, very often	4	3.0
newcomers out of	Yes, often	14	10.5
market	Yes, but seldom	18	13.5
	Yes, but very rarely	20	15.0
	No, never	75	56.4
Picking up	Yes, very often	0	0
business ideas	Yes, often	11	8.3
	Yes, but seldom	20	15.0
	Yes, but very rarely	20	15.0
	No, never	81	60.9

7. Working Part-Time or Full-Time? On the Impact of Family Context and Institutional Arrangements on Atypical Work: A Cross-National Comparison of Female Self-Employment in Western and Eastern Europe

Robert Strohmeyer and Vartuhi Tonoyan*

INTRODUCTION

Although the number of self-employed women has grown recently in most of the OECD countries (OECD 2001), gender-specific differences in self-employment rates (the 'gender gap') still persist, with women being significantly less likely to become self-employed than men. Attempts to explain gender-specific variations in self-employment have mainly focused on the determinants of women's and men's entry into entrepreneurship. However, previous approaches toward understanding recent increases in female self-employment have largely neglected to investigate the actual character and the quality of the jobs of self-employed women (for exceptions see Arum 1997, Arum and Müller 2004, Kraus et al. 2006).

In contrast, recent evidence has shown that women's long-standing increase in self-employment has been accompanied by an expansion of women's commitment to part-time work (see Leicht and Strohmeyer 2005 for a descriptive overview). Against this background, this study sets out to explore in depth why women become increasingly engaged in part-time self-employment across Western, Eastern and Southern Europe. In this context, women's choice of part-time self-employment is understood as a response to the individuals' personal characteristics on the one hand and the country's institutional environment (political, economic and sociocultural institutions) on the other. More exactly, when examining the impact of individual variables on part-time self-employment, we mainly concentrate on the respondent's family composition (number and age of small children in the household and the presence of a partner or husband). A special focus is put on the question of whether women's choice of part-time self-employment can be attributed to their wish to reconcile work and family responsibilities. However, attributing women's choice of engaging in part-time self-employment solely to their wish to remain flexible fails to provide explanations for international discrepancies in part-time self-employment across European countries. Another important question thus arises in this context, namely, whether women's choice of part-time self-employment is also institutionally bound. Moreover, does part-time self-employment vary across different institutional contexts in Western and Eastern Europe, that is, countries with varying economic and political rules and organizations as well as sociocultural norms (Shane 2003)?

This study is organized as follows. First we give definitions of part-time self-employment. This is followed by the presentation of the theoretical model as well as hypotheses highlighting the impact of individual and institutional determinants on women's choice to enter part-time self-employment. The next section introduces empirical data and describes the methods of this study. Then we present empirical results. The final section summarizes our findings and concludes with implications for research and policy.

PART-TIME SELF-EMPLOYMENT: ON DEFINITION AND TYPES

Before developing specific hypotheses concerning the impact of single determinants on part-time self-employment, we first want to give a definition of part-time work. Analysing previous research, it becomes clear that there is no all-encompassing definition of part-time work which could be employed in cross-country research on industrialized countries. In official statistics, such as those of the European Commission, part-time work is considered to be any reduction of working time in relation to regular full-time work. However, this definition seems to be problematic for our research study: on the one hand, part-time work conceals a considerable diversity between countries, industries and occupations (Hakim 1997, p. 30), and on the other hand, this definition is not applicable to self-employed people, since a standard measure of working hours does not exist for the self-employed. Keeping this in mind, we therefore prefer a fixed threshold to define part-time work. Aware of the fact that this threshold is rather arbitrary, we define part-time self-employment as a form of gainful occupation for less than 35 hours per week.

As pointed out by Hakim (1997, pp. 23–33), the term 'part-time' encompasses a broad range of working forms and working arrangements. Hakim (1997) argues that a conceptual framework which differentiates between various types of part-time jobs across industrialized countries has to be advanced to understand the attractions of part-time employment for an employee or employer. In this study, a slightly modified classification by Hakim (1997) (for employees) is employed to distinguish between three possible types of women's part-time self-employment, namely 'reduced hours' self-employment (30–35 hours a week), 'half-time' self-employment (15–29 hours a week) and marginal self-employment (10–14 hours a week).

THE MICRO-LEVEL PERSPECTIVE: EXPLAINING WITHIN-COUNTRY DIFFERENCES IN PART-TIME SELF-EMPLOYMENT

Family Context: Presence of Young Children

According to Sainsbury (1994), public policies aimed at supporting women's integration into the labour markets, even those adopted by the egalitarian welfare states in Scandinavia, have not been effective enough to change the household division of labour between women and men dramatically. Across all industrial countries, women still bear the main responsibility for childrearing, independent of the type of welfare regime and country-specific family and child policies (Stier et al. 2001, p. 1734). Recent research suggests that this is partially due to prevailing (conservative) social norms towards the division of labour in the household. Across most European societies, the majority of women and men still accept and even prefer the sexual division of labour that allocates domestic responsibilities to the female and the income-earning role to the male (Hakim 1997, p. 38). However, family obligations and especially the presence of small children restrict women's involvement in the labour market. This implies that if women were voluntarily to choose the responsibility for household chores and if they wanted to be economically active at the same time, they would have to find adequate (flexible) forms of employment (for example part-time self-employment or home-based work) which demanded a lower work input and enabled authority and control over work schedules and places of work.

Part-time work is thus considered an important way of incorporating women into the labour market, since it is perceived as a solution for coping with women's multiple roles as mothers and workers. According to Pfau-Effinger (2004, 2005), part-time jobs are attractive to women because of the 'gender contract', a phenomenon which describes prevailing norms and rational calculations about the sexual division of labour within the family, with housework and childrearing being ascribed to women, and work outside the home and earning income to men. Therefore, women's self-selection into part-time jobs may reflect their rational decision to enjoy higher flexibility in order to combine work and family activities (Becker 1981). In this regard, previous research has provided empirical support for the hypothesis that self-employment is a form of occupation which provides women (and especially mothers) with flexibility in terms of their workplaces and work schedules (for US evidence see studies by Carr 1996, Heller Clain 2000, Lombard 2001, and Boden 1996, 1999; for a cross-country comparison see Lohmann 2001, 2004). Following this strand of argument, we put forward the hypothesis that part-time self-employment may be preferred over full-time self-employment, because it allows women higher flexibility in terms of combining work and family responsibilities:

Hypothesis 1: The likelihood of engaging in part-time self-employment is dependent on the presence of small children in one's household. Generally, the presence of a small child increases the probability of engaging in part-time self-employment to reconcile work and family responsibilities.

Family Context: Presence of Partner

Marriage is assumed to be a valuable asset for both spouses (Becker 1965, 1976). Collectively, a married couple can put up more financial, human and social capital to achieve a certain goal. One could argue that the likelihood of a self-employed woman engaging in part-time work is strongly linked to the occupational status and workload of her spouse or partner. More exactly, the decision to choose household work (as opposed to participating in the labour market) depends on the availability of the partner's specific resources. In this context, the amount of time needed for the production of a certain output or service as well as the individual's specific human capital are considered to be valuable goods. Moreover, opportunity costs of undertaking a certain activity (either participating in the labour market or performing household work) play a crucial role.

Against this background, one could assume that the decision to engage in part-time self-employment is linked to the presence of a partner or spouse. Assuming that a married couple jointly maximizes the expected (monetary and non-monetary) benefits of the family, it is logical to expect that the household division of labour will be based on the productivity of each partner (in both the household and the labour market). More specifically, it seems to be very intuitive to assume that having a spouse or partner as the family's main wage earner would positively impact upon the self-employed woman's willingness to engage in part-time self-employment. In doing so, the self-employed woman will not only be able to remain economically independent of her husband or partner, but will also take on the responsibilities of fulfilling family and household tasks, for example raising children, cooking, cleaning or caring for elderly people in the household. In contrast, not having a partner or husband may decrease the likelihood of engaging in part-time self-employment due to lower expected income from a part-time job.

Hypothesis 2: Having a partner or husband increases the probability of engaging in part-time self-employment. In contrast, not having a partner or husband decreases the probability of entering part-time self-employment.

THE MACRO-LEVEL PERSPECTIVE: TYPES OF WELFARE STATES IN EUROPE

However, does the presence of small children in one's household have the same consequences for the likelihood of becoming involved in part-time self-employment across Western and Eastern Europe? An important question in this context is why self-employed women are more likely to become engaged in part-time self-employment in some countries than in others. In this regard, we argue that the welfare states' institutional environments (Shane 2003, pp. 146–60; Strohmeyer et al. 2005), and particularly policies regulating women's reconciliation of family and work (political environment), economic environment (societal wealth or GNP per capita) and sociocultural values and norms concerning the household division of labour and women's role in the society (sociocultural environment), have an important bearing on women's choice to enter part-time self-employment.

It is well documented that welfare states differ in the supply of publicly supported measures (such as childcare coverage, maternity leave entitlement, voluntary family leave, flexible arrangement of working time and social tax policies) which indirectly influence women's participation in the labour market (Sainsbury 1994, Gornick et al. 1997, Korpi 2000, OECD 2001, pp. 129–66). Conservative welfare states such as (West) Germany, Austria and the Netherlands largely support a traditional male breadwinner model (or secondary female breadwinner model). Priority is given to general family support, in the form of cash child allowance, family tax benefits for small children and tax benefits for mothers staying at home, for example. Public daycare services exist predominantly for older children (above three years old), but not for smaller ones (under 3 years old). Full-time childcare is rather limited in such welfare states. Lohmann (2001, p. 6) argues that one has to differentiate between East and West Germany as far as the role of the welfare state in the support of female employment is concerned. Although East Germany has (more or less) adopted the Western economic and political system since the reunification in 1990, there are still large differences both in the public provision of childcare for the youngest children and in public attitudes towards female participation in the labour market. Compare, in this context, 2 per cent of children under three years old as well as 60 per cent of those aged between three and six years old in publicly funded childcare in West Germany with 16 per cent of children under three years old and 87 per cent of children aged between three and six years old in publicly funded childcare in East Germany (Engelbrech and Jungkunst 2001, p. 2; Spieß et al. 2002).

In contrast, social democratic welfare states in Scandinavia largely support a dual-earner model, gender equality and women's active participation in the labour market. A long paid maternity leave, the existence of public daycare services for very young children (0–2 years old) and full-time childcare in nursery schools enable mothers to remain flexible, thus without being handicapped by the presence of small children in the household. Consequently, women's involvement in the labour market is high. A favourable institutional context for women's participation in the labour market can be seen in Sweden, where full-time childcare is the rule rather than the exception, with 60 per cent of Swedish nursery children attending publicly supported all-day childcare institutions. Higher female participation rates as well as women's higher involvement in full-time jobs are typical for the welfare states in Scandinavia. Interestingly, France shows similar patterns to the Scandinavian-type 'dual-earner' models, with governmental policies actively supporting the employment of mothers, granting broad coverage of public childcare (full-time nursery schools) and issuing rather generous parental leave policies (Lohmann 2001, p. 6; Laulom 2004, pp. 85–121).

Similar to the social democratic welfare states' in Scandinavia, former Socialist countries largely supported equal gender participation in the labour market, with women being as likely to engage in full-time activities as men (Drobnic 1997). The existence of public daycare services for small children and full-time childcare in nursery schools have enabled mothers to reconcile work and family responsibilities. However, there is a lack of research on the contemporary institutional infrastructure in Eastern Europe, that is, there are no reliable statistics which would provide information on the institutional infrastructure (such as full-time nursery schools, day nurseries and so on) of the new EU member states. Little is also known about prevailing social norms and values concerning the woman's role in Eastern Europe. On the one hand, one could assume that the Socialist legacy of the dual-earner model may have left long-lasting effects on societal values, thus encouraging women to engage in full-time activities. On the other hand, one may argue that the Socialist ideology on gender equality has been imposed on the citizens by the state 'from above', thus not reflecting the latter's true conservative social values and norms (compare the revival of conservative, Catholic values in Poland as well as the prevalence of traditional values in Hungary, Slovenia and the Czech Republic; Drnakova 2006, pp. 17–19).

Finally, liberal and laissez-faire welfare states like the US or the UK maintain policies orientated towards stimulating individuals to forge their own destiny. Public involvement in family policies is weak. Childcare facilities are provided on a private basis, and no public support for the provision of childcare facilities (or other family support-orientated services) exist (Gustafsson and Wetzels 1997, p. 120). Moreover, parental leave in the UK is short, with very small income compensation (Esping-Andersen 1990, Gustafsson and Wetzels 1997, p. 118).

Against this background, one could assume that the effect of having children on the probability of engaging in part-time self-employment will vary substantially between different institutional arrangements. Since conservative welfare states in Western Europe largely foster a traditional male breadwinner model, the impact of children on a woman's decision to engage in part-time self-employment will be the strongest in this type of welfare state. In contrast, the share of self-employed women working part-time will be the lowest in the new EU member states, given the lower societal wealth (lower GNP per capita) and consequently weaker financial situation of Eastern European households. Equally, poorly designed political support for childcare after the collapse of the Socialist system in Eastern Europe may reinforce women's likelihood to become engaged in full-time self-employment.

Hypothesis 3: The share of women's part-time self-employment will vary substantially between welfare states with different institutional (political, economic and societal) environments.

Hypothesis 3a: The share of women having children and therefore being engaged in part-time self-employment will be the highest in conservative welfare states. In contrast, the share of women having small children and therefore being involved in part-time self-employment will be the lowest in post-Socialist countries in Eastern Europe.

DATA, VARIABLES AND METHODS

The database is the European Labour Force Survey (Eurostat 2005). A total of 85 000 self-employed women (aged between 20 and 64), working either part-time or full-time in non-agricultural sectors, are analysed in this study. Twenty-five Western and Eastern European countries were chosen and classified into five regional groups (see Table 7.1).

The dependent variable measures whether the respondent works on a part-time or full-time basis. In line with Hakim (1997), we define part-time self-employment as a form of gainful occupation which encompasses less than 35 hours per week. Independent variables refer to the respondent's age (proxy for working experience), occupation, industry (manufacturing, service, trade and so on) and family composition, the latter describing the presence of children and a partner or husband in the household.

Heckman Probit Model

The rationale behind the use of the Heckman probit model is similar to the error correction procedure known as the 'Heckman correction model' which is commonly used in econometrics to control for the sample selectivity bias in Mincerian types of earnings equation (see Heckman 1979). In the latter type of model, the selectivity term is used to correct the estimates of the regression coefficients in the earnings equation of employed workers for the existence of jobless individuals, that is, unemployed or economically inactive people with different characteristics.

The difference between a Heckman correction model and Heckman probit model is that in the former the dependent variable of the main equation is not a continuous, but a dummy variable, which takes the value 1 if the self-employed woman works on a part-time basis, and the value 0 if she works on a full-time basis. To control for the possible sample selection bias (which results from the exclusion of those who have chosen to be an employee rather than self-employed), the beta-coefficients of the main probit regression model are corrected by a term estimated simultaneously by the maximum likelihood technique in the Heckman selection equation. The dependent variable of the 'selection equation' takes the value 1 if the individual has chosen to be self-employed and the value 0 if she has become an employee. The Heckman estimation is thus a two-stage equation model. The first equation, the selection, predicts the probability of having entered self-employment (value 1) as opposed to having entered dependent employment (value 0). The second equation, the main estimation model, estimates the determinants of the self-employed woman's choice of part-time work (versus full-time work), while correcting simultaneously for the sample selection bias.

Table 7.1   Share of Female Part-Time Self-Employed and Part-Time Employees* (%)

	Self-Employed	Employees
DK	32.3	38.1
FI	27.4	21.5
NO	40.3	43.4
SE	32.1	35.9
AT	33.2	45.1
BE	25.7	47.7
D-West	38.2	48.4
FR	17.8	34.9
IE	41.1	41.4
LU	29.3	42.1
NL	68.2	77.2
GR	10.5	20.1
IT	32.3	38.2
PT	21.5	11.6
ES	14.7	23.9
CZ	13.7	7.4
EE	25.4	10.4
HU	15.0	8.1
IS	40.9	34.3
LT	16.3	16.2
LV	21.7	12.7
PL	13.3	18.4
SI	4.7	7.1
D-East	14.0	30.6
SK	8.3	5.5

Notes: * Part-time is defined as work for 'less than 35 hours a week'.

Source: The European Labour Force Survey (Eurostat 2005); Authors' calculations.

Why is it important to control for the sample selection bias? Ignoring the sample selection bias, that is, the problem that the dependent variable (part-time self-employment) is observed for a restricted, non-random sample (more exactly, only for those respondents who have already chosen to be self-employed but ignoring those who have become employees), would lead us to an overestimation of the predicted values, thus generating misleading conclusions about the significance of the independent variable(s) (Heckman 1979).

Marginal Effects

Furthermore, we estimate marginal effects, that is, changes in the predicted probabilities of the dependent variable, namely, the probability of being part-time self-employed, associated with the changes in the explanatory variable for all 19 countries investigated (Greene 2003). The objective of this method is to examine whether having a child and a partner ('family effect') increases the probability of engaging in part-time self-employment in conservative welfare states more strongly than in Eastern European countries, as predicted in Hypotheses 3 and 3a. A further advantage of this method is that in comparison to probit model coefficients marginal effects can easily be interpreted as changes in predicted probabilities.

Marginal effects are calculated using estimates of a discrete (Heckman probit) choice model. The dependent variable predicts the probability of being part-time self-employed (versus full-time self-employed), thus representing a discrete choice model, when all but one independent variable are held constant.[1] This single independent variable is a dummy, which takes the value 1 if a self-employed woman has a family, that is, both a child (aged either 0–9 or 10–19 years old) and a partner, and the value 0 if she has no family, that is, neither child nor partner. First, the probability of being part-time self-employed (versus full-time self-employed) is calculated, taking into account that a self-employed woman does not have either a partner or a child ('no family'). Second, the effects of having a child (either aged 0–9 or 10–19 years old) and having a partner ('family effect') are estimated for the probability of being part-time self-employed. The marginal effect of 'having a family' (versus 'not having a family') is then an algebraic difference between the predicted probabilities of being part-time self-employed and having a family on the one hand, and the probability of being part-time self-employed and not having a family on the other.

EMPIRICAL FINDINGS

Development of Part-Time Self-Employment in EU-15 Countries

Figure 7.1 compares a ten-year development (1995–2005) of women's and men's part-time self-employment and full-time self-employment in the EU-15 countries. It becomes evident that women's part-time self-employment cannot be treated as a marginal issue of the EU-15 countries' labour markets, but has become a pervasive type of occupation during this time period. Representing an increase of 54 percentage points, women's part-time self-employment grew more rapidly than women's full-time self-employment (15 percentage points) during 1995–2005. Surprisingly, one also observes an increasing trend in men's part-time self-employment: Compared to men's full-time self-employment (an increase of 4 percentage points), men's part-time self-employment grew considerably during 1995–2005, representing a difference of 54 percentage points.

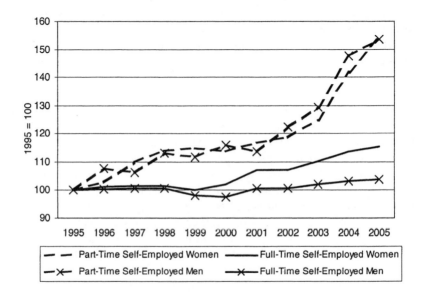

Notes: * based on respondents' own assessment.

Source: European Labour Force Survey (Eurostat 2005); Authors' calculations.

Figure 7.1   Development of Part-Time* Self-Employment in EU-15 Countries

Table 7.1 depicts East–West differences in the share of women's part-time self-employment. The Netherlands is on the top of the ranking, with an outstanding 68 per cent of self-employed women working part-time. Equally, a large share of about 40 per cent of self-employed women are engaged in part-time work in Ireland as an economically liberal welfare state. Moreover, part-time self-employment is quite a widespread phenomenon, comprising about one-third of all self-employed women, in both corporatist welfare states in Western Europe and social democratic states in Scandinavia. More precisely, the share of self-employed women working part-time comprises 38 per cent in West Germany, 33 per cent in Austria, 32 per cent in Denmark and Sweden, 29 per cent in Luxembourg, 27 per cent in Finland and 26 per cent in Belgium. In sharp contrast, countries with the lowest share of part-time self-employment are found in Eastern Europe and the Baltic region, with Slovenia (5 per cent), Slovakia (8 per cent), Poland (13 per cent), the Czech Republic (14 per cent) and Hungary (15 per cent) being cases in point. Part-time self-employment is also very low in East Germany (14 per cent). Equally, part-time self-employment is less widespread in Southern Europe: Only 11 per cent, 15 per cent and 21 per cent of self-employed women work on a part-time basis in Greece, Spain and Portugal respectively.

Furthermore, a simple correlation analysis between the country's share of female part-time self-employed and the share of female part-time employees shows a high correlation (Pearson r: 0.86). With the exception of France, Belgium and Estonia, one observes that most countries lie close to the regression line, thus implying that the higher the country's ratio of part-time employees (to total employees), the higher its ratio of part-time self-employed (to the total number of self-employed), and vice versa. We assume that this very high and positive interdependence between the country's share of (women's) part-time self-employment and (women's) part-time employment points to the existence and importance of country-specific institutional environments that affect these two forms of gainful occupation in the same way.

Marginal, Half-Time and Reduced-Hours (Part-Time) Self-Employment: East–West Comparison

However, as pointed out by Hakim (1998), part-time work encompasses different qualities and types of work across different countries. More precisely, one has to differentiate between three types of part-time work, namely marginal work, half-time jobs and reduced-hours work. One must be cautious about equating marginal part-time work – usually less than 15 hours a week and thus often referring to unskilled work – with part-time work that makes up half of an average full-time job (15–30 hours a week). In the same vein, the comparison between marginal work and reduced-hours work (30–35 hours a week), the latter deviating only slightly from full-time work, does not seem theoretically justifiable (see Figure 7.2).

Looking at Figure 7.3, it becomes clear that marginal part-time self-employment shows the same pattern as overall part-time self-employment in Eastern and Western Europe. More specifically, the highest percentage of marginal self-employment can be found in the Netherlands, where almost every fourth self-employed woman works in a marginal job. Moreover, a disproportionately high percentage of self-employed women are also engaged in marginal jobs in West Germany (14.1 per cent), Austria (10.19 per cent), Norway (10.1 per cent) and Ireland (9.7 per cent). At the same time, marginal part-time work does not play a crucial role in most Southern European and Eastern European countries.

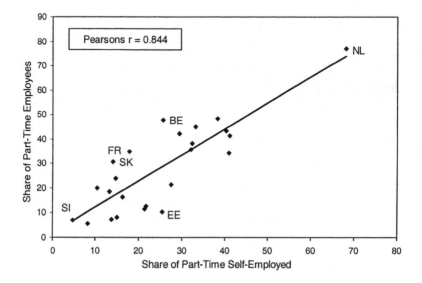

Source: European Labour Force Survey (Eurostat 2005); Authors' calculations.

Figure 7.2   Correlation between Women's Share in Part-Time Self-Employment and Women's Share in Dependent Employment across 25 European Countries

On the other hand, the majority of female entrepreneurs are involved in 'half-time' self-employment, encompassing between 15 and 30 hours a week. In contrast, a kind of part-time self-employment, almost as work-intensive as a full-time job and therefore described as 'reduced-hours self-employment' can be found in the Netherlands (12.7 per cent), Ireland (9.0 per cent) and Scandinavian countries – with Denmark (12.2 per cent), Sweden (9.4 per cent), Finland (9.2 per cent) and Norway (8.9 per cent) being cases in point.

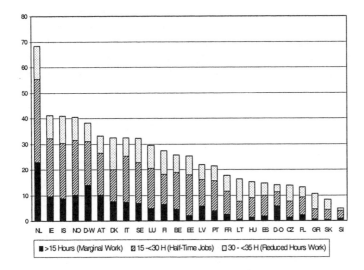

Source: European Labour Force Survey (Eurostat 2005); Authors' calculations.

Figure 7.3 Marginal Self-Employment, Half-Time Self-Employment and Reduced-Hours Self-Employment: East–West Comparison

Results from Regression Analysis (Heckman Probit Model)

Can small children be considered an underlying factor of women's part-time self-employment, when controlling for other factors such as the presence of a partner, the respondent's age, the existence of a second job and firm characteristics (firm size, firm industry and firm age)? Are children still an important determinant of women's choice to enter part-time self-employment, when correcting for the sample selection bias as well as taking into account country-specific institutional differences in Western and Eastern Europe?

Looking at the results for 19 Western and Eastern European countries[2] obtained from the Heckman probit model, the following can be summarized (see Table 7.2). First, having a young child (aged between 0 and 9 years) is closely associated with part-time self-employment in 15 out of the 19 countries investigated. Countries in which the presence of a young child does not impact upon the self-employed woman's decision to engage in part-time work are Belgium, Greece, Latvia and the Slovak Republic.

Interestingly, the values of the beta-coefficients (significance at the 1 per cent level) of the independent variable 'children aged between 0 and 9 years' are the highest in conservative welfare states, such as the Netherlands (0.769),

Germany (0.606) and Austria (0.468), as assumed in Hypothesis 3a. Equally, part-time self-employment seems to be a solution for the reconciliation of work and family responsibilities in Ireland. This is consistent with the hypothesis that economically liberal welfare states with weak public support for childcare force self-employed women to engage in part-time work to meet work and family duties.

Table 7.2   Heckman Probit Estimation: Part-Time versus Full-Time Self-Employment

Country	Children 0–9 years	Children 10–19 years	Partner
Austria	0.468**	0.122	0.395**
Belgium	0.055	0.045	0.105
Germany–West	0.744**	0.368**	0.303**
Germany–East	0.620**	0.324+	-0.139
France	0.236**	-0.111	0.249**
Ireland	0.474**	0.085	0.249**
Luxembourg	0.371*	0.603**	0.374**
The Netherlands	0.769**	0.246**	0.443**
Greece	0.068	0.092	0.000
Italy	0.338**	0.195**	0.070**
Portugal	0.270**	-0.085	0.018
Spain	0.272**	0.030	0.166**
Czech Republic	0.477**	-0.109	0.121
Estonia	0.468**	0.122	0.395**
Hungary	0.358**	0.139*	-0.076
Lithuania	0.346*	0.294*	-0.074
Latvia	-0.665	0.012	-0.079
Poland	0.347**	-0.045	-0.423**
Slovenia	0.746*	-0.290	-0.503
Slovak Republic	-0.141	0.159	0.348*

Notes:
* Significant at 5 %
** Significant at 1 %
Selected results; other variables controlled for refer to education, age, holding a second job, employer versus own-account worker, industry and duration of self-employment.

Source: European Labour Force Survey (Eurostat 2005); Authors' calculations.

In the same vein, small children are an apparent reason for engaging in part-time self-employment in all Mediterranean welfare states but Greece. The strongest effect can be observed in Italy (0.338), followed by Spain (0.272) and Portugal (0.270).

On the other hand, young children affect the self-employed woman's decision to engage in part-time work in Eastern European countries such as Estonia (0.468), the Czech Republic (0.477), Hungary (0.358) and Poland (0.347) as well, which seems to be counter-intuitive at this stage, thus rejecting the hypothesis of the 'Socialist dual-earner model' in the new EU member states.

At the same time, the effect of older children (aged between ten and 19 years) on part-time self-employment is significant only in six out of the 19 countries investigated. Apparently, caring for older children does not require as much time and effort as caring for young children (up to nine years old). Interestingly, countries where older children affect women's decisions to engage in part-time self-employment are primarily conservative Western European welfare states, namely the Netherlands (0.246), Luxembourg (0.603) and Germany (0.249). This again supports the hypothesis that women's part-time self-employment in conservative welfare states can be considered a response to both conservative social norms and public policies encouraging women to be a secondary breadwinner, thus taking on the main responsibility for family-related tasks.

Marginal Effects of Family Structure on Part-Time Self-Employment: Do Institutions Matter?

As shown in Figure 7.4, the marginal effects of the family on part-time self-employment are strongest in conservative welfare states in Western Europe, that is, West Germany (0.580), the Netherlands (0.533), Luxembourg (0.353) and Austria (0.245). The marginal effect of the family on the likelihood of engaging in part-time self-employment is 0.242 in Ireland. On the other hand, the marginal effects of the presence of children and partner on the probability of engaging in part-time self-employment are very modest in Southern Europe, ranging from 0.041 for Portugal to 0.026 for Greece, for example. The exception to the rule is Italy, where the marginal effect of the family on part-time self-employment (0.207) is almost as strong as in Ireland, for instance.

In sharp contrast, the marginal effects of the family on women's part-time self-employment are weakest in Eastern Europe. More specifically, the probabilities of being a self-employed part-timer 'without family' are 0.068 and 0.018 in Hungary and the Czech Republic respectively, while the probability of being a self-employed part-timer 'with family' is 0.145 and

0.056, thus representing a very modest increase of 0.077 for Hungary and 0.038 for the Czech Republic respectively. Similarly, no marginal differences can be observed for the Slovak Republic (0.003), Latvia (0.000), Lithuania (-0.008), Poland (0.022) or Slovenia (-0.003). This implies that the inclination for women to become engaged in part-time self-employment does not increase in the new EU member states if they are bound by family restrictions such as the presence of a small child and a partner.

This leads us to conclude that cross-country differences in women's part-time self-employment are certainly a result of different institutional environments.

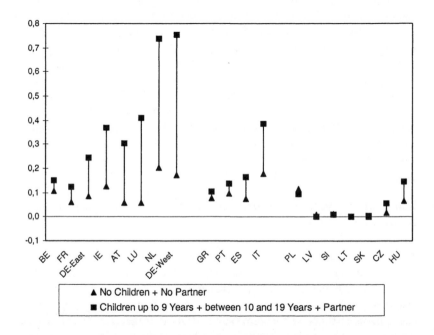

▲ No Children + No Partner

■ Children up to 9 Years + between 10 and 19 Years + Partner

Notes:
The length of the line from (triangle) bottom to (square) top shows the marginal effect of having a family.
Predicted probabilities are conditional on selection of being self-employed.

Source: European Labour Force Survey (Eurostat 2005); Authors' calculations.

Figure 7.4   Marginal Probability of Working Part-Time (versus Full-Time) as an 'Average' Self-Employed Woman with and without Family

SUMMARY AND DISCUSSION

When analysing gender-specific differences in entrepreneurship, previous research has mainly focused on the quantitative aspects of female- and male-owned small ventures, such as those relating to women's and men's entry rates into self-employment as well as performance differences of their firms. In sum, gender-specific deviations in self-employment rates ('gender gap') or firm performance (employment and sales growth, firm innovativeness and so on) have been the main topics around which previous (gender-related) research has revolved. However, previous research has largely failed to examine the actual character and quality of the work of self-employed people (for exceptions see Arum 1997 or Arum and Müller 2004). More specifically, we do not know whether the increase in women's self-employment (across most industrialized countries of Western Europe) has been accompanied by an increasing trend in women's commitment to part-time self-employment as an atypical work form (Lewis 2001, Hakim 1997), thus representing an increasing 'marginalization' of their work (Arum 1997, Arum and Müller 2004).

To fill this gap, we have advanced an alternative approach, focusing on the qualitative aspect of women's self-employment. One of the central findings of our study is that the recent increase in the number of self-employed women across EU-15 countries between 1995 and 2005 is largely associated with an increasing 'marginalization' of their work. While women's part-time self-employment grew by 54 per cent, women's full-time self-employment experienced only an increase of 15 per cent during 1995–2005. We thus clearly observe a trend towards 'atypical' or 'non-standard' work (Lewis 2001) which cannot be treated as a marginal issue either by social science scholars or by those promoting self-employment at the political level. Equally, we notice a dramatic increase of 54 per cent in men's part-time self-employment during the same period, as opposed to a moderate growth of men's full-time self-employment of only 4 per cent. This implies that policies crudely equating (women's and men's) self-employment with an increasing professionalization in the labour market and thus neglecting the distinct character of their quality of work will be inadequate.

What factors underlie women's choices to enter part-time self-employment? To answer this question, we have analysed the impact of individual and country-specific institutional (or macro-structural) characteristics on the decision of engaging in part-time self-employment. A special focus of this study has been put on the self-employed woman's family context. More precisely, it has been acknowledged that the presence of (young) children as well as the presence of a partner or husband are likely to affect the woman's choice to do atypical work. Moreover, it has been hypothesized that the impact of the family context on part-time self-employment is strongly influenced by the country-specific institutional make-up, that is, country-specific political, economic and sociocultural environments (Shane 2003, Strohmeyer et al. 2005). More specifically, it has been assumed that the effect of the household context (young children, partner) on part-time self-employment will be strongest in conservative welfare-type states such as the Netherlands, (West) Germany and Austria, because of the weakly designed institutional support for female participation in the labour market in these countries as reflected in the absence of full-time nursery schools and day nurseries as well as tax benefits for wives staying at home and caring for children. Besides, higher rates in women's part-time self-employment in conservative welfare states may reflect these countries' traditional values that ascribe the role of main breadwinner to the men, but only a secondary breadwinner role to the women. In sharp contrast, it has been suggested that the effect of family on the choice of atypical work will be weakest in the new EU member states, taking into account distinct institutional environments (for example lower societal wealth) in countries such as Poland, Hungary, Slovenia, Slovakia, the Czech Republic, Latvia, Lithuania and Estonia.

Indeed, our empirical results have substantiated most hypotheses advanced in this study. Looking at the micro level, the presence of a (young) child increases the likelihood of engaging in part-time self-employment, a result which is remarkably stable across most countries investigated in Western and Eastern Europe. Atypical work thus seems to allow for relative flexibility in the choice of work schedule, apparently reflecting women's striving to reconcile family (childcare) and work responsibilities. Moreover, the probability of becoming involved in part-time self-employment is strongly associated with the presence of a partner or husband in one's household. More precisely, not having a partner forces a self-employed woman to engage in full-time self-employment. In contrast, having an economically active partner impacts upon the likelihood of being part-time self-employed both positively and strongly significantly. This holds true for both Western and Eastern European countries.

However, the family effect on part-time self-employment differs between various institutional settings, that is, within Western Europe (on the one hand) as well as between Eastern, Southern and Western Europe (on the other). More specifically, the probability of engaging in part-time work is shown to be strongest in conservative welfare states (such as West Germany, Austria and the Netherlands), which largely encourage women to be mainly responsible for the care and upbringing of children. Put differently, self-employed women in conservative welfare states in Western Europe pursue part-time work to accommodate obligations of child-upbringing. As shown by descriptive statistics, the share of female self-employed working part-time is about 60 per cent in the Netherlands, 38 per cent in West Germany, 33 per cent in Austria and 29 per cent in Luxembourg. Moreover, this finding was supported when adjusting for control variables (age, educational level, firm characteristics) and controlling for the 'sample selection bias' in the Heckman probit model.

There are however exceptions to the rule. As predicted theoretically, French policies fostering active female participation in the labour markets (and thus resembling dual-earner models of Scandinavian governments) have apparently created an institutional environment which is supportive for women's full-time self-employment. Moreover, East Germany displays a disproportionately low share of women's part-time self-employment (14 per cent). Evidently, the favourable political environment in East Germany (with a large share of publicly supported nursery schools and day nurseries; Spieß et al. 2002) enables women to engage in full-time self-employment.

However, some inconsistencies in our study also emerged. For example, we find a surprisingly strong effect of family on part-time self-employment in Italy, which differs strongly from the typical effects of the remaining Mediterranean welfare states in Southern Europe (Spain, Greece) in scope and rather resembles a pattern found in Western European conservative states. By the same token, the Czech Republic is a clear outlier of the typical Eastern European pattern of women's part-time self-employment, since the effect of the family composition on the likelihood of being part-time self-employed is disproportionately high for the Czech women, again resembling the pattern found in Western European welfare states which support traditional male breadwinner models.

CONTRIBUTIONS AND LIMITATIONS

This study makes several critical contributions to (female) entrepreneurship research. First, it shows an increasing importance of part-time self-employment as an atypical work form for self-employed women in both Western and Eastern Europe. Second, it deciphers the micro-level determinants of part-time self-employment, focusing on the importance of the family context (children and partner) for self-employed women's choice to do part-time work. Third, and most importantly, it contributes to the understanding of international differences in women's part-time self-employment, pointing to the importance of the welfare states' institutional arrangements (political, economic and sociocultural environments) in Western and Eastern Europe. Fourth, it extends the understanding of similarities and differences of female self-employment in Eastern and

Western Europe, combining micro and macro levels of analysis.

The main limitation of our study is that it does not provide answers to the question of whether self-employed women chose to work part-time voluntarily or are rather forced into part-time self-employment due to unfavourable market conditions (for example weak demand for products and services in certain industries). We were also unable to test the applicability of our hypotheses for social-democratic 'dual-earner' welfare states in Scandinavia and liberal welfare states in the USA and the United Kingdom because of a lack of information on self-employed women's family context variables in the European Labour Force Survey (Eurostat 2005). Another limitation is shared with previous research studying the impact of welfare state institutions on societal outcomes, that is, on the country's share of part-time self-employed women in our context. More precisely, we have not controlled for the impact of (political, economic and social) institutions on atypical work directly by employing multi-level hierarchical models (for the use of this statistical tool of analysis for women's potential entrepreneurship see Strohmeyer et al. 2005, for example) but only indirectly through utilizing 'bridging hypotheses' (Coleman 1990) between micro- and macro-units of analysis.

NOTES

*	The authors gratefully acknowledge the financial support of the Fritz-Thyssen foundation. They also thank Christoph Weichert for his excellent research assistance on this study.
1.	Other factors apart from children which affect women's choice to engage in part-time self-employment are working experience, holding a second job and firm characteristics (firm size, firm age and firm industry). Full results are available upon request.
2.	The number of countries investigated dropped from 25 to 19 due to a lack of information on the household configuration of four Scandinavian countries, namely, Denmark, Sweden, Finland and Norway. Additionally, we had to exclude Cyprus and Iceland due to the small sample size.

REFERENCES

Arum, R. (1997), 'Trends in male and female self-employment: growth in a middle class or increasing marginalization of the labour force?' *Research in Stratification and Mobility*, **15**, 209–38.
Arum, R. and W. Müller (2004), 'The Reemergence of Self-Employment: Comparative Findings and Empirical Propositions', in R. Arum and W. Müller (eds), *The Reemergence of Self-Employment: A Comparative Study of Self-Employment Dynamics and Social Inequality*, Princeton, NJ: Princeton University Press, pp. 426–54.
Becker, G.S. (1965), 'A theory of the allocation of time', *Economic Journal*, **75**, 493–

517.

Becker, G.S. (1976), *The Economic Approach to Human Behavior*, Chicago, IL: UP.

Becker, G.S. (1981), *A Treatise on the Family*, Cambridge, MA: Harvard University Press.

Boden Jr., R.J. (1996), 'Gender and self-employment selection: an empirical assessment', *Journal of Socio-Economics*, **25** (6), 671–82.

Boden Jr., R.J. (1999), 'Flexible working hours, family responsibilities, and female self-employment', *American Journal of Economics and Sociology*, **58** (1), 71–84.

Carr, D. (1996), 'Two paths to self-employment? Women's and men's self-employment in the United States', *Work and Occupation*, **23** (1), 26–53.

Coleman, J.S. (1990), *Foundations of Social Theory*, Cambridge, MA: Harvard University Press.

Drnakova, L. (2006), 'Cultural values in transition environment: assessment based on international social survey programme data', Center for Economic Research and Graduates Educations at the Charles University, Discussion Paper, No. 159, http://www.cerge-ei.cz.

Drobnic, S. (1997), 'Part-time work in Central and Eastern European countries', in H.-P. Blossfeld and C. Hakim (eds), *Between Equalization and Marginalization: Women Working Part-Time in Europe and the United States of America*, New York: Oxford University Press, pp. 71–90.

Engelbrech, G. and Jungkunst, M (2001), Erwerbsbeteiligung von Frauen: Wie bringt man Beruf und Kinder unter einen Hut? in: IAB Kurzbericht 7/2001, Nürnberg, website: http://doku.iab.de/kurzber/2001/kb0701.pdf.

Eurostat (2005), *LFS User Guide: Labour Force Survey: Anonymised Data Sets*, European Commission Eurostat.

Esping-Andersen, G. (1990), *The Three Worlds of Welfare Capitalism*, Cambridge: Polity Press.

Gornick, J.C., M.K. Meyers and K.E. Ross (1997), 'Supporting the employment of mothers: policy variation across fourteen welfare states', *Journal of European Social Policy*, **7** (1), 45–70.

Greene, W.H. (2003), *Econometric Analysis*, 5th edition, London: Prentice Hall.

Gustafsson, S. and C. Wetzels (1997), 'Family policies and women's labour force transitions in connection with childbirth', *Vierteljahrshefte zur Wirtschaftsforschung*, **1**, 118–24.

Hakim, C. (1997), 'A sociological perspective on part-time work', in H.-P. Blossfeld and C. Hakim (eds), *Between Equalization and Modernization. Women Working Part-Time in Europe and the United States of America*, New York: Oxford University Press, pp. 23–70.

Hakim, C. (1998), *Social Change and Innovation in the Labour Market*, London: Routledge.

Heckman, J. (1979), 'Sample selection bias as a specification error', *Econometrica*, **47**, 153–61.

Heller Clain, S. (2000), 'Gender differences in full-time self-employment', *Journal of Economics and Business*, **52** (6), 499–513.

Korpi, W. (2000), 'Faces of inequality: gender, class and patterns of inequalities in different types of welfare states', *Social Politics*, **7** (2), 127–91.

Kraus, V., V. Tonoyan and R. Strohmeyer (2006), 'Are self-employed women a marginal work force? A cross-national comparison between Israel and Germany', paper presented at the RC 28 ISA Committee on Stratification and Social Mobility, Nijmegen, the Netherlands, 11–14 May.

Laulom, S. (2004), 'France: part-time work – no longer an employment policy tool', in S. Sciarra, P. Davies and M. Freedland (eds), *Employment Policy and the Regulation of Part-Time Work in the European Union: A Comparative Analysis*, Cambridge: Cambridge University Press, pp. 85–121.

Leicht, R. and R. Strohmeyer (2005), 'Women's self-employment in Europe: catching-up at a crawl', in L. Hagbarth (ed.), *Entrepreneurial Spirit in Cities and Regions*, Denzlingen: Hagbarth Publications, pp. 53–60.

Lewis, S. (2001), 'Restructuring workplace cultures: the ultimate work–family challenge?' *Women in Management Review*, **16** (1), 21–9.

Lohmann, H. (2001), 'Self-employed or employee, full-time or part-time? Gender differences in the determinants and conditions for self-employment in Europe and the US', Discussion Paper, No. 38, Mannheim Centre for European Social Research.

Lohmann, H. (2004), 'Berufliche Selbständigkeit von Frauen und Männern im internationalen Vergleich – Welche Rolle spielt die Vereinbarkeit von Familie und Erwerbstätigkeit?', in G. Schmid, M. Gangl and P. Kupka (eds), *Arbeitsmarktpolitik und Strukturwandel: Empirische Analysen, BeitrAB 286*, Nuremberg: Institut für Arbeitsmarkt- und Berufsforschung, pp. 205–26.

Lombard, K.V. (2001), 'Female self-employment and demand for flexible, nonstandard work schedules', *Economic Inquiry*, **39** (2), 214–37.

OECD (2001), 'Balancing work and family life: helping parents into paid employment', in OECD (ed.), *Employment Outlook 2001*, Paris: OECD, pp. 129–64.

Pfau-Effinger, B. (2004), 'Socio-historical paths of the male breadwinner model: an explanation of cross-national differences', *British Journal of Sociology*, **55** (3), 377–99.

Pfau-Effinger, B. (2005), 'Culture and welfare state policies: reflections on a complex interrelation', *Journal of Social Policy*, **34** (1), 3–20.

Sainsbury D. (1994), 'Women's and men's social rights: gendering dimensions of welfare states', in D. Sainsbury (ed.), *Gendering Welfare States*, London: Sage Publications, pp. 150–70.

Shane, S. (2003), *A General Theory of Entrepreneurship: The Individual-Opportunity Nexus*, Cheltenham, UK and Northampton, MA, USA: Edward Elgar.

Spieß, C.K., F. Büchel and J.R. Frick (2002), 'Kinderbetreuung in West- und Ostdeutschland: Sozioökonomischer Hintergrund entscheidend', *Wochenbericht des DIW Berlin*, 31/02, www.diw.de/deutsch/produkte/publikationen/wochenberichte/docs/02-31-2.html, 20 December 2006.

Stier, H., N. Lewin-Epstein and M. Braun (2001), 'Welfare regimes, family-supportive policies, and women's employment along the life-course', *American Journal of Sociology*, **106** (6), 1731–60.

Strohmeyer, R., V. Tonoyan and W.W. Wittmann (2005), 'Gendered and cross-country differences in the perceived difficulty of becoming self-employed: the impact of individual resources and institutional restrictions', *Frontiers of Entrepreneurship Research*, Wellesley, MA: Babson College.

8.   Is Modesty Attractive? Study of the Present and Future States of the Entrepreneurial Skills of Finnish Small and Medium-Sized Entrepreneurs

Mikki Valjakka

INTRODUCTION

Owner-entrepreneurs are the power centres of their companies and are responsible for the financial capital. They are concerned with both the company's economic and intellectual capital. Their own know-how has not been researched deeply. The work of the entrepreneur is quite fragmented, with the time taken to concentrate on a single task being often only a matter of minutes. Technology, although freeing the entrepreneur from place and time, can add to the feeling of fragmentation of time and cause more stress.

Stress is also caused by the requirement level being too high because of a lack of know-how. The knowledge competency of owner-entrepreneurs and their personnel is one of the most important factors of competitiveness. The possession of knowledge has become a more important factor for success – even a critical one. Companies' investments in training have increased year by year, because of a lack of qualified employees able to do several jobs. New, competitive products and services can be developed only based on the latest know-how.

The problems of an entrepreneur can be divided into three groups. The first consists of the problems caused by the entrepreneur. These are, for instance, lack of professional skills, creativity, courage and confidence in his or her own skills. The second group consists of the problems caused by the company, such as business operations or managing employees. The third group consists of the problems caused by the environment, such as the requirements of the public sector. Knowledge can also be divided into the operative level (daily working), tactical level (drawing up the budget) and strategic level (planning and inauguration of new operational strategies).

There is no consensus as to the minimum entrepreneurial skills. Even general items concerning many entrepreneurs are difficult to define because of the different kinds of demands depending on the branches of activity and environment. Additionally, the phase of the life cycle and the size of a firm (the resources available) set different demands on knowledge.

The synonym for know-how here is competency. The word 'competency' is considered to include the idea of knowing how to conduct business, of being able to improve and renew one's capabilities and implement the tasks and core thoughts of the leadership of learning (Kirjavainen and Laakso-Maninen 2000, p. 13).

In this study the entrepreneurial skills are defined as two kinds of competency: that of creating value and that of enabling contingency. The ability to create good customer relationships, competency to master the technology and competency to develop products or services, as well as production and logistical competences, belong to value-creative competences. The competency to direct and steer business operations, the competency to develop personnel and the competency to master knowledge are all competencies which enable contingency (Hannus et al. 1999, p. 5).

The success of management depends on success in many factors. A good level of know-how application is one of the success factors. This study aims to shed light on the present and future states of entrepreneurial skills. What does entrepreneurial know-how mean? How can it be classified? Is it primarily readiness to tolerate stress and uncertainty – or what? What level of know-how is sufficient or good? Is renewal capability relevant?

The success of society depends on the success of companies, therefore it is important to study and try to enhance the skills (competences) and learning of the owner-entrepreneur. The prerequisite for enhancement is identifying the knowledge, know-how and capabilities needed and also the possible lack of competence. All this increases the consciousness of the needs and wishes of entrepreneurs, and increases their readiness to be leaders. The balance between the entrepreneur's capability and hopes increases the chances of leading a healthy life mentally and physically, the ability to work well and also the feeling of satisfaction. For these reasons it makes sense to research entrepreneurial skills.

OBJECTS AND QUESTIONS

It is important for the quality of life of owner-entrepreneurs to have a feeling of control over their own lives. It means that they have sufficient time for the important tasks and a feeling of harmony between what they want or aim to do and what they are actually doing. A lack of knowledge leads to a feeling of stress and lack of time. This study aims to chart and analyse the judgements of entrepreneurs regarding their present and future entrepreneurial skills. This chapter aims to answer the following questions:

1. What is the level of the entrepreneurial skills and know-how (present state)?
    a. What is the level of capacity for self-renewal?
    b. Are there any differences based on age, gender or education?
2. What is the level of the entrepreneurial skills and know-how (future state)?
    a. Are there any differences based on age, gender or education?

This chapter aims to shed more light on the profile of a Finnish SM entrepreneur and increase the amount of research. The perspective is centred on the individual, or, to be more precise, on the entrepreneur.

METHODOLOGY

This study follows the quantitative and descriptive tradition. The data were gathered using a questionnaire, which was sent by e-mail to 3253 e-mail addresses of owner-entrepreneurs. These e-mail addresses were provided by two Finnish enterprise organizations in two provinces in Finland. A total of 660 owner-entrepreneurs returned the questionnaire, of which 656 were accepted, the response rate being 20.2 per cent. So the sample consists of 656 observations, including 163 female and 493 male owner-entrepreneurs.

The skills were examined and analysed by calculating the means, the explorative factor analysis was used to test and confirm the statements and the Mann-Whitney U test was used for the comparisons.

The entrepreneurial skills (the present and future states) were rated using a four-grade scale: low (D = 1), satisfactory (C = 2), good (B = 3) and excellent (A = 4). When calculating the means, the figures up to 0.49 gave low (D), figures 1.50–2.49 gave satisfactory (C); figures 2.50–3.49 good (B) and 3.50 upwards excellent (A).

ABOUT ENTREPRENEURIAL SKILLS

The ability to produce new ideas and quickly put them into practice is decisive for success. Critical knowledge factors are a sense of development trends, and the ability to master processes, share knowledge and build innovative teams (Edvinsson 1999, p. 14). The afore-mentioned skills/competences pose great challenges for an entrepreneur and several entrepreneurs in this study long for support in developing their mental resources. Many of them also lack the ability to judge their own proficiencies. One prerequisite for learning is the identification of deficiencies in one's own abilities and proficiencies.

This study focuses on Finnish owner-entrepreneurs, so in the survey it was natural to chart the entrepreneurial skills based on the 'demands for the vocational qualification of an entrepreneur' (Allardt et al. 1984, p. 7). According to Allardt et al., in order to manage as an entrepreneur one must master certain thematic entities and be able to complete knowledge and bring it up to date, as well as develop personal characteristics so that learning can be best exploited.

To carry out this study, the entrepreneurial skills/competences which have been focused on are the nine themes listed below. The contents of the themes (single areas of competence) are shown in Appendix 1. It should also be emphasized that the analysis below describes the levels of the skills/competences according to the respondents' own estimations.

The 64 areas of competence to be examined are divided into nine themes (see Appendix):

1. Collaboration and communication (8 statements)
2. Learning (5 statements)
3. Certain competences/skills (10 skills)
4. Planning and managing operations (5)
5. Development of customer- and market-oriented functions (5)
6. Development of human resources (5)
7. Development of financial administration (9)
8. Computer and teleinformatic skills (12 skills)
9. Language skills (5 languages).

ABOUT CAPACITY FOR SELF-RENEWAL

An enterprise's capability for continuous self-renewal arises spontaneously from (systemic) consciousness, the opportunity to interact and personal influence (Ståhle 1998). The capacity for self-renewal requires the ability to change and instantly to adopt new ways of acting. This provides the trust between the owner and the employees (strong commitment), motivation and networking. The entrepreneur should be able to create an atmosphere in which sharing information and communication between all the employees happens automatically. From an entrepreneur's perspective the capacity for self-renewal means that he or she is able to make good strategic choices and decisions instantly and at an appropriate time.

The most important features and factors of capacity for self-renewal in this study are culture of openness, willingness to learn, innovativeness (including the willingness to change and strategic competency), networking and branch-specific knowledge.

In this study the culture of openness entails trust and natural collaboration between individuals, free expression of opinions and free flow of sufficient information. In addition it provides the understanding and knowledge of the company's vision and goals at all levels, so that it is clear to all employees why they are doing what they are doing and what their goals are.

Companies that emphasize learning also encourage employees to carry out tasks in new ways and constantly produce new ideas, the tolerance for disparity is appreciated, professional specialization is important and appreciated, and training is often systematically planned.

Innovativeness is also close to the capacity for self-renewal. In this study innovativeness means the ability to create useful changes originating from a new idea to be carried out by the value chain of a company. Often the above-mentioned changes, that is, innovations, are the result of complicated, interactive, constant processes conditional upon networking. In an innovative company an atmosphere favourable to change is predominant and the new theoretical know-how and knowledge of the processes of one's business sector will be created. Working life is characterized by constant changes and the speed of reaction is important. Changes often cause resistance among employees, and the entrepreneur needs the ability to handle this. Changes occur best through conversations with employees and the entrepreneur is constantly asking the personnel for new ideas, as well as deciding together with the employees what actions should be taken and how they should be implemented. An innovative company with a favourable attitude towards change constantly emphasizes combining the skills of innovation, problem solving and teamwork. Innovativeness also provides an atmosphere where there is trust (everyone is involved in the company's visions). Trust means allowing employees to work independently.

Networking is the third feature and a factor concerning the capacity for self-renewal. Networking is also one of the most important success factors in modern business. Understanding the importance of networking and gravitating towards co-operation among companies has become a fundamental factor of success.

'Networking changes all the economic (and social) structures of a company. The global economy means a new kind of competition and new competitors while companies and states are participating in a new form of production, commerce, capital and labour' (Bauman 1998, p. 11). The basic aims of networking are, for example, to share risk, gain faster access to new markets, adopt new technologies, improve the efficiency of the delivery chain and also combine complementary knowledge and skills (Powell 1990, Miettinen et al. 1999, adapted).

In line with the above, networking is defined in this study as the activity between two or more companies, a joint will and effort to do at least one of the following: share risks, facilitate the access to new markets and also cut access time, adopt new technologies, improve the efficiency of the delivery chain, and combine skills and knowledge complementary to each other. Networking can also mean the co-operation between several networks, the co-operation between a company and public sector, work with clusters in the same business sector or personal relationships (for instance between private self-employed individuals). The companies operating in a network bond bilaterally: structurally and/or socially and/or strategically. Networking also provides the entrepreneur with confidentiality and an ability to interact.

In addition to many other characteristics and skills, an owner-entrepreneur also needs strong branch-specific knowledge, without which it is hard to be competitive. Branch-specific knowledge is defined as having the theoretical knowledge and also knowing the methods and processes of one's own industry. Knowledge of the production or service process is a prerequisite for planning, following and managing as well as forecasting.

FINDINGS

The median respondent is male, aged 43, married with 2–3 children, 'O'-level to college-level training and has worked for 12 years as an entrepreneur. The entrepreneur profile is shown in Table 8.1.

The 64 areas of competence examined were divided into nine themes (see p. 138) and the content of each theme is found in the Appendix. The entrepreneurial skills (the present and future states) were rated using a four-grade scale: low (D), satisfactory (C), good (B) and excellent (A).

Table 8.1   Entrepreneur Profile

Variable	N = 656	%
Respondents: women 163		24.8
men 493		75.2
Age groups:		
53 or older	53	8
43–52	237	36
33–42	246	38
32 or younger	120	18
Marital status:		
single	37	6
married/cohabiting	581	89
widowed/divorced	35	5
not available	3	0.5
Education:		
elementary school	91	14
middle school	264	40
matriculation	204	31
not available	97	15
Qualification:		
vocational school	94	14
college level	294	45
lower academic degree	100	15
higher academic degree	61	9
not available	107	16
Years as entrepreneur:		
over 25	152	23
16–25	168	26
6–15	115	18
5 or less	138	21
not available	83	13

The Present State of Entrepreneurial Skills

Table 8.2 shows the order of the nine themes. The theme for which the entrepreneurs rated themselves most highly was 'Planning and managing operations'. 'Collaboration and communication' came second and 'Certain competences/skills' third. The theme for which they rated themselves least highly was 'Language skills', with 'Computer and teleinformatic skills' coming second to last and 'Human resources' third last.

The mean of the means (2.34) is only 'satisfactory' and no single statement or skill was 'excellent'. The very best figure (3.39) was knowledge of the production or service process, belonging to 'Planning and managing operations'.

Table 8.2   Entrepreneurial Skills. The Means of the Present State. Range 1–4

n = 656			
Order	Alpha	Means	
1. Planning and managing operations	0.764	2.96	good
2. Collaboration and communication	0.894	2.93	good
3. Certain competences/skills	0.897	2.91	good
4. Learning	0.893	2.84	good
5. Finance	0.847	2.60	good
6. Customer- and market-oriented functions	0.764	2.50	good
7. Human resources	0.847	2.32	satisfactory
8. Computer and teleinformatic skills	0.894	2.07	satisfactory
9. Language skills	0.689	1.61	satisfactory
Mean of the means		2.34	

Table 8.3 shows the eight areas where entrepreneurs rated themselves most highly. Three of these areas of competence belong to 'Computer and tele-informatic skills' and the rest to other themes.

Table 8.4 shows the eight areas of competence where entrepreneurs rated themselves least highly. The skills in foreign languages are 'low' and three 'Computer and teleinformatic skills' are fairly 'satisfactory'.

Table 8.3 The Eight Most Highly-Rated Individual Skills. Range 1–4

Variable	Figure
Knowledge of production and/or service processes (PLANNING AND MANAGING OPERATIONS)	3.39
E-mail (COMPUTER AND TELEINFORMATIC SKILLS)	3.33
Relevance of profitability, liquidity, financial stability and productivity (FINANCE)	3.30
The Internet (COMPUTER AND TELEINFORMATIC SKILLS)	3.25
Emphasizing the importance of vocational special skills (LEARNING)	3.23
Favouring free flow of information (COLLABORATION AND COMMUNICATION)	3.16
Text-processing program (COMPUTER AND TELEINFORMATIC SKILLS)	3.09
Stress tolerance (CERTAIN COMPETENCES/SKILLS)	3.07

Table 8.4 The Eight Least Highly-Rated Individual Skills. Range 1–4

Variable	Figure
Russian (LANGUAGES)	1.06
French (LANGUAGES)	1.07
German (LANGUAGES)	1.40
Production management system (COMPUTER AND TELEINFORMATIC SKILLS)	1.53
Advertising programmes (COMPUTER AND TELEINFORMATIC SKILLS)	1.89
Payroll computation (COMPUTER AND TELEINFORMATIC SKILLS)	1.90
Accounting programme (COMPUTER AND TELEINFORMATIC SKILLS)	1.94
Ability to devise plans for personnel and implement them (HUMAN RESOURCES)	2.00

The influence of age
The respondents were distributed into four classes: 53 or older (class 1, n = 48), 43–52 (class 2, n = 222), 33–42 (class 3, n = 242) and 32 or younger

(class 4, n = 119). The Mann-Whitney U test was used for the comparisons. Here only the differences between the oldest (class 1) and the youngest (class 4) classes will be presented.

A significant difference was found in six skills belonging to 'computer and teleinformatic skills', as shown in Table 8.5. All six skills were rated more highly by the youngest class (4). In 'Language skills' the youngest were better at English (p = 0.000) while the oldest were better at German (p = 0.036). The oldest were better at devising plans for personnel and implementing them ('Human resources') (p = 0.013).

The influence of gender
There were 161 female and 470 male respondents. Significant differences were found in five of the nine themes. The Mann-Whitney U test was used for the comparisons.

Significant differences in favour of women were found in naturalness of appearance (p = 0.027) ('Collaboration and communication'); theoretical knowledge of one's own industry (p = 0.002) and teamwork skills (p = 0.000) both belonging to 'Certain competences/skills'; the skills in interactive, productive salesmanship and customer service (p = 0.004) and knowledge of customer contentment (p = 0.002), both belonging to 'Customer- and market-oriented functions', and also managing accounting and taxation (p = 0.044) and ability to control pension, accident and unemployment insurance (p = 0.003) ('Finance').

Table 8.5   Differences in Computer and Teleinformatic Skills: Oldest versus Youngest

Computer and Teleinformatic Skills	p=
The Internet	0.004
E-mail	0.001
Text processing program	0.001
Spreadsheet program	0.016
Calendar software	0.005
Graphics processing	0.039

In 'Computer and teleinformatic skills' women were better at the Internet (p = 0.000), e-mail (p = 0.000), text-processing programmes (p = 0.000), advertising programmes (p = 0.013) and production management systems (p = 0.002). In foreign languages women were better at Swedish (p = 0.001),

English (p = 0.000), German (p = 0.029) and French (p = 0.000). None of men rated themselves more highly than the women with regard to these skills.

The influence of education

Education was distributed among four levels: vocational (class 1, n = 94), college level (class 2, n = 294), lower academic degree (class 3, n = 100) and higher academic degree (class 4, n = 61) (the whole group). Only the differences between class 2 (college level, n = 266) and higher academic degree oldest class (4, n = 60) will be presented here. The Mann-Whitney U test was used for the comparisons.

One significant difference was found concerning computer programs for accounts payable and receivable (p = 0.033) ('Computer and teleinformatic skills'), where respondents with a college-level education were better. All other differences, or 17 in five themes, were better known by respondents with a higher academic degree: clarity of communication (p = 0.007), expressing opinions and forwarding information (p = 0.033), constantly requesting new ideas and proposals (p = 0.031) and favouring a free flow of information (p = 0.008), all belonging to 'Collaboration and communication'; encouraging employees to take risks (p = 0.006) ('Learning'); general knowledge (p = 0.003), theoretical knowledge of one's own industry (p=0.045), teamwork skills (p = 0.022), innovation skills (p = 0.009), problem-solving skills (p = 0.041) and analysing skills (p = 0.011) ('Certain competences/skills'). Respondents with a higher academic degree also rated their ability to use leadership skills to remove resistance to change (p = 0.043) ('Human resources') more highly and, in 'Languages', rated themselves more highly with regard to Swedish, English, German and French (all p = 0.000).

The Future State of Entrepreneurial Skills

The four-step scale was also used for the future state: I know it (= 0), I would like to know it slightly better (= +1), moderately better (= +2) and much better (= +3).

In the future state we must be content with only six themes. The bigger the figure, the less one wishes to enhance the competency/skill and the smaller the figure the more one wishes to enhance the skill.

The number one priority for further knowledge was the 'Finance' theme and the second was 'Planning and managing operations'. Of all the themes concerning further knowledge 'Human resources' was the least important. Only slightly more important than 'Human resources' was 'Computer and teleinformatic skills'. Table 8.6 shows the order of six themes.

Table 8.6   Entrepreneurial Skills. The Means of the Future State.
Range 1–4

n = 656 order	Alpha	Means
1. Finance	0.952	2.94
2. Planning and managing operations	0.935	2.95
3. Customer- and market-oriented functions	0.890	2.96
4. Language skills	0.824	3.07
5. Computer and teleinformatic skills	0.946	3.09
6. Human resources	0.938	3.12
Mean of the means		3.02

Table 8.7 shows the list of eight individual skills that needed most improvement. Finnish SM entrepreneurs seemed to fret most over insufficient knowledge of the English language, followed in second place by knowledge of regulations, company forms, company reorganization and contract regulations, where they need further knowledge most.

Table 8.7   Requiring Further Knowledge (Most). Eight Individual Skills.
Range 1–4

Variable	Figure
English LANGUAGES	2.60
Knowledge of regulations, company forms, company reorganization and contract regulations FINANCE	2.73
Knowledge of accounting and taxation FINANCE	2.74
Swedish LANGUAGES	2.80
Ability to interpret market research and competitor analyses CUSTOMER- AND MARKET-ORIENTED FUNCTIONS	2.82
Skills in mapping out risks PLANNING AND MANAGING	2.84
Familiarity with pension, accident and unemployment insurance FINANCE	2.85
Ability to forecast functions PLANNING AND MANAGING	2.86

Table 8.8 shows the eight skills needing least improvement. Further studies of Russian and French are least needed, as Table 8.8 shows. (Table 8.4 showed that they were also the two skills rated least highly.) Four of the 'Computer and teleinformatic skills' were also thought to need improving.

The influence of age

Only the differences between the oldest (class 1, n = 53) and the youngest (class 4, n = 120) will be presented here. The Mann-Whitney U test was used for the comparisons.

The oldest wanted significantly to their improve knowledge of regulations, company forms, company reorganization and contract regulations (p = 0.018), belonging to 'Finance', and also Swedish ('Languages'). The youngest would like to be better at 'Computer and teleinformatic skills': the Internet (which came fourth in the list of skills rated most highly, as Table 8.3 showed) (p = 0.004), text-processing programs (p = 0.016) and spreadsheet programs (p= 0.037).

Table 8.8   Requiring Further Knowledge (Least). Eight Individual Skills. Range 1–4

Variables	Figure
Russian LANGUAGES	3.53
French LANGUAGES	3.52
Production management system COMPUTER AND TELEINFORMATIC SKILLS	3.28
Software account payable and receivable COMPUTER AND TELEINFORMATIC SKILLS	3.23
Accounting program COMPUTER AND TELEINFORMATIC SKILLS	3.22
Payroll computation COMPUTER AND TELEINFORMATIC SKILLS	3.21
Knowledge of production and/or service processes PLANNING AND MANAGING	3.20
Ability to use leadership skills to remove resistance to change HUMAN RESOURCES	3.20

The influence of gender

Women n = 163, men n = 493. The Mann-Whitney U test was used for the comparisons.

Women wanted to be better at six competences/skills: 'Human resources' in five skills: ability to devise plans for personnel and implement them (p =

0.020), ability to use human resources development discussion in personnel management (p = 0.003), ability to use leadership skills in the enhancement of team spirit (p = 0.000), ability to use leadership skills to remove resistance to change (p = 0.001) and ability to attend to the well-being of the personnel (p = 0.000). Additionally women would like to be better at the ability to use the services of accountants, accounting companies or such when planning, controlling and directing the company economy (p = 0.004) ('Finance').

Men did not want to be significantly better at any of the skills/competences examined.

The influence of education

Only the significant differences between class 2 (college level, n = 266) and class 4 (higher academic degree, n = 60) will be presented here. The Mann-Whitney U test was used for the comparisons.

The respondents with a college-level education wanted to be better at French ('Languages') (p = 0.007).

Those with a higher-level education wanted to be better at eight skills: skills in critical evaluation of the current state of the company (p = 0.031), ability to forecast functions (p = 0.018), skill in mapping out risks (p = 0.035) ('Planning and managing operations'); payroll computation (p = 0.009), computer programs for accounts payable and receivable (p = 0.005) and accounting programs (p = 0.031) ('Computer and teleinformatic skills'); and also in Swedish (p = 0.049) and English (p = 0.014) ('Languages').

The level of capacity for self-renewal

Culture of openness. According to the factor analysis, six of the areas of competence in 'Collaboration and communication' measure the culture of openness: clarification of the individuals' and the company's objectives, favouring natural co-operation, favouring free flow of information, concern over the availability of sufficient information, expressing opinions and forwarding information, and clarity of communication (vision + objectives). When comparing the mean (2.99) of the statements measuring culture of openness to the mean (2.93) of the theme (that is, 'Collaboration and communication') it can be seen that only the figure (2.71) for clarity of communication (vision + objectives) was smaller than the mean of the whole theme. The method of functioning is open in the respondents' enterprises and the level was good (2.99).

Willingness to learn. According to the factor analysis, all five areas of competence belonging to the theme 'Learning' (emphasizing the importance of vocational special skills, emphasizing the value of diversity, encouraging employees to establish new ways to act, encouraging employees to think creatively and take risks and methodicalness of training) measured the willingness to learn.

The level of the respondents' willingness to learn seemed to be in quite good order. Methodicalness of training (2.33 versus the mean of the theme as a whole 2.84) needs to be developed most. Attention should also be paid to encouraging the employees to establish new ways to act (2.71 versus the mean 2.84 of the theme as a whole). The level of willingness to learn was good (2.78).

Innovativeness. Innovativeness was measured by five areas of competence from 'Certain competences/skills': problem-solving skills, theoretical knowledge of one's own industry, knowledge of methods in one's own industry, teamwork skills and innovation skills. Only the actual innovation skill (2.73 versus the mean of the whole theme, 2.91) needs improvement. The level of innovativeness was good (2.93).

Positive attitude towards change and networking. Here, in contrast, there were areas of competence from four different themes that measured a positive attitude towards change and networking, as shown in Table 8.9. The positive attitude towards change and networking does not seem to be good – all the skills need improvement. The biggest difference to the means is found in constantly requesting new ideas and proposals (-0.44). The level of the positive attitude towards change and networking was satisfactory (2.34) (Table 8.9).

Industry-specific knowledge. Industry-specific knowledge was measured by three areas of competence: management skills in planning, controlling and directing company economy ('Finance'), knowledge of production and/or service processes ('Planning and managing') and ability to forecast functions ('Planning and managing'). Only the ability to forecast functions (2.81 versus the mean of themes, 2.84) needs improvement. The level of industry-specific knowledge was the best of all those mentioned above, the mean being 3.07. The capacity for self-renewal seems to be good with the mean being fairly good (2.82).

Table 8.9   Positive Attitude towards Change and Networking

Theme	Mean of Theme	Area of Competence	Figure for the Skill	Differ -ence
Human resources	2.32	Ability to use human resources development discussions in personnel management	2.08	- 0.24
Human resources	2.32	Ability to use leadership skills to remove resistance to change	2.30	
Finance	2.60	Ability to define indicators for surveying the business	2.33	- 0.27
Customer- and market-oriented functions	2.50	Ability to form and maintain networks	2.49	
Collaboration and communication	2.93	Constantly requesting new ideas and proposals	2.49	- 0.44
Mean of the means	2.53	Mean	2.34	

CONCLUSIONS

In answer to the question: What is the level of entrepreneurial skills and know-how (present state and future state)? it can be seen that the level of the respondents' entrepreneurial skills in most of the themes examined is more or less good – no theme was excellent – nor did the respondents want to be excellent.

'Planning and managing operations' was rated most highly (and knowledge of production or service process was the best single skill) and 'Collaboration and communication' came second. Ability to use e-mail, the Internet and text-processing programs from 'Computer and teleinformatic skills'; understanding the relevance of profitability, liquidity, financial stability and productivity in company operations from 'Finance'; and emphasizing the importance of vocational special skills and favouring free flow of information from 'Learning' were also good. These enterprises do not suffer from a poor flow of information. The ability to tolerate stress was also good.

Skills especially important for good economic results as well as the computer and teleinformatic skills needed in everyday life are strongly emphasized. An explanation for this could be that the enterprises are quite small. Small entrepreneurs are familiar with the production and often do it themselves.

Why were none of the themes or skills 'excellent'? One feature typical of Finns, and a Finnish national virtue, is modesty. Finns seldom stress how good they are and boasting is frowned upon. An old saying goes that 'Modesty is attractive'. Is it a question of cultural difference? Or low self-esteem?

In addition to poor self-esteem, Finns have been characterized as a silent nation, or a nation which keeps its mouth shut in many languages. The theme of 'Languages' (Russian, French and German) was therefore rated least highly. Even the languages considered to be important, that is, Swedish and English, were only satisfactory. The second-worst was 'Computer and teleinformatic skills'. Finns are in the lead in worldwide comparisons of the use of mobile phones and computers. This gives us reason to believe that the poor teleinformatic skills are not the real truth, but rather a question of excessive modesty.

In addition, in the future state the skills important for achieving financial results were emphasized and the respondents did not want to be excellent in any of the skills.

Special interest was focused on the culture of openness, willingness to learn, innovativeness, a positive attitude towards change and networking and industry-specific knowledge which constituted the capacity for self-renewal. In answer to the question: 'What is the level of the capacity for self-renewal?' it can be seen that a culture of functioning openly is mostly good, and the willingness to learn is also good. Likewise, innovativeness is quite good. In contrast, the positive attitude towards change and networking does not seem to be characteristic of the respondents. Industry-specific knowledge is good, but the ability to forecast functions needs improvement. The level of the capacity for self-renewal was fairly good.

In answer to the question: 'Are there any differences based on age, gender or education concerning entrepreneurial skills, in both the present and future state?' it can be seen that the youngest respondents have a better grasp of English and also of six 'computer and teleinformatic skills'. The natural explanation for this is a change in the Finnish school system at the beginning of the 1960s.

In the present state women evaluated their level to be better with regard to 16 skills compared to men, and six in the future state. What does this say about women? Women scarcely have better self-esteem than men. Do women exaggerate their abilities? If the result is true, how is the better know-how of women shown? Are there more women than men in the top positions of society? Are the enterprises owned by women more successful? Or is society wasting women's knowledge resources?

Education significantly influenced 17 skills for those with a higher academic degree and one those with a college level education.

To summarize, the respondents seem to be satisfied with having only a good level of the skills and know-how most commonly needed and do not wish to be excellent. Or is it rather a question of modesty (the typical Finnish national virtue) and poor self-esteem, which is also said to be typical of Finns?

The old Finnish proverb 'Modesty is attractive' (*Vaatimattomuus kaunistaa*) seems to be true with regard to the results of this study.

REFERENCES

Allardt, E., E. Asp, I. Heikkonen, H. Rautkallio and J. Vuorinen (1984), *Yrittäjäkoulutus Suomessa*, Mikkeli: Yritystoiminnan kehittämissäätiö, Suomen Yrittäjäin Keskusliitto ry, Länsi-Savo Oy.

Bauman, Zygmunt (1998), 'Postmodernisuuden ja etiikan epäpyhä allianssi', *Aikuiskasvatus*, **1**, 11. (Interviewed by Tuomas Nevanlinna.)

Edvinsson, Leif (1999), 'Henkisen omaisuuden hillitön ryntäys' *Tukholma Fakta*, **1**, 14.

Hannus, Jouko, Jan-Erik Lindroos and Tapani Seppänen (1999), *Strateginen uudistuminen osaamisen ajan toimintaympäristössä*, Helsinki: Hakapaino Oy.

Kirjavainen, Paula and Ritva Laakso-Manninen (2000), *Strategisen osaamisen johtaminen: yrityksen tieto ja osaaminen kilpailuedun lähteeksi*, Helsinki: Edita.

Miettinen, R., J. Lehenkari, M. Hasu and J. Hyvönen (1999), *Osaaminen ja uuden luominen innovaatioverkoissa*, Tutkimus kuudesta suomalaisesta innovaatiosta. (Study of six Finnish innovations) SITRA, Helsinki: Taloustieto Oy.

Powell, W.W. (1990), 'Neither market nor hierarchy: network forms of organization', in B. Staw and L.L. Cummings (eds), *Research in Organizational Behavior*, Greenwich, CT: JAI Press, pp. 295–336.

Ståhle, Pirjo (1998), *Supporting a System's Capacity for Self-Renewal*, Helsinki: University of Helsinki.

APPENDIX

The Research Focus: The Fields (Themes) of Entrepreneurial Skills and the Contents within the Fields

1. *Collaboration and communication skills (8)*
   Favouring free flow of information
   Favouring natural co-operation
   Concerned about the availability of sufficient information
   Expressing opinions and forwarding information
   Naturalness of appearance, lack of stress during performance
   Clarification of the individuals' and the company's objectives
   Clarity of communication (vision + objectives)
   Constantly requesting new ideas and proposals

2. *Learning (5)*
   Emphasizing the importance of special vocational skills
   Emphasizing the value of diversity
   Encouraging employees to establish new ways to act
   Encouraging employees to think creatively and take risks
   Methodicalness of training

3. *Certain competences and skills (10)*
   Stress tolerance
   Problem-solving skills
   Theoretical knowledge of one's own industry
   General knowledge
   Knowledge of methods in one's own industry
   Negotiation skills
   Analysing skills
   Teamwork skills
   Innovation skills
   Physical state

4. *Planning and managing company operations (5)*
   Knowledge of production and/or service processes
   Skills in critical evaluation of the current state of the company
   Organizational and management skills
   Ability to forecast functions
   Skills in mapping out risks

5. *Development of customer- and market-oriented functions (5)*
   Interactive, productive salesmanship and customer service skills
   Customer satisfaction-related skills
   Ability to form and maintain networks
   Skills in segmenting customers by profitability
   Ability to interpret market research and competitor analyses

6. *Development of human resources (5)*
   Ability to attend to the well-being of the personnel
   Ability to use leadership skills in the enhancement of team spirit
   Ability to use leadership skills to remove resistance to change
   Ability to use human resources development discussions in personnel management
   Ability to devise plans for personnel and implement them

7. *Development of financial administration (9)*
   Understanding of the relevance of profitability, liquidity, financial stability and productivity in company operations
   Management skills in planning, controlling and directing the company economy
   Ability to use the services of accountants, accounting companies or such when planning, controlling and directing the company economy
   Ability to interpret annual accounts and other economic reports and key figures
   Ability to use profit and loss accounts, balance sheets and financial budgets as planning tools
   Ability to define indicators for surveying the business
   Familiarity with pension, accident and unemployment insurance
   Knowledge of accounting and taxation
   Knowledge of regulations, company forms, company reorganization and contract regulations

8. *Skills in information technology (12)*
   E-mail
   The Internet
   Text-processing programs
   Spreadsheet
   Calendar software
   Graphics processing
   Database (card index programs)
   Software accounts payable and receivable
   Accounting programs
   Payroll computation
   Production management system
   Advertising programs

9. *Language skills (5)*
   English
   Swedish
   German
   French
   Russian

9. Performance and Survival of Technology Firms: The Impact of Intellectual Property

Wolfgang Bessler and Claudia Bittelmeyer

INTRODUCTION

Innovation as measured by intellectual property should have a significant impact on the long-run performance and success of technology firms.[1] Although the positive effect of innovation on value creation is intuitively appealing, it is much more difficult to provide empirical evidence that an increase in innovative activity will lead to a higher firm value. One of the difficulties is to find adequate measures for innovation on the one hand and for firm performance on the other hand. Possible innovation variables that are observable are R&D expenditure, patents and patent indicators. Stock prices are usually a good proxy for capturing the market value of firms and the valuation effects of events and specific factors. With respect to the impact of technology and growth opportunities, we would expect that the valuation effects are more pronounced for start-up firms and especially for firms that raised new equity by going public. Hence, it is important and challenging to provide empirical evidence on the superior long-run financial performance and on the higher probability of survival for initial public offerings (IPOs) that concentrate on innovation and have relatively more intellectual property. The major research question is whether firms that filed for patents outperformed those firms with no patented technology and whether they were less likely to file for bankruptcy.

In the empirical analysis we include all German firms that went public on the Neuer Markt in Germany during the period from 1997 to 2003. Because the Neuer Markt was created by the Deutsche Börse as a special market segment for high-technology firms, these initial public offerings are an interesting sample for analysing the effects of innovation on firm performance. Moreover, this high-tech stock market attracted a large number of start-up firms over a short period of time and was characterized by extreme swings in valuation and market performance. In the empirical analysis we test the hypothesis that the long-run performance of IPOs is related to the number of filed patents. This relationship is analysed by calculating buy-and-hold abnormal returns (BHAR) for the first two years after going public. Finally, we broaden the perspective on the positive impact of innovation on firm performance by investigating the long-run success and survival of individual firms. We test the hypothesis that the quality of intellectual property has a significant impact on the survival probability of IPOs. We distinguish between those IPOs that either filed for bankruptcy or were acquired and those that stayed independent. In the analysis the patent quality is measured by the empirical patent value indicators such as the number of IPC classes (International Patent Classification), the family size, the number of backward and forward citations, and the frequency of cited articles. In order to gain a better understanding of the importance of patent quality we also investigate whether the two groups of successful and bankrupt firms have patents that are either of higher or lower quality, respectively.

Our findings provide significant empirical evidence that intellectual property as measured by the number of patents has a positive impact on firm valuation. In particular we find that IPOs with patents generate a superior short- and long-run performance compared to firms without patents. As revealed in most studies on IPOs, the performance first increases over a certain period of time and then starts to diminish. In our study, however, the valuation effects are much more pronounced. There are various explanations for these stock price reactions over time and for the differences between IPOs with and without patents. Most likely, there is an overvaluation of growth opportunities for firms with patents during the first year after going public. It is possible that these firms were able to employ patents to signal convincingly their quality in a situation where in fact there was no positive impact on current and future cash flows. Moreover, there are other factors that may influence the performance, such as venture capital, mandatory and tax lock-up periods and bank ownership. In the empirical analysis on bankruptcy we find evidence that surviving firms filed for more patents and have patents that are of a higher quality as measured by the patent indicators.

The rest of the chapter is organized as follows. In the next section we review the literature with respect to innovation and the importance of innovation for firm performance. In the section on data both the stock market data and the patent data are described. The methodology and the empirical results for the long-run stock price performance are presented in the section on intellectual property and the long-term performance of IPOs. In the subsequent section we analyse the impact that intellectual property has on the survival probability of initial public offerings. The final section concludes this study.

REVIEW OF THE LITERATURE

There is a vast amount of literature related to measures of innovation on the one hand and the impact of innovation on firm performance on the other. Performance measures usually range from productivity and accounting numbers to stock market performance. In this section we review the relevant literature for a variety of innovation measures as well as for the impact of innovation on stock market performance.

Measuring Innovation

When measuring the impact that innovation has on firm value, it is usually difficult to find an accurate indicator for the firm's innovation potential. In the next two sections we discuss the advantages and disadvantages of R&D expenditure and patents as possible innovation indicators.

R&D as an innovation measure

Because the expenditure on research and development (R&D) is often used as a measure for the firm's intangible assets, this is also often used as a proxy for innovative activity. When R&D expenditure is used as a proxy for innovation, there are usually some inherent shortcomings. In a study for the pharmaceutical industry Grabowski and Vernon (1994) point out that the failure rate is extremely high, in that only 30 per cent of all R&D projects generate a positive net present value. Moreover, the use of R&D expenditure as an innovation measure does not allow for differentiating between successful and failed projects. In a comparison of the stock market reaction to successful and unsuccessful R&D projects, Shortridge (2004) concludes that these results could be biased due to the fact that only successful projects lead to a positive capital market reaction. So the finding that R&D is a value driver could be misleading. More importantly, R&D expenditure is not fully disclosed in the traditional German accounting reports (HGB). Nevertheless, Ramb and Reitzig (2005) find empirical evidence that the impact of R&D expenditure on the market value of the firm is higher when the firms report under the traditional German accounting standards (HGB) compared to US GAAP (Generally Accepted Accounting Principles) or IAS/IFRS (International Accounting Standards / International Financial Reporting Standards). This finding is quite surprising because reporting R&D

expenditure under HGB is voluntary. Moreover, internally generated intangible assets have to be reported at production cost. They can be reported at market value only when they are externally acquired. To cope with this dilemma, the rules and regulations of the Neuer Markt introduced higher listing requirements in Germany. These IPOs had to publish their financial statements by following either IAS/IFRS (International Financial Reporting Standards) or US GAAP. However, a large number of firms did not fulfil these requirements appropriately (Glaum and Street 2003), resulting in some problems with respect to the completeness and accuracy of the R&D database.

Patents as an innovation measure

As an alternative to R&D, patents have been used to measure innovation. Griliches (1990) regards patents as one output in the knowledge production function, whereas R&D expenses are used as an input. Firms that apply for a patent have to pay for the application and the granting procedure as well as the annual renewal. Because the costs for international patents can be especially high, Licht and Zoz (1998) conclude that only valuable ideas are worth being patented. The study by Ramb and Reitzig (2004) compares the relevance of information that is contained in accounting and patent data. They find that there is a stronger positive relationship between the number of filed patents and the market value of the firm than between R&D and intangible accounting information and firm value. Consequently, the number and quality of a firm's patents should be a better measure of the quality of a firm's innovative activity than R&D expenditure. Most importantly, the patent database appears to be of higher quality than the R&D database, because patents are publicly available and most patent offices publish the application date, the publication date and the patent code independently of the status of the patent.

Performance and Innovation

Performance measures usually range from productivity and accounting numbers to stock market performance. In this section we review the literature that employs stock market performance to analyse the value relevance of innovative activity. An interesting approach is employed by Chung et al. (2005) who analyse for the US market the premium that investors are willing to pay for firms that employ intangible assets. The empirical findings support these ideas in that more innovative firms have a higher offering price as well as larger initial returns (higher underpricing) at the time of the IPO. Nevertheless, these highly innovative firms also reveal negative BHAR after two years, which is in accordance with the usual negative long-run performance of IPOs. However, the underperformance of these innovative IPOs is smaller than that of other IPOs. Guo et al. (2006) also find evidence that innovation, as measured by R&D intensity, is positively related to both the underpricing and the long-run performance. They suggest that due to the additional risk of R&D the valuation of high-R&D firms should be lower and the expected return higher compared to low-R&D firms. They conclude that in general the investor's optimism should be lower for R&D firms, which results first in a higher underpricing but subsequently in a higher long-run performance. They use the alpha (intercept) from the Fama-French model as the abnormal return measure and find support for their hypothesis. These findings are in accordance with Eberhardt et al. (2004), who report a long-run outperformance when firms increase their R&D expenditure.

Other studies that focus on established firms expand the model structure to multi-factor asset pricing models by including additional R&D and patent variables. For example, al-Horani et al. (2003) are able to improve the explanatory power of the three-factor Fama-French model by including an additional R&D factor. Hirschey and Richardson (2004) and Deng et al. (1999) include weighted patent counts in the market model. In one of the first studies including continental Europe, Hall and Oriani (2004) find evidence for different valuation effects of R&D expenditure and knowledge stock in continental European countries than in Anglo-Saxon ones. When controlling for the ownership structure of the company, the results confirm previous findings. Booth et al. (2006) take a different research direction and offer interesting insights into the importance of the financial system. They find empirical evidence that technology and innovation are more rapidly priced in a financial market-oriented system than in a bank-oriented financial system. This result is interesting for our own research because the opening of the Neuer Markt was one initiative to complement the traditional bank-oriented system in Germany with a more capital market-oriented approach.

DATA

Initial Public Offerings

The data that are used in our empirical analysis are patent counts and daily stock price data for the initial public offerings in Germany as well as the NEMAX All Share Index of the Neuer Markt. Historically, the German capital market was small relative to the size of the economy and did not offer great opportunities for start-up firms to raise additional equity by going public. Over the period from 1983 to 1997 the annual number of new listings was between nine and 33 (Bessler and Thies 2007). Given the size and focus of the German economy on innovation and technology, this was a very small number. With the bull market and the technology boom in the late 1990s, IPOs suddenly became tremendously popular and an important financing source for start-up technology firms. There were 329 firms that went public during the period from 1997 to 2003. Because of different patenting behaviour and specific patent rights in other countries we concentrate in our empirical analysis on the 288 German IPOs. Stock prices were provided by Reuters and all IPO information such as issuing date and offer size are from Deutsche Börse AG.

Between 1997, the year of the opening of the Neuer Markt, and 1999 there were 184 (162) firms[2] that went public. Between 2000 and 2003 another 145 (126) firms went public. Obviously, 1999 and the first three months of 2000 can clearly be labelled as a hot issue market. The Neuer Markt is a perfect example of the valuation problems of start-up technology firms that usually exist at the time of the IPO but also of the market timing abilities of firms. As shown in Figure 9.1, the NEMAX All Share Index rose from about 500 index points in March 1997 to 8583 index points in March 2000. This is an increase of about 1600 per cent within three years. Subsequently, the index declined from its peak to a level of 353 on 8 October 2002, a decline of 96 per cent. Consequently, the Deutsche Börse closed the Neuer Markt segment in 2003 in response to this decline, but also due to several company scandals and legal problems.

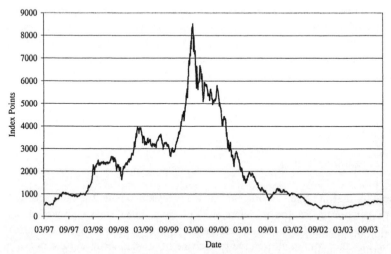

Figure 9.1   Performance of the Nemax All Share Index in Index Points

Thus, the attempt to overcome the traditional bank-based financial system in Germany by creating a new stock market segment for innovative growth firms was clearly not a long-run success. Nevertheless, the hot issue market of 1998 and 1999 and the cold issue market thereafter were unique for the German stock market (Bessler and Kurth 2005). Thus, this market environment offers a great opportunity to investigate the valuation effects and long-run performance of high-tech firms in extreme bull and bear markets.

Patent Data

The data for patents and patent value indicators that we employ in the second part of the study are from the Derwent Innovation Index from Thomson Financial (Derwent 2003). The patent data cover the period from 1980 to 2003. Later data were not available at the time of the analysis (May 2005) due to the publication time lag of 18 months imposed by the regulation of the patent offices. We include all patent applications filed by these IPOs. This number includes all filings with the patent offices, which are applications, granted patents and filings for other property rights. The patent count is identified by the patents and applications of the firm. The patents are counted by their patent number, which is used as an identifier. Furthermore, the patent number reveals the country which the patent protection was applied for. In addition to the national patents there are European patents filed with the European patent office and global applications filed with the World Intellectual Property Organization (WIPO). The patent count for each firm equals the number of patents applied for by the specific firm and also includes all patents by wholly owned subsidiaries as listed in the *Hoppenstedt Aktienführer*.

Our data analysis reveals that 90 firms in our sample have patents. They filed for 6255 applications. This includes all documents published by the patent offices.[3] Of these patents 29 per cent were applied for with the German patent office, 19 per cent with the European patent office, 16 per cent with the US patent office and 13 per cent with the WIPO.[4] When we include only the earliest patent in a patent family as the priority patent, 72 per cent of all patents are filed with the German patent office and 17 per cent with the US patent office.[5] During the period of three years before and three years after the IPO, 86 firms filed applications with a patent office. There were 4448 applications altogether.

In the next two sections we present our empirical analysis. In the following section the methodology, the data and the empirical findings for the long-run performance analysis are presented. In the penultimate section we discuss the methodology and the data and present the empirical findings for the survival analysis.

INTELLECTUAL PROPERTY AND THE LONG-RUN PERFORMANCE OF IPOS

Methodology

The major theme of this analysis is that firms with more intellectual property should have a superior long-run performance. For this we first test empirically whether firms with more intellectual property outperformed the market index, where intellectual property is approximated by the number of patents. Subsequently, we investigate whether the IPOs with patents significantly outperformed the group of IPOs without patents. To measure the long-run performance we employ buy-and-hold abnormal returns (BHAR). BHAR are calculated by first calculating holding period returns (BHR) for a single stock i for time period T as follows:

$$BHR_{i,T} = \left[\prod_{t=1}^{T} (1 + R_{i,t}) \right] - 1 \qquad (9.1)$$

where $R_{i,t}$ is the return of stock i at time t, and T is the time period for which the BHR is determined. For an equally-weighted portfolio of stocks the return is calculated as:

$$dBHR_{P,T} = \frac{1}{N} \sum_{i=1}^{N} BHR_{i,T} \qquad (9.2)$$

where $dBHR_{P,T}$ is the average BHR of the portfolio, N is the number of stocks in the portfolio, and T is the time period for which the BHR is calculated. Finally, buy-and-hold abnormal returns (BHAR) are calculated in that the return of the benchmark is subtracted from the IPO return.

$$BHAR = \frac{1}{N} \sum_{i=1}^{N} \left[\left(\prod_{t=1}^{T} (1 + R_{i,t}) \right) - \left(\prod_{t=1}^{T} (1 + R_{M,t}) \right) \right] \qquad (9.3)$$

The advantage of this method is that the terminal values of the two strategies, that is, investing in an IPO or investing in the benchmark, are directly comparable. Thus, BHAR compare real investment strategies over a defined period. The NEMAX All Share Index is used as a benchmark. This market-weighted performance index includes all companies that are listed at the Neuer Markt.

Because returns are highly skewed, both parametric and non-parametric tests are employed to test for the statistical significance of our findings. We compare the BHAR of four different sub-groups: (1) IPOs with patents; (2) IPOs with no patents at all; (3) IPOs with more than the median number of patents; and (4) IPOs with less than the median number of patents. To test whether the returns of the sub-samples differ significantly we apply a pairwise parametric t-test for the differences between means and a nonparametric Wilcoxon test for the differences of the medians. To test whether the BHAR are significantly different from zero we employ the t-test as well as the Wilcoxon test.

Empirical Results

The long-run valuation effects of the two groups of IPOs are analysed by using buy-and-hold abnormal returns. The BHAR for both the group of IPOs without patents (190 firms) and the group of IPOs with patents (80 firms) are presented in Figure 9.2.

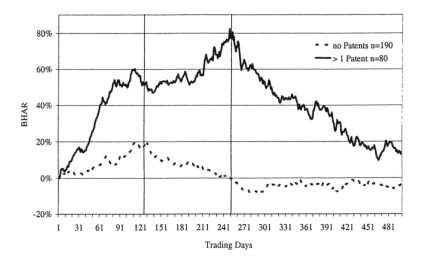

Figure 9.2   BHAR of the Group with Patents (Solid Line) and the Group without Filed Patents (Dotted Line) for the First 500 Trading Days (2 Years)

Nine firms are excluded from the sample because of lack of data due to bankruptcy. One firm (EM.TV) is excluded because of an extreme performance of over 11 000 per cent. We also exclude eight firms which only have a single patent to avoid borderline interpretations. In empirical capital market research, buy-and-hold-abnormal returns (BHAR) are the standard measure for the relative performance of long-run stock returns when analysing initial public offerings. In this study BHAR are calculated by using the NEMAX All Share Index as a proxy for the market performance. The BHAR for both groups – IPOs without patents (190 firms) and IPOs with patents (80 firms) – are presented in Figure 9.2.

After the first six and 12 months of trading the group of initial public offerings with patents has BHAR of 51.06 per cent (51.93 per cent for all)[6] and 77.16 per cent, respectively. In contrast, the group of initial public offerings without patents has a performance of 15.72 per cent and 0.2 per cent after six and 12 months, respectively. The difference in returns between these groups is statistically significant, indicating that firms with patents outperformed firms without patents over that period. These empirical findings support the notion that technology and innovation were reflected in the valuation of IPOs in Germany and that innovation was an important factor for achieving a superior performance. Interestingly, the performance of both groups diminishes after 12 months. Thus, after 24 months of trading the performance for both groups is lower than for the six- and 12-month periods.

One possible explanation for this relative underperformance is the overvaluation of all IPOs during the first year after going public. After two years the BHAR for the group of IPOs with more than one patent is 13.99 per cent (41 per cent for all) whereas the IPOs without patents have a negative performance of -4.06 per cent. The BHAR of the two groups (41 per cent and -4.06 per cent) are significantly different at the 10 per cent level (t-test). Although both groups show a similar decline in market values over time, it appears that the IPOs with patents outperformed the IPOs without patents in both the short and long term.

Although there is ample empirical evidence of short-term outperformance and long-run underperformance for IPOs in most capital markets, the strong abnormal performance of IPOs over the first six- and 12-month periods, independent of patents and technology, seems surprising at first. However, this may be explained by the special legal and tax environment in Germany. There was a six-month mandatory lock-up period at the Neuer Markt for certain investor groups such as venture capitalists and management (Bessler and Kurth 2006a, 2006b). Moreover, there is an exemption from capital gains taxation for private investors after a 12-month holding period (Bessler and Kurth 2007). Both regulations had a significant impact on investors' transaction behaviour and especially on sell decisions. As a consequence, we observe different valuation effects, especially a run-up before the end of both periods and a decline thereafter. Overall, there is significant evidence of a positive relationship between intellectual property (patents) and firm performance for IPOs at the Neuer Markt in Germany.

In order to gain additional insights into the valuation effects of innovation we further separate the group of firms with patents into two sub-groups of approximately the same size where the median (25 patents) is the cut-off point. The performance of the group (40 firms) with fewer patents (2–25) is 47.08 per cent after 123 trading days and -0.01 per cent after 500 trading days, respectively. In contrast, the performance of the group (40 firms) with more patents (26 and over) is 55.03 per cent after 123 trading days and 28.77 per cent after 500 trading days. The results are presented in Table 9.1.

Table 9.1   BHAR after 123 and 500 Trading Days with Respect to the Patenting Behaviour

		BHAR 123 in %		t Diff. MW z Diff. Med.	BHAR 500 in %		t Diff. MW z Diff. Med.
	N	Mean	Med.		Mean	Med.	
> 0 patents	88	51.93***	13.74***	2.74***	41.00	-2.54	1.77*
no patents	190	15.72**	-10.22	3.12***	-4.06	-10.96***	2.83***
> 1 patent	80	51.06***	15.33***	2.62***	13.99	-2.54	1.02
no patents	190	15.72**	-10.22	3.19***	-4.06	-10.96***	2.86***
> 25 patents	40	55.03***	30.93***	2.36**	28.77	3.48	1.37
no patents	190	15.72	-10.22	3.17***	-4.06	-10.96***	3.01***
2–25 patents	40	47.08**	12.11	1.76*	-0.01	-6.44	0.14
no patents	190	15.72**	-10.22	1.72*	-4.06	-10.96***	1.37
> 25 patents	40	55.03***	30.93***	0.32	28.77	3.48	1.03
2–25 patents	40	47.08**	12.11	1.22	-0.01	-6.44	1.77*

Notes:
*** Significant at the 1% level
** Significant at the 5% level
* Significant at the 10% level

The differences are substantial but not significant. Overall the empirical evidence suggests that patents have a positive impact on the performance of IPOs, in the short as well as the long term. Further differentiation by the number of patents does not offer additional insights, at least not in this framework. Although there is convincing evidence of the positive impact of patents on firm valuation and performance, it seems interesting to extend our empirical analysis by investigating the impact that patents may have on the long-run survival probability of firms that went public.

INTELLECTUAL PROPERTY AND SUCCESS OF TECHNOLOGY FIRMS

The objective of the second part of our study is to provide additional insights into the effects that patents have on the success and survival of initial public offerings or on the exit, where market exit is defined as either being acquired or having filed for bankruptcy.

Literature Review

Obviously, there are various approaches for measuring the success of a firm. They range from accounting-based measures and operating performance to financial performance (Devinney et al. 2005). A different approach is to estimate the probability of success or failure of an enterprise. Although the risk of failure of a firm is dependent on the business cycle and many other factors, there is empirical evidence that on average the risk of failure has increased over the last decade, especially for firms that went public. Fama and French (2004), for example, find in a study of NASDAQ firms that the probability of success of IPOs has decreased over time. This implies that the risk that the investor will lose all his money by investing in IPOs has increased. Of those firms that went public during the period from 1973 to 1979, 47.1 per cent were operating for more than ten years. For the period from 1980 to 1991 only 38.2 per cent of the IPOs were still operating after ten years.[7] This raises the question for the investor of whether it is possible not only to increase the average rate of return by investing in innovative firms but at the same time to reduce the risk of failure. This question is addressed in this section.

External debt ratings by rating agencies such as Moodys and Standard & Poors and internal ratings by banks as required under Basel II are indicators of the probability that the firm may not be in a position to make the scheduled interest payments and the repayment of the face value at maturity. The most prominent models are the Z-Score model (Altman 1968) and the Zeta model (Altman et al. 1977), which are based on discriminant analysis. Most of the time, however, measures of innovative activities are not included in these models for estimating the survival rate or the probability of bankruptcy. Nevertheless, Rammer (2005, p. 7) interprets the results of the Mannheimer Innovation Panel (MIP) such that firms that invest in and concentrate on research and development have a higher probability of success, that is, continuing operations, than firms with lower R&D activities.

A number of other studies also find evidence that innovative firms have a higher probability of success than less innovative firms. However, these studies often differ with respect to the approach they use for measuring innovation. For the United States, Hall (1987) finds a positive relation between R&D activities and the survival of a firm. Surprisingly, this effect diminishes when patent filings are included. By using information about innovation from the CIS (Community Innovation Survey) questionnaire, Cefis and Marsili (2005) find evidence that innovative firms have a higher probability of survival. Cockburn and Wagner (2005) analyse the success of 356 IPOs at NASDAQ that operate in the intangible sensitive software industry. Their findings suggest that firms with a larger number of patent filings have a lower probability of bankruptcy, supporting the notion that patents are an important factor for success. This positive relationship between intellectual property and success is also supported in a study by Audretsch and Lehmann (2004) for IPOs at the Neuer Markt in which they employ patent counts as the innovation measure. In contrast to their study, our empirical analysis is more detailed in that we include various patent value indicators instead of only the number of patents. These patent indicators are explained and discussed in the next section. Thus, the objective of this section is to investigate the relationship between innovation and the probability of bankruptcy for IPOs at the Neuer Markt. The hypothesis is that firms that file for bankruptcy have lower innovative activities. As a proxy for innovative activity we use patent counts and patent value indicators.

Methodology

As before, we separate the IPOs into two groups. Group 1 includes all firms that went public but exited the market later on (up to May 2005). Group 2 includes all firms that went public but continued to operate up to the end of the observation period (May 2005). We follow the approach employed in other studies (for example Agarwal and Audretsch 2001) and use the filing for bankruptcy and the acquisition by another firm as a measure for the market exit.

We investigate whether the two groups are different with respect to the success of their intellectual property activity. One problem that usually comes up in such a study is the fact that the value distribution of patents is skewed. When valuing patents by using renewal data, Schankerman and Pakes (1985) find evidence of a highly skewed distribution. Scherer (1998), Harhoff et al. (1999) and Scherer and Harhoff (2000) support the results of a skewed distribution by analysing the value distributions of royalties, new ventures that are dependent on patents, renewal fees and survey data. This skewed value distribution is not surprising but makes the patent valuation more difficult. Thus, the use of patents as the only innovation measure could be problematic, because patent counts could be too imprecise as a measure.

Further, valuing technology requires very specific knowledge and skills. Moreover, the valuation of a patent is challenging due to the fact that there is no accepted methodology or common approach for patent valuation. We approach this problem by employing patent value indicators. A survey of these issues is provided in Reitzig (2003). He also analyses the value relevance of the patent indicators in an empirical study. In the following section we present the indicators that we employ in this study.

Following the approach by Lerner (1994) and Austin (1993), we employ the number of IPC classes which a patent is allocated to as an indicator. In an event study Austin (1993) provides empirical evidence that patents that are allocated to a larger number of IPC classes are valued more positively by the market. In addition Lerner (1994) finds positive valuation effects for those venture capital investments in which a firm is able to increase the average number of IPC classes a patent belongs to.

Putnam (1996) highlights the relevance of patent families and triadic patents whereas Ramb and Reitzig (2004) use the family size as an indicator for patent value. We employ the family size as an indicator for the 'geographic' breadth of a patent. Citation indicators have been used to measure the overall quality of a patent. Especially forward citations (these are patents that cite a specific patent) but also backward citations (these are patents that a specific patent cites) as well as citation to the non-patent literature (cited articles) seem to contain important information about the private and social value of patents (Bloom and Van Reenen 2002, Hall et al. 2005, Harhoff et al. 1999, Harhoff et al. 2003, Reitzig 2003). Hence, we analyse whether the two groups of IPOs are different with respect to their intellectual property. In addition to the patent counts we employ as patent value indicators the IPC classes, family size, and backward and forward citations as well as cited articles.

Data

Of the 288 German IPOs that went public 73 firms filed for bankruptcy or were acquired and are therefore included in Group 1. Consequently, 215 firms survived and belong to Group 2. The information about firm performance and firm exit was gathered from *Hoppenstedt Aktienführer*, from 'ad hoc information services', and from Deutsche Börse AG. The patent count and the patent indicators are from the Derwent Innovation Index. The Derwent Innovation Index consists of the Derwent World Patent Index and the Derwent Citation Index. The Derwent World Patent Index includes the IPC classes, the family size, the backward citations and the cited articles. The citation index allows the search for the forward citations. On average, the firms have 21.72 entries at the patent offices. The patents of a firm are included on average in 4.02 IPC classes. A patent family of a firm has an average of 4.85 entries. Finally, a firm's patent has, on average, 1.98 backward citations, 0.07 cited articles, and receives 1.84 forward citations.

Empirical Findings

First we analyse whether the capital market was able to anticipate the failure of the firms and had already valued these firms lower, beginning with the time of the IPO and up to two years after the IPO. These results are compared with the group of firms that do not file for bankruptcy. In Figure 9.3 we present the BHAR for the two groups. At first glance there is no obvious difference in the performance of the two groups. This empirical finding suggests that the capital market is not in a position to differentiate between those IPOs that are successful in the long term and those that eventually will file for bankruptcy.

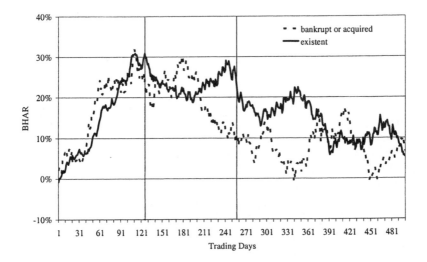

Figure 9.3   BHAR of the Firms of Group 1 (Bankrupt or Acquired) (Dotted Line) and Firms of Group 2 (Existent) (Solid Line) for the First 500 Trading Days (2 Years)

Because previous research indicates that the age of a firm has an impact on the performance and on the probability of failure of IPOs (Cefis and Marsili 2005), we investigate whether the two groups of IPOs differ with respect to age. We analyse whether the age distributions for the time period up to the initial public offering of the firms are different for these two groups. In fact we test for the homogeneity of the groups by using the Kolmogorov-Smirnov test with respect to age. We find no statistical evidence to reject this homogeneity hypothesis, meaning that the two groups are not different.

As an alternative the investor could use the patenting activities of an IPO to estimate the survival probability of a firm in order to reduce the probability of losing all the money invested in a specific IPO. This approach can only be successful if firms that file for patents have a lower probability to file for bankruptcy. We now analyse the patenting behaviour for both groups. The results from our analysis are presented in Table 9.2. Of the 288 German IPOs in our sample, 90 IPOs (31 per cent) filed at least for one patent. Of the 73 firms that went bankrupt and therefore belong to Group 1, 19 firms filed for at least one patent. For Group 2 we find that of the 215 firms belonging to that group, 71 firms filed for at least one patent. The relative figures for both groups are 26 per cent and 33 per cent, respectively. Furthermore, firms belonging to Group 1 filed for 6.14 patents on average whereas firms belonging to Group 2 filed for an average of 27.01 patents. At first glance these figures suggest that there is a clear difference in patenting behaviour (Table 9.2).

Table 9.2   Patenting Behaviour of the Firms in Group 1 (Insolvent) and Group 2 (Solvent)

	N	Share	With Patents	Share
Group 1	73	22%	19	26%
Group 2	215	65%	71	33%
Foreigners	41	12%		
Sum	329	100%	90	31%

	Patents	Years with Patents	Patents p.a.
Group 1	6.14	4.05	1.52
Group 2	27.01	7.69	3.51
$P(t > T)$	0.03	0.01	

To control further for the patent effect, we examine the number of patents filed for per year (patents p.a.) as well as the number of years the firm filed for a patent. The results are all robust (Table 9.2).

Another explanation for the difference in patent counts could be that firms that filed for bankruptcy belong to a sector which was heavily influenced by the stock market crash or that does not usually file for patents due to various reasons. Again, we cannot reject the homogeneity hypothesis according to the results of the Kolmogorov-Smirnov test indicating that there is no special industry effect in the data. In addition to the patent counts, we employ the quality indicators for both groups to analyse whether they are different. To do this we use the average frequency of an indicator per firm per patent. With respect to the IPC classes the patents of the bankrupt group are in three IPC classes and the patents of the successful firms are in more than four classes. The family size of the successful firms is on average 5.16 whereas the family size of the failed firms is 3.68. The patents of the successful firms are cited on average 2.12 times, whereas this number for the patents of the failed IPOs is only 0.82. For the backward citations we find that on average the patents of the firms belonging to Group 1 (bankrupt) cite 1.18 patents whereas the patents of the firms belonging to Group 2 (still operating) cite 2.21 patents. Furthermore, the patents of the firms still operating cite more articles (0.08 versus 0.01). Thus, they are more involved in R&D which spills over into a better performance. The means of the indicators are all different at the 10 per cent level (Table 9.3).

Table 9.3   Patent Quality of the Patents of Firms in Group 1 (Insolvent) and Group 2 (Solvent)

	Patents	IPC	Family Size	Backwards	Forwards	Cited Articles
Group 1 - mean	6.14	3.08	3.68	1.18	0.82	0.01
Group 2 - mean	27.01	4.27	5.16	2.21	2.12	0.08
P(t > T)	0.03	0.08	0.04	0.10	0.03	0.05
D	0.41***	0.34**	0.29	0.31*	0.33**	0.46***

Note: D = Test statistic of the test for homogeneity – H_0 distributions are homogeneous.

In addition to the analysis of the means we extend the analysis by testing the homogeneity of the distributions. Again we use the Kolmogorov-Smirnov test and investigate whether the two groups are equal for the following three hypotheses: (1) the distribution of the patent counts are equal; (2) both distributions are equal with respect to the indicators IPC classes and size of the patent family; and (3) the distributions are equal with respect to the number of forward and backward citations and the frequency of cited articles. Because the empirical analysis of the means indicates that the firms with the higher patent quality are less likely to be insolvent, a difference in the distribution should be interpreted in supporting these previous results. The relative frequencies for the patent counts and cited articles of Groups 1 and 2 are presented in Figure 9.4. It appears that the distribution of the patents of the successful firms in Group 2 covers a wider range. So we can reject the first hypothesis that the patent counts are equal (D = 0.41, α = 0.01).

This result supports our previous findings that the number of patents has a positive impact on the long-run performance of IPOs at the Neuer Markt. The findings for the second and third hypotheses with respect to patent breadth and citations are not as clear-cut. In fact the distributions of the patent breadth of both groups (IPC) are significantly different (D = 0.34, α = 0.01) but the test for the equality of the distribution with respect to the family size cannot be rejected at any significance level. The forward citations are significant at the 5 per cent level whereas the backward citations are significant at the 10 per cent level. Interestingly, the hypothesis that the two distributions of the frequency of cited articles are equal can be rejected at the 1 per cent significance level (Figure 9.4 and Table 9.3).

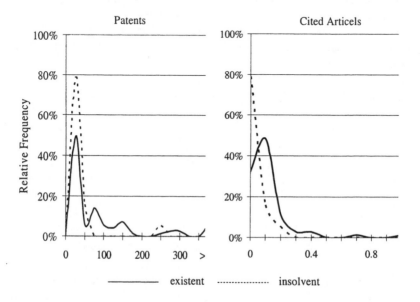

Figure 9.4   Probability Function of the Patent Counts and Cited Articles for the Insolvent and Solvent Firms

CONCLUSIONS

In this study we investigate the impact of the patenting behaviour on the performance of German firms that went public at the Neuer Markt during the period from 1997 to 2003. The main focus of the empirical analysis is to examine whether companies that filed for patents outperformed those companies with no patented technology. Because the Neuer Markt was a stock exchange segment especially for high-technology firms and patents are usually considered a good measure for technical innovation, the German initial public offerings (IPOs) are ideal for analysing the impact of intellectual property on firm value. In the empirical analysis we measure performance by using buy-and-hold abnormal returns (BHAR) for the first two years after going public. Overall the empirical analysis provides convincing evidence that intellectual property has a positive impact on the value and long-run performance of technology firms. In particular, the abnormal performance of IPOs with patents is positive and significantly higher than that of IPOs without patented technology after 123 and 500 days of trading. The major result of this study is that innovation as measured by patents is an important factor that has a positive impact on the long-run performance of initial public offerings in Germany.

Moreover, we find some empirical evidence that the patenting behaviour has a significant impact on the success or bankruptcy of firms. The results suggest that there is a significant difference in the patenting behaviour between the group of firms that exit the market and the group of firms that still operate. The firms that failed had fewer patents and patents of lower quality. Thus, intellectual property as measured by patents is an important factor that has a positive impact on the long-run performance and survival of start-up technology firms that went public.

NOTES

1. Innovative enterprises are firms that have the ability to introduce new products to the market (innovation) in a regular manner. One prerequisite for innovation is investments in R&D and the protection of this intellectual property by filing for patents (intellectual property rights, for example patents). In our study we use innovation as the more general expression for R&D and patents. Later on in our empirical study we use intellectual property and patents in particular because of the advantage of using patents instead of R&D expenses.
2. The figures in parentheses indicate the number IPOs of German firms.
3. In this study we do not differentiate between statuses of the patents, for example application and granted. In another study, we find evidence that the results are similar when only granted patents are considered (Bessler and Bittelmeyer 2006).
4. Eight per cent, 7 per cent and 2 per cent of the patents were applied for with the Australian, Japanese and Korean patent offices, respectively. The other 6 per cent are patents that have been filed with 25 different offices.
5. Seven per cent of the priority registrations are with the European patents office, 1 per cent with the WIPO and 1 per cent in Japan. The other 2 per cent of registrations are with ten different patent offices.
6. Figures in parentheses are the means if we also include the firms that applied for only one patent. When we calculate the BHAR by using the DAX as the market index we find the following results for firms without patents and more than one patent: 123 trading days: no patents: 22 per cent versus patents: 45 per cent; 250 trading days no patents: -3 per cent versus patents: 65 per cent; 500 trading days no patents: -36 per cent versus patents: -10 per cent.
7. For an analysis of bank IPOs in the United States see Bessler et al. (2006). Their analysis reveals that there is a high exit rate (acquisition and failure) for banks that went public. Only 20.2 per cent of the 431 banks that went public between 1971 and 1997 were still operating

ten years after the IPO. This figure is only 14 per cent for bank IPOs for the hot issue period between 1983 and 1988.

REFERENCES

Agarwal, R. and D.B. Audretsch (2001), 'Does entry size matter? The impact of the life cycle and technology on firm survival', *Journal of Industrial Economics*, **49**, 21–43.

Al-Horani, A., P.F. Pope and A.W. Stark (2003), 'Research and development activity and expected returns in the United Kingdom', *European Finance Review*, **7**, 27–46.

Altman, E.I. (1968), 'Financial ratios, discriminant analysis and the prediction of corporate bankruptcy', *Journal of Finance*, **23**, 589–609.

Altman, E.I., R. Haldeman and P. Narayanan (1977), 'ZETA analysis: a new model to identify bankruptcy risk of corporations', *Journal of Banking and Finance*, **1**, 29–54.

Audretsch, David B. and Erik E. Lehmann (2004), 'The effect of experience, ownership, and knowledge on IPO survival: evidence from the Neuer Markt', Discussion paper 04/10, Diskussionspapier der Forschergruppe Heterogene Arbeit: Positive und Normative Aspekte der Qualifikationsstruktur der Arbeit, Konstanz.

Austin, D.H. (1993), 'The value of intangible assets – an event-study approach to measuring innovative output: the case of biotechnology', *American Economic Review*, **83**, 253–8.

Bessler, W. and C. Bittelmeyer (2006), 'Innovation and the performance of technology firms: evidence from initial public offerings in Germany', working paper, University of Giessen, Germany.

Bessler, W. and A. Kurth (2005), 'Exit strategies of venture capitalists in hot issue markets: evidence from Germany', *Journal of Entrepreneurial Finance and Business Ventures*, **10** (August), 27–51.

Bessler, W. and A. Kurth (2006a), 'Die Auswirkungen der Spekulationssteuer auf die Verkaufsentscheidungen der Anleger in Deutschland', *Zeitschrift für Bankrecht und Bankwirtschaft*, **18** (1), 1–15.

Bessler, W. and A. Kurth (2006b), 'Lock-up Verträge und Bewertungseffekte bei Initial Public Offerings am Neuen Markt', working paper, University of Giessen.

Bessler, W. and A. Kurth (2007), 'Agency problems and the performance of venture-backed IPOs in Germany: Exit strategies, lock-up periods, and bank ownership', *European Journal of Finance*, 13 (1), 29–63.

Bessler, W., J.P. Murtagh and D. Siregar (2006), 'Dividend Policy of Bank Initial Public Offerings', Chapter 7, in M. Bagella, L. Becchetti and I. Hassan (eds), *Transparency, Governance and Markets*, Elsevier, pp. 189–219.

Bessler, W. and S. Thies (2007), 'The long-run performance of initial public offerings in Germany', *Managerial Finance*, forthcoming.

Bloom, N. and J. Van Reenen (2002), 'Patents, real options and firm performance', *Economic Journal*, **112** (March), C97–C116.

Booth, G.G., J. Juttila, J. Kallunki, M. Rahiala and P. Sahlström (2006), 'How does the financial environment affect the stock market valuation of R&D spending?' *Journal of Financial Intermediation*, **15**, 197–214.

Cefis, E. and O. Marsili (2005), 'A matter of life and death: innovation and firm survival', *Industrial and Corporate Change*, **14**, 1167–92.

Chung, K.H., M. Li and L. Yu (2005), 'Assets in place, growth opportunities, and IPO returns', *Financial Management*, **34** (3), 65–88.

Cockburn, I.M. and S. Wagner (2005), 'Intellectual property and the survival of internet related NASDAQ-IPOs', working paper, TU Munich.

Deng, Z., B. Lev and F. Narin (1999), 'Science and technology as predictors of stock performance', *Financial Analyst Journal*, (May/June), 20–32.

Derwent (2003), *Derwent Innovation Index*, London: Thomson Scientific.

Devinney, T.M., P.J. Richard, G.S. Yip and G. Johnson (2005), 'Measuring organizational performance in management research: a synthesis of measurement challenges and approaches', working paper, Australian Graduate School of Management, Sydney.

Eberhart, A.C., W.F. Maxwell and A.R. Siddique (2004), 'An examination of long-run abnormal stock returns and operating performance following R&D increases', *Journal of Finance*, **59**, 623–50.

Fama, E.F. and K.R. French (2004), 'New lists: fundamentals and survival rates', *Journal of Financial Economics*, **73**, 229–69.

Glaum, M. and D.L. Street (2003), 'Compliance with the disclosure requirements of Germany's new market: IAS versus US GAAP', *Journal of International Financial Management and Accounting*, **14**, 64–100.

Grabowski, H.G. and J.M. Vernon (1994), 'Returns to R&D on new drug introductions in the 1980s', *Journal of Health Economics*, **13**, 383–406.

Griliches, Z. (1990), 'Patent statistics as economic indicators: a survey', *Journal of Economic Literature*, **28**, 1661–707.

Guo, Re-Jin, Baruch Lev and Charles Shi (2006), 'Explaining the short- and long-run IPO anomalies by R&D', *Journal of Business Finance and Accounting*, **33**, 555–79.

Hall, B.H. (1987), 'The relationship between firm size and firm growth in the US manufacturing sector', *Journal of Industrial Economics*, **35**, 583–606.

Hall, B.H., A. Jaffe and M. Trajtenberg (2005), 'Market value and patent citations', *RAND Journal of Economics*, **36**, 16–38.

Hall, B.H. and R. Oriani (2004), 'Does the market value R&D investment by European firms? Evidence from a panel of manufacturing firms in France, Germany, and Italy', working paper, University of California at Berkeley.

Harhoff, D., F. Narin, F.M. Scherer and K. Vopel (1999), 'Citation frequency and the value of patented inventions', *Review of Economics and Statistics*, **81**, 511–15.

Harhoff, D., F.M. Scherer and K. Vopel (2003), 'Citations, family size, opposition and the value of patent rights', *Research Policy*, **32**, 1343–63.

Hirschey, M. and V.J. Richardson (2004), 'Are scientific indicators of patent quality useful to investors?' *Journal of Empirical Finance*, **11**, 91–107.

Lerner, J. (1994), 'The importance of patent scope: an empirical analysis', *RAND Journal of Economics*, **25**, 319–33.

Licht, G. and K. Zoz (1998), 'Patents and R&D: an econometric investigation using applications for German, European and US patents by German companies', *Annales D'Economie et de Statistique*, **49/50**, 329–60.

Putnam, J.D. (1996), *The Value of International Patent Rights*, Ann Arbor, MI: UMI Dissertation Services.

Ramb, F. and M. Reitzig (2004), 'A comparative analysis of the explanatory power of balance sheet and patent information for the market values of German firms', working paper, Copenhagen Business School.

Ramb, F. and M. Reitzig (2005), 'Comparing the value relevance of R&D reporting in Germany: standard and selection effects', discussion paper, Deutsche

Bundesbank, Series 1: Economic Studies, (36/2005).

Rammer, C. (2005), 'FuE-Verhalten von jungen Unternehmen in Deutschland - eine Panelanalyse für den Zeitraum 1998–2003', working paper, ZEW, (8).

Reitzig, M. (2003), 'What determines patent value? Insights from the semiconductor industry', *Research Policy*, **32**, 13–26.

Schankerman, M. and A. Pakes (1985), 'Estimates of the value of patent rights in European countries during the post-1950 period', *Economic Journal*, **96** (384), 1052–76.

Scherer, F.M. (1998), 'The size distribution of profits from innovation', *Annales D'Economie et de Statistique*, **49/50**, 495–516.

Scherer, F.M. and D. Harhoff (2000), 'Technology policy for a world of skew-distributed outcomes', *Research Policy*, **29**, 559–66.

Shortridge, R.T. (2004), 'Market valuation of successful versus non-successful R&D efforts in the pharmaceutical industry', *Journal of Business Finance and Accounting*, **31**, 1301–26.

10. Academic Founders and Business Opportunity Generation: An Empirical Analysis based on Italian Academic Spin-Offs

Riccardo Fini and Rosa Grimaldi

INTRODUCTION

The important role that academic spin-offs have in supporting economic and technological growth has been widely acknowledged (Shane 2004). Academic spin-offs are companies created to exploit technological knowledge originating within universities. Such a definition includes cases in which university employees start a company on the basis of either a university-assigned technology (licence) or a more generic technological knowledge (non-university-assigned). It also encompasses situations in which the university elects to provide the rights to the technology to an external, independent entrepreneur, a non-university employee, who initiates a new company (Radosevich 1995).

Universities, which are aware of the important contribution that academic spin-offs can give to economic and technological development, have been increasingly supporting their creation and growth. Many studies have been devoted to understanding factors spurring their creation and growth, and have addressed the mechanisms put in place by universities, ranging from business plan competitions, university incubators, technology transfer offices (Colombo and Delmastro 2002, Grimaldi and Grandi 2001) to the characteristics of the local contexts in which these companies are settled (Degroof and Roberts 2004, Florida 1999) and the characteristics of academic founders and the founding teams (Roberts 1991, Grimaldi and Grandi 2003).

Despite the growing interest around academic spin-offs, there is little evidence on the nature of academic entrepreneurs and their behaviour in university technology transfer. More specifically the issue of business opportunity identification is central to entrepreneurship (Wright et al. 2004). Knowledge (and information), cognitive and behavioural differences help to explain why certain individuals recognize and develop opportunities while others do not (Venkataraman 1997).

In this chapter, we tackle this important issue for policy makers, university administrators and would-be entrepreneurs. The recognition of opportunities for commercially exploiting technological knowledge is the first step in a new venture creation process. The ability to connect specific knowledge and a commercial opportunity requires a set of skills, aptitudes and circumstances that may not be evenly distributed (Venkataraman 1997).

In this chapter we address this issue first through the analysis of the literature, by offering a review of previous studies that have analysed the factors influencing the ability of new venture founders to recognize and develop opportunities. Drawing on the literature, we develop a framework which is specific to academic spin-off founders and in which we distinguish two main phases of the opportunity recognition process. The first is 'opportunity recognition', during which an opportunity is recognized. In this phase the academic founder's ability to spot an opportunity depends on factors relating to his or her previous knowledge (previous experience) and personal characteristics (personal traits). Then follows a second phase in which the academic founder plays a more proactive role and he or she starts developing (shaping) the opportunity by matching the ideas initially spotted with the concrete characteristics of the environment around him or her, including those of his or her university of origin.

Then we present a descriptive empirical analysis based on a database of 47 Italian academic spin-offs, originating from five universities settled in the Emilia Romagna region in Italy, which has been identified by the EU Commission as one of the leading regions in Europe for its increasing number of research start-ups. Data were gathered through a questionnaire addressed to academic founders in order to explore their characteristics, their previous experience and the factors that in their opinion have most influenced their ability to identify opportunities for commercially exploiting their technologies. Overall we received data from 88 academic founders. We sent the questionnaire to every academic founder, for an overall number of 88 completed questionnaires. Academic founders provided self-reported data based on their own experience and involvement in a new venture creation process. In addition to personal information, through the survey academic founders also provided information about the support that they received from the environment in which they operate and from their universities of origin.

The chapter is organized as follows: in the next section we review the literature which has addressed the issue of 'opportunity identification' and 'opportunity development'. In the section on research design we present the methodology and provide some information about the regional context that we investigated. The subsequent section illustrates the empirical analysis. We first provide descriptive statistics relating to some issues influencing opportunity recognition and development, and then we develop a principal component analysis aimed at identifying some possible aggregations of these issues. In the final section we conclude by discussing the empirical evidence.

BUSINESS OPPORTUNITY GENERATION PROCESS

Business Opportunity

Opportunities are core to entrepreneurial processes. There is growing interest in business opportunity generation and several authors have started researching and publishing in this important area. A business opportunity can be defined in several ways. According to Wickham (2001) it may be seen as a potential to serve customers differently and better than they are being served at present. Shane (2003) defines a business opportunity as a situation in which a person can create a new means–ends framework for recombining resources that the entrepreneur believes will yield a profit. Shane and Venkataraman (2000) argue that 'entrepreneurial opportunities' are situations in which new goods, services, raw materials and organizing methods can be introduced and sold at a greater price than their cost of production.

An opportunity may appear as an 'imprecisely-defined market need' (Kirzner 1997). As the market needs become more defined, the opportunity progresses from its elemental form and a business concept or idea begins to emerge which identifies the type and amount of resources, and the benefits and value brought to particular users (Ardichvili et al. 2003). Eventually, as the opportunity develops into its most elaborated form, formal cash flows, schedules of activities, and resource requirements are added. These additions enable the business idea to be transformed into a business plan.

So far we define business opportunity as a situation in which individuals identify new ways to combine their resources and competences and exploit them to generate a profit.

Business Opportunity Theories

Research on entrepreneurship falls into three schools of thought (Shane 2000), each with different assumptions about the process of entrepreneurial opportunity detection.

Equilibrium theories assume that everyone can recognize all entrepreneurial opportunities and that fundamental attributes of people (rather than information about opportunities) determine who becomes an entrepreneur. Because an equilibrium framework does not allow people to recognize opportunities that others do not see, equilibrium theories explain entrepreneurship by identifying individuals who prefer to become entrepreneurs.

Psychological theories explicitly assume that fundamental attributes of people, rather than information about opportunities, determine who becomes an entrepreneur; moreover this process depends on people's ability and willingness to take action. Researchers from this perspective argue that discovery depends on relative differences between people in their willingness and/or ability to search for and identify opportunities. Stiegler (1952) and Caplan (1999) argue that opportunity identification is the output of a successful rational search process. Shaver and Scott (1991) argue that entrepreneurs identify opportunities as a result of superior information-processing abilities, search techniques or scanning behaviour. According to this perspective, human attributes – need for achievement (McClelland 1961), willingness to bear risk (Brockhaus and Horowitz 1986), self-efficacy (Chen et al. 1998), internal locus of control and tolerance for ambiguity (Begley and Boyd 1987) – lead some people and not others to choose entrepreneurship.

Austrian theories assume that people cannot recognize all entrepreneurial opportunities and that information about opportunities, rather than fundamental attributes of people, determine who becomes an entrepreneur. The whole process depends on factors other than people's ability and willingness to take action. According to this theory, people possess different information, which leads them to see different values in a given commodity or service and offer different prices to obtain it. Kirzner (1997) argues that discovery of opportunities is neither a result of a deliberate search for information nor a result of pure chance. This view of opportunity discovery as happening without deliberate searching is shared by several authors (Ioannides 1999, Streit and Gerhard 1992).

An Integrative Framework

According to Alsos and Kaikkonen (2004), opportunities begin unformed and become developed through time. They may begin as simple concepts and become more elaborate as developed by the entrepreneur. The opportunity detection process is a process of forming and transforming, and change is a fundamental part of it. Opportunities can therefore best be described as processes of opportunity generation or development (see the framework provided in Figure 10.1). In accordance with (and drawing on) previous contributions, we present a framework which sees the creation of a new venture as the last phase of a process that starts with 'opportunity recognition', passes through 'opportunity development and exploitation' and eventually ends in the creation of a new venture. The creation of successful businesses follows a successful opportunity exploitation process. This includes recognition of an opportunity and its development (Ardichvili et al. 2003).

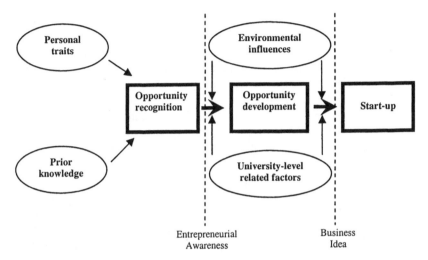

Figure 10.1   Framework

Opportunity recognition

According to Ardichvili et al. (2003), De Koning (1999) and Hills (1995) an opportunity recognition can be viewed as a result of three different processes: (1) spotting market needs and/or underemployed resources; (2) recognizing a fit between market needs and specified resources; and (3) creating a new fit between separate needs and resources in the form of business concepts. Opportunity recognition ends with the awareness of the existence of an opportunity for commercial exploitation (what several authors in the literature refer to as 'entrepreneurial awareness'). Entrepreneurs' personal traits and prior knowledge are seen as antecedents of entrepreneurial awareness (Shane 2000, Gaglio and Taub 1992).

With regard to personal traits, two of them have been shown to be related to successful opportunity recognition (Ardichvili et al. 2003): first, the connection between optimism and higher opportunity recognition has been observed by a number of scholars. Studies by Krueger and Dickson (1994) and Krueger and Brazeal (1994) show that entrepreneurial optimism is related to self-efficacy beliefs. Guth et al. (1991) see optimism as an 'inside view' of the potential success of the venture, largely based on the entrepreneurs' evaluation of their abilities and knowledge. The second personality trait is that of creativity. Hills et al. (1997) found that 90 per cent of entrepreneurs that they surveyed found creativity to be very important for opportunity identification.

In relation to prior knowledge, Shane (2000) argues that entrepreneurs discover opportunities related to the information that they already possess. They discover opportunities because prior knowledge triggers recognition of the value of the new information (Shane 2000). Each person's idiosyncratic prior knowledge allows them to recognize certain opportunities but not others. According to Shane three major dimensions of prior knowledge are important: prior knowledge of markets, prior knowledge of ways to serve markets and prior knowledge of customer problems. Shane argues that general business experience, industry experience, functional experience in marketing, product development and management, and previous start-up experience all provide some of the information and skills that increase the likelihood of opportunity exploitation.

Prior knowledge, in addition to being affected by previous experience, also comes from the network of relations (Alsos and Kaikonnen 2004). McGrath (1996) holds that entrepreneurs with access to a large and well-functioning network will probably have access to a large number of good 'shadow options'. Singh et al. (1999) also suggest that a large social network with many weak ties going beyond close friends and family relates positively to idea identification and opportunity recognition.

Opportunity development
Eventually the 'entrepreneurial awareness' turns into a more concrete 'business idea' as it undergoes the opportunity development phase. By business idea we refer to the complex of products or services, knowledge, competencies, market and technologies which are necessary to run a business (Normann 1977). According to Normann, the business idea (BI) is the unifying principle of a complex system. It expresses concrete conditions of an enterprise, its organization, its actors, processes and strategies.

The opportunity development process is iterative as an entrepreneur is likely to conduct evaluations several times at different stages of development; these evaluations could lead to recognition of additional opportunities or to adjustments to the initial vision. As this more precise and differentiated business idea matures, it grows into a business plan, also including financial models, estimating the value created and how that value might be distributed among shareholders. As an opportunity develops into its most elaborate form, formal cash flows, schedules of activities, and resource requirements are added. In this phase potential entrepreneurs become more actively involved. The influences that they receive from the external environment – incentives, access to resources, and so on – and/or from the local context in which they move and operate, are fundamental to shaping their initial 'entrepreneurial awareness' into a concrete business idea.

Academic entrepreneurs and opportunity recognition and development

In this study we deal with opportunity recognition and development in the specific case of academic spin-off founders. With regard to the framework described above, some of the 'prior knowledge' factors affecting opportunity recognition come to mirror academics' past experience, their prior knowledge and their networks. Several characteristics of their research activities (basic versus applied research, industry-financed research), their networks (relations with firms, with universities and/or other external institutions and so on) and, more generally, their previous experience are likely to influence their ability to recognize opportunities.

As for the opportunity development phase, in addition to support mechanisms offered by the context in which academics move and operate (including infrastructure availability in the regions and the presence of public and private research institutions, venture capitalists, business angels, companies operating in the same sector, science parks, and individuals and organizations which are key to new venture creation), there are also other specific incentives put in place by universities. More specifically, the resources and the support necessary for transforming an initial entrepreneurial awareness into a business idea may be found in the context in which they operate. If we consider that all over the world universities have been encouraging the exploitation of research results through the creation of academic spin-offs, and that specific policies and support mechanisms have been implemented to this purpose, it is reasonable to assume that these university-level support mechanisms are likely to influence the development of a business idea by academics. These support mechanisms include procedures that universities can set up within their organizations to foster academic start-ups and range from specific internal regulations to business plan competitions, university-affiliated business incubators, availability of university venture capital funds and establishment of Technology Transfer Offices, and so on. More details on factors affecting academics' opportunity recognition and development will be provided in the empirical part of this chapter.

RESEARCH DESIGN

The Research Context

Our research is based on the academic spin-offs of the Emilia Romagna region, which has been identified by the EU Commission as one of the leading regions in Europe for its increasing number of research start-ups and, more generally, for its proactive role in supporting research-to-industry technology transfer. Located in the north of Italy, Emilia Romagna has an extension of about 22 100 km^2 and 4.1 million inhabitants, with a pro capita GDP among the highest in Europe. The Emilia Romagna region has the fourth largest R&D workforce and expenditure of all the regions in Italy, with almost 16 000 researchers and 1416 million euros devoted to R&D expenditure in 2004 (ISTAT, 2004).

In November 2003 the Emilia Romagna region adopted its first programme for industrial research, innovation and technology transfer (PRRIITT), aiming at fostering applied research through new collaborations between public research and private sectors, the creation of new research laboratories and the creation of research spin-offs. It is the very first case of an Italian region with its own law concerning innovation. This law has given emphasis, among other things, to new research-based venture creation. In fact, part of the yearly budget is dedicated to the creation of new companies from research.

These regional initiatives have followed legislative changes at national level aimed at creating the conditions necessary for an effective commercialization of research results through academic spin-offs. Moreover, the majority of Italian universities and public research centres have adopted within their organizations spin-off regulations to lay down rules about duties and rights for the actors involved, to define the practices to be followed, and to allocate specific tasks to those university administrators who are supposed to be in charge of technology transfer activities.

The Sample

We included in our analysis all the companies created in order to exploit technological knowledge originating within universities; our definition of academic spin-offs includes companies which have either the university or at least one academic (full, associate or assistant professor, PhD student, research fellow or technician) among the founders. The research was carried out on a regional basis with a focus on the Emilia Romagna region. The regional population of academic spin-offs consists of 50 firms, spun off from the five universities settled in the region, University of Bologna, University of

Ferrara, University of Modena e Reggio Emilia, University of Parma and University Cattolica of Milan in Piacenza.

Through the websites of the five universities, regional technology transfer offices (Spinner Points) and university technology transfer offices (where available) we have been able to retrieve basic information about each company, such as names and telephone and e-mail contacts. Moreover, for each company we identified the names and contact information of the leading academic founders. In our sample there was only one academic spin-off with a university sharing equity but with no academic founders. In this particular case we contacted a non-academic founder to gather general information and data at the company level, which we included in the descriptive analysis relating to companies. After the first round of e-mails on 31 May 2005, a second reminder targeting the non-respondents on 2 September 2005, and several phone calls, we were able to arrange appointments with 47 academic spin-off founders. More specifically, we carried out face-to-face interviews with 45 of them, and telephone interviews with the remaining two. All of the interviews were conducted through a structured questionnaire (described in the next section) running for an average of one hour. During the face-to-face interviews we also gathered e-mail addresses of other academic founders (when more than one academic founder was involved in the new venture), to whom we submitted a shorter electronic version of our questionnaire (only those sections gathering personal-level data) in order to have specific information about their opportunity recognition and opportunity development processes. Out of a total population of 150 academic founders (relating to the 47 companies in our sample), at the end of the data-gathering process we had 86 completed questionnaires and two incomplete ones, which, after few phone calls, were completed and included in the analysis. The data collection was closed in December 2005 with a total number of 88 completed questionnaires (corresponding to an overall response rate of 58.6 per cent, with 88 complete and usable questionnaires out of 150), 48 of which were based on face-to-face interviews, and 40 on electronic surveys. In Tables 10.1, 10.2 and 10.3 we provide descriptive statistics for both the sample of 47 companies (for example business sector, founding year) and the sample of 88 academic founders (for example university affiliation, academic status and gender). For the latter we highlighted four main areas reflecting specific fields in which they carry out their research: Biotechnology (20.4 per cent), Information and Communication Technology – ICT (23.9 per cent), Advanced Mechanics (25 per cent) and Others (30.7 per cent). In the first group we included Biomedical, Biotechnology, Pharmaceutical and Micro-biological fields, in the second one all the ICT-related topics, in the third one Advanced Mechanics and Materials, and in the last one all the remaining fields. All four sectors were well represented, revealing a well-balanced research activity amongst the academic founders.

Table 10.1   Year of Establishment, Incubation and Industries of Academic Spin-Offs

Year of Establishment	Number of Firms	Frequency (%)
2005	9	19.1
2004	11	23.4
2003	13	27.7
2002	3	6.4
2001	5	10.6
2000	3	6.4
1999	3	6.4
Incubation		
Incubated in a university incubator	8	17
Incubated in a department	24	51
Not incubated	15	32
Industries		
ICT	6	12.7
Food	3	6.4
Materials and environmental services	9	19.2
Electronic	12	25.5
Mechanics and automation	3	6.4
Biotechnology	10	21.3
General services and consultancy	4	8.5

Table 10.1 shows that academic spin-offs operate in the following sectors: ICT, food, materials and environmental services, electronics, mechanics and automation, biotechnology, general services and consultancy.

Table 10.2   Output and Size for Academic Spin-Offs

Output	Mean	SD	Median
Patent applications (since start up)	0.7	1.44	0
Products introduced (since start up)	1.9	3.18	1
Forthcoming products (in 2006)	0.9	3.00	0
Process introduced (since start up)	0.2	0.85	0
Forthcoming processes (in 2006)	0.1	0.66	0
Commercial collaborations (since start up)	1.9	3.79	1
Technological collaborations (since start up)	1.9	1.92	2
Size			
Number of founders (2005)	6.3	3.4	6
Number of employees (2005)	0.8	1.9	0
Number of *pro tempore* employees (2005)	2.1	3.49	1

Table 10.3   Descriptive Statistics for Founders of Academic Spin-Offs

	A. Academic Founders' Population	B. Academic Founders' Sample	Difference Tests (between A and B)
Status			
Fully enrolled academics (full, associate and assistant professors)	97	51	
Pro tempore academics (research grants, PhD students, *pro tempore* professors and research collaborators)	43	31	$\chi^2 (2) = 4.68$
Technicians (admin. and lab.)	10	6	
Total	150	88	
University affiliation			
Bologna	82	46	
Ferrara	30	20	
Modena e Reggio	10	9	$\chi^2 (4) = 5.673$
Piacenza	5	2	
Parma	18	11	
Total	145*	88	
Gender (% males)	82.5	86.3	$\chi^2 (1) = 2.17$

Note: * Five founders belong to universities other than the five regional ones.

A comparison of the whole sample of academic founders and respondents on the basis of certain individual-level characteristics (including gender, academic position and university of affiliation) did not highlight any significant differences (see Tables 10.3 and 10.4).

Table 10.4   Contingency Analysis of Academic Status by University of Affiliation

Universities	Fully Enrolled Academics	Pro Tempore Academics	Tech-nicians	Difference Tests
University of Bologna population and (sample)	58 (31)	18 (12)	6 (3)	Population χ^2 (8) = 10.23
University of Ferrara population and (sample)	17 (8)	10 (9)	3 (3)	
University of Modena e Reggio population and (sample)	7 (6)	3 (3)	0 (0)	
University of Parma population and (sample)	11 (5)	6 (6)	1 (0)	(Sample) χ^2 (8) = 8.67)
University of Piacenza population and (sample)	1 (1)	4 (1)	0 (0)	

The Questionnaire

Based on the theoretical and empirical research on academic spin-offs and, more specifically, the opportunity recognition and opportunity development processes, we constructed a survey to collect data directly from academics involved in the creation of new technology-based firms.

The survey consisted of eight sections aimed at gathering different information at both the company level and academic founders level, including general information on the firms and data on company performance, relationship networks, sources and amount of financing and academic founders. We also gathered information on the incentives and motivations for academic entrepreneurs to get involved in the creation of new companies and on the obstacles faced in creating them. Finally we gathered information on academic entrepreneurs' personal characteristics, previous experience and scientific productivity, and investigated the sources of entrepreneurship ideas.

While the importance and relevance of the different topics covered within the questionnaire emerged clearly from a review of the literature and the public debate on the role and involvement of university researchers in supporting the creation of new companies, there were no fully developed and validated scales for measuring the corresponding constructs. For the development and selection of the items included in the different sections, we first carefully analysed studies that followed a similar approach in order to derive a first set of possible items. In particular, in relation to factors fostering academics to create new companies, from Roberts (1991), Shane (2004), McQueen and Wollmark (1991), Zucker et al. (1998) we derived some items related to the academic founders' personal characteristics. Second, we used our knowledge of the existing literature to extend this initial set of items to include other aspects related to the characteristics of the local context in which companies operated (Roberts and Malone 1996) and the role of specific university-level support mechanisms (OECD 2003, Baldini et al. 2004). We also relied on Watson et al. (1995) and Stuart and Abetti (1987), who, in their studies on new venture creation, made extensive use of self-reported data to describe characteristics of individuals, institutions and external context, and so on. Concerning the opportunity recognition literature we drew on Ardichvili et al. (2003), Shane (2000) and Kirzner (1997).

Finally, we used a small-scale field test to gather data on whether questions were phrased in an unambiguous manner or not, and to find out if other relevant aspects could be included in the different parts of the questionnaire. More specifically, we contacted the founders of four academic spin-offs, who provided very helpful insights with regard to the questionnaire's completeness and clarity, as well as an evaluation of the time needed to complete it. No major inconsistencies emerged from this pre-test phase.

Methods

In the empirical analysis we first provided descriptive statistics for some of the items dealing with both the opportunity recognition process and the opportunity development process.

In relation to opportunity recognition, we asked academic founders to rank on a 1–7 Likert scale factors that most affected their ability to recognize business opportunities. More specifically, and with regard to the framework of Figure 10.1, we investigated the effect of five items relating to prior knowledge. We did not gather information relating to academic personal traits and therefore we will not touch on this in the empirical analysis.

As for opportunity development, we asked academic founders to rank on a 1–7 Likert scale the relevance of five items relating to environmental factors and of eight items relating to university-level related factors.

Then, we developed a principal component analysis in order to analyse whether there were some items, measuring the same construct, that could be collapsed into more aggregated indicators. The scales were submitted to PCA using varimax rotation to ensure maximal loading of each scale on one factor. Rotation was orthogonal and was uncorrelated throughout the rotation process and obtains theoretically significant factors. A loading threshold of 0.5 for component identification was used (Hair et al. 1995) as was a Kaiser-Meyer-Olkin measure of sampling adequacy level around 0.6 (Tabachnik and Fidell 2001).

EMPIRICAL ANALYSIS

Descriptive Statistics

In Table 10.5 we provide additional descriptive statistics relating to the 88 academic entrepreneurs interviewed relating to their previous activities at universities. As for the patent activity of academic founders, we found that it was not equally distributed among the founders, revealing various outliers with more then ten patents and almost half of the sample without patent activity. Then we provide descriptives for a set of six items targeting prior activities in which each academic founder was involved. The analysis revealed a high commitment to all of them with particular emphasis devoted to basic and applied research activities. The answers were given on a 1–7 Likert scale.

Table 10.5   Descriptive Statistics Relating to Academic Founders' Prior Activities

	Mean	SD	Median
Patents number	1.68	4.49	0
Prior activities			
Applied research	5.61	1.82	6
Basic research	4.67	2.00	5
Collaboration with other universities	4.55	2.27	5
Research supported by private institutions	4.31	2.29	5
Collaboration with private firms	4.30	2.33	5
Consultancy	3.48	2.16	4

Then we investigated the sources of opportunity recognition for academic founders. Table 10.6 reports all the items that we investigated. It also shows that academic founders' industry networks and personal investments in applied research activities were the most relevant factors relating to the 'prior knowledge' and influencing their ability to recognize a business opportunity.

Table 10.6   Factors Affecting Opportunity Recognition and Development

Prior Knowledge	Mean	SD	Median
Industry network	5.35	1.80	6
Prior investments in applied research activities	4.86	1.93	6
Prior working experience	3.26	2.19	3
Prior investments in basic research activities	2.71	1.88	2
Managerial competences	2.56	1.72	2
Existence of a market demand for commercially exploiting the technology	5.10	1.65	5.5
Environmental influences			
Sector opportunity for commercial exploitation	4.63	1.62	5
Supportive local context	4.11	1.89	4
Supportive academic environment	4.10	1.92	4
Supportive institutional context	3.36	1.99	3
University-level related factors			
Possibility to be hosted in academic incubators or departments	4.67	2.36	6
Possibility to use academic laboratories and infrastructures	4.67	2.17	5
Availability of university-level spin-off regulations	3.27	2.14	3
The university invests in equity	2.71	1.95	2
Availability of a business plan competition	2.13	1.81	1
Availability of a technology transfer office (TTO)	1.96	1.68	1
University patented technology	1.87	1.70	1
Availability of university-level patent regulation	1.32	1.07	1

In relation to the items affecting the opportunity development process, as shown in Table 10.6, among the 'environmental influences', the most relevant were those relating to the existence of opportunities for commercial exploitation (existence of market demand for commercially exploiting the technology, and opportunities offered by the sector for commercial exploitation). All items were perceived in a positive way, reporting high means ranging from 3.36 to 5.10 and medians from 3 to 5. In relation to 'university-level related factors', the most relevant factors were the possibility to be incubated within universities (access to logistics infrastructure) and the possibility to use academic laboratories and facilities. It is interesting to note the low relevance which has been given to items like the availability of a university-level patent regulation and of a university patented technology. This suggests that in the Italian context, university investments in patent protection do not influence and foster academics' opportunity exploitation process

Principal Component Analysis

Table 10.7 reports the PCA results for items relating to prior knowledge which are likely to be sources of opportunity recognition. Overall, the extraction procedure separated this first set of items relating to prior knowledge into three factors. The first encompassed two items, 'prior working experience' and 'managerial competences', both strongly loading on the factor that we labelled 'prior business experience'.

Table 10.7   PCA Results for Prior Knowledge

Factors	Items	Factor 1	Factor 2	Factor 3
Prior business experience	Prior working experience	0.88	-0.01	-0.03
	Managerial competences	0.83	0.21	0.06
Industry experience	Prior investments in applied research activities	0.13	0.83	-0.17
Basic research experience	Industry network	0.06	0.77	0.31
	Prior investments in basic research activities	0.01	0.04	0.96
Component (rotation sums of square loadings)		1.51	1.34	1.06
Proportion of variance explained (%)		30.22	26.98	21.20
Cumulative proportion of variance explained (%)		30.22	57.20	78.41
Kaiser-Meyer-Olkin measure of sampling adequacy level				0.56

The second factor, which we named 'industry experience', was characterized by two items relating to prior investments in applied research activities, and the industry network. Both items strongly characterize the social and industry network of academic founders. We finally labelled the last extracted factor 'basic research experience', which encompassed only a single item relating to academics' prior investments in basic research activities.

As for 'environmental influences', which are likely to affect opportunity development, we obtained two factors: the first one grouped responses to different aspects concerning the opportunity for commercial exploitation. It encompassed two items: commercial opportunity offered by the sector and the existence of a market demand for commercially exploiting the technology. The second factor, which we labelled 'support coming from the external context' in which firms operate, encompassed three items: supportive institutional context, fertile local context and supportive academic environment. We will comment more on these results in the final section. Table 10.8 reports PCA results for environmental influences.

Table 10.8   PCA Results for Environmental Influences

Factors	Items	Factor 1	Factor 2
Opportunity for commercial exploitation	Existence of a market demand for commercially exploiting the technology	0.88	-0.03
	Sector opportunity for commercial exploitation	0.75	0.21
Support coming from the external context	Supportive academic environment	0.09	0.80
	Supportive institutional context	-0.01	0.70
	Supportive local context	0.37	0.54
Component (rotation sums of square loadings)		1.51	1.34
Proportion of variance explained (%)		30.22	26.98
Cumulative proportion of variance explained (%)		30.22	57.20
Kaiser-Meyer-Olkin measure of sampling adequacy level			0.59

In relation to university-level related factors, which are likely to affect the opportunity development process, we obtained three factors (reported in Table 10.9). The first one, which we labelled 'university patent protection', encompassed two items: the availability of university-level patent policies and the existence of a university patented technology on which the new firm would be based. The second factor that we extracted included a set of items all related to 'university support services'; more specifically it encompassed the existence of a technology transfer office (TTO), the existence of a business plan competition, the possibility for the university to invest in equity and the availability of a university-level spin-off regulation/policy. This factor clearly identifies some 'intangible' support mechanisms offered by most universities to facilitate entrepreneurial processes.

Table 10.9   PCA Results for University-Level Related Factors

Factors	Items	Factor 1	Factor 2	Factor 3
University patent protection	Availability of university-level patent regulation	0.85	-0.02	-0.03
	University patented technology	0.79	0.22	0.20
University support services	Availability of a technology transfer office (TTO)	0.20	0.72	-0.17
	Availability of a business plan competition	-0.23	0.65	0.11
	The university invests in equity	0.36	0.57	0.20
	Availability of university-level spin-off regulation	0.45	0.57	0.27
Access to university infrastructures	Possibility to be hosted in academic incubators or departments	0.01	0.20	0.84
	Possibility to use academic laboratories and infrastructures	0.15	-0.06	0.83
Component (rotation sums of square loadings)		1.81	1.71	1.61
Proportion of variance explained (%)		22.73	21.48	20.20
Cumulative proportion of variance explained (%)		22.73	44.21	64.41
Kaiser-Meyer-Olkin measure of sampling adequacy level				0.68

The third and last factor, which we labelled 'access to university infrastructures', encompassed two factors: the possibility to be incubated within universities (access to logistic infrastructure) and the possibility to use academic laboratories and facilities which strongly loaded on this factor. In relation to the descriptive statistics, presented in Table 10.6, these two items were perceived as the most important university-related factors influencing the opportunity development process.

DISCUSSION

This chapter represents an attempt to investigate the factors affecting business opportunity generation in the specific case of academic founders. Drawing on the existing literature we have described a model which distinguishes two important phases for opportunity generation: opportunity recognition and opportunity development. We have focused on the main sources of opportunity recognition and opportunity development for would-be academic entrepreneurs. In the empirical section we provided descriptive statistics of some items which appear to influence academics' opportunity recognition and opportunity development abilities. We also develop a principal component analysis with the aim of collapsing some items measuring the same constructs into aggregated indicators.

The analysis of the effects of items relating to academics' prior knowledge on opportunity recognition shows that industry experience is considered a relevant source of opportunity recognition. More specifically, industry experience is an aggregated indicator (which we obtained through PCA) encompassing, as sources of opportunity recognition, academics' industrial network and their prior investments in applied research activities. These two items have the highest means. This result shows that relations with industry may be important in triggering entrepreneurial processes. Both items reflect personal-level characteristics, that is, academics' personal ties with industrial partners and their personal investments in applied research activities. The two items are strongly correlated, which makes sense if we consider that applied research activities are often oriented to solving specific problems and/or addressing specific requirements coming from the market. This confirms previous results by Shane (2000), illustrating that prior knowledge of markets, of customer problems and of how to serve a market does influence opportunity discovery processes.

Even if almost all academic founders are actively involved in some basic research activities, this does not represent a source of opportunity recognition. Moreover, the dimensions related to academics' prior business experience are not fundamental to the opportunity recognition process, confirming that almost all the Italian academic founders started their careers as academics without previously focusing on different business activities. This may be seen as a peculiarity of the Italian system, where the labour market is rigid and does not reward (foster) people coming from business and moving into academia.

In relation to the second phase of the proposed framework we have distinguished two sets of factors influencing the opportunity development phase: environmental influences and university-related factors. Among the most important items affecting the opportunity development process are the existence of a market demand for commercially exploiting the technology, and sector opportunity for commercial exploitation, both loading on a unique factor that we named 'opportunity for commercial exploitation'. It is clear how the best environmental influences, in fostering and developing entrepreneurship opportunities, are characterized by a real interest coming from the market and by sector commercialization opportunities. This confirms previous studies by Mowery et al. (2001), who argue that in the US the increasing growth of university licensing income cannot only be explained by changes in university incentives structures. Reasons must be sought in the increasing opportunities for practical exploitation offered by the context in which academic spin-offs operate. In a similar way previous studies based on the US context have shown, among the determinants of academic spin-offs, the opportunities for commercial exploitation offered by specific industries like ICT, biotechnology and computer software (Lowe 2002, Shane 2004).

Finally, focusing on the university-level related factors, we notice that on average they are perceived as less important than the other environmental influences. The only exception is represented by the items we labelled "Possibility to be hosted in academic incubators or departments" and "Possibility to use academic laboratories and infrastructures", which have the highest means. It is interesting to note that 68 per cent of the firms included in our sample are hosted within a department or a university incubator. The high values of means and medians of these two items suggest that the possibility to access physical infrastructure represents an important factor for academics in developing their business ideas. This might be a peculiarity of academic start-ups: Thursby et al. (2001) found that half of the inventions licensed were only proofs of concept at the time of licence. In a more recent study Thursby and Thursby (2003) show that 71 per cent of the inventions licensed by American universities could not be successfully commercialized without faculty co-operation in further development. Similar findings are supported by Lowe's case-studies (2002). These studies show that in their early stages it might be important for these academic spin-offs to maintain close links with their universities of origin for a full development of their technologies.

Our study presents some limitations. First, we relied on self-reported perceptions, which may increase the possibility of response bias. It is also important to notice that all respondents are currently involved in the firms, which are still in business. These responses, therefore, might suffer from *ex post* rationalization of behaviour and intentions, which is typical of cross-sectional questionnaires.

An interesting extension of the study would be the analysis of the factors relating to the 'personal traits' dimension, which we included in our framework but did not investigate from an empirical point of view. In a similar way, it would be interesting to explore, within the 'prior knowledge' dimension, other factors that the literature has addressed as relevant – likewise knowledge of customers, knowledge of specific markets and relations with specific companies – with other organizations that might contribute to nurturing academics' prior information/knowledge. Another interesting extension of the chapter would be also to introduce to the analysis academic would-be entrepreneurs who failed in the process (who either recognized an opportunity without turning it into a concrete business idea, or developed the opportunity into a business idea but never started up a new venture). This would be of interest insofar as it offers the possibility of exploring the obstacles and factors hampering the business opportunity development processes.

REFERENCES

Alsos, G.A. and V. Kaikkonen (2004), 'Opportunity recognition and prior knowledge: A study of experienced entrepreneurs', 13th Nordic Conference on Small Business Research.

Ardichvili, A., R. Cardozo and S. Ray (2003), 'A theory of entrepreneurial opportunity identification and development', *Journal of Business Venturing*, **18**, 105–23.

Baldini, N., R. Grimaldi and M. Sobrero (2004), 'Institutional changes and the commercialization of academic knowledge: a study of Italian universities' patenting activities between 1965 and 2002', Cresco Working Paper no. 11.

Begley, T. and D. Boyd (1987), 'Psychological characteristics associated with performance in entrepreneurial firms and smaller businesses', *Journal of Business Venturing*, **2** (1), 279–93.

Brockhaus, R. and P. Horowitz (1986), 'The psychology of the entrepreneur', in D. Sexton and R. Smilor (eds), *The Art and Science of Entrepreneurship*, Cambridge, MA: Ballinger, pp. 25–48.

Caplan, B. (1999), 'The Austrian search for realistic foundation', *Southern Economic Journal*, **65** (4), 823–38.

Chen, C., P. Greene and A. Crick (1998), 'Does entrepreneurial self-efficacy distinguish entrepreneurs from managers?' *Journal of Business Venturing*, **13** (4), 295–316.

Colombo, M. and M. Delmastro (2002), 'How effective are technology incubators? Evidence from Italy', *Research Policy*, **31**, 1103–22.

De Koning, A. (1999), '*Conceptualizing Opportunity Recognition as a Socio-Cognitive Process*', Stockholm: Centre for Advanced Studies in Leadership.

Degroof, J.J. and B.E. Roberts (2004), 'Overcoming weak entrepreneurial infrastructures for academic spin-off ventures', *Journal of Technology Transfer*, **29**, 327–52.

Florida, R. (1999), 'The role of the university: leveraging talent, not technology', *Issues in Science and Technology*, **15** (4), 67–73.

Gaglio, C.M. and R.P. Taub (1992), 'Entrepreneurs and opportunity recognition', in N.C. Churchill, S. Birley, W.D. Bygrave, D.E. Muzyka, C. Wahlbin and W.E. Wetzel (eds), *Frontiers of Entrepreneurship Research*, Babson Park, MA: Babson College, pp. 136–47.

Grimaldi, R. and A. Grandi (2001), 'The contribution of university business incubators to new knowledge-based ventures: some evidence from Italy', *Industry and Higher Education*, **15** (4), 239–50.

Grimaldi, R. and A. Grandi (2003), 'Exploring the networking characteristics of new venture founding teams: a study of Italian academic spin-offs', *Small Business Economics*, **21**, 329–41.

Guth, W.D., A. Kumaraswamy and M. McErlean (1991), 'Cognition, enactment, and learning in the entrepreneurial process', in N.C. Churchill, W.D. Bygrave, J.G. Covin, D.L. Sexton, D.P. Slevin, K.H. Vesper and W.E. Wetzel (eds), *Frontiers of Entrepreneurship Research*, Babson Park, MA: Babson College.

Hair, J., R. Anderson, R. Tatham and W. Black (eds) (1995), *Multivariate Data Analysis with Readings*, 4th edition, Upper Saddle River, NJ: Prentice-Hall.

Hills, G.E. (1995), 'Opportunity recognition by successful entrepreneurs: a pilot study', *Frontiers of Entrepreneurship Research*, Wellesley, MA: Babson College, pp. 103–21.

Hills, G., G.T. Lumpkin and R.P. Singh (1997), 'Opportunity recognition: Perceptions and behaviours of entrepreneurs', *Frontiers of Entrepreneurship Research*, Wellesley, MA: Babson College, pp. 203–18.

Ioannides, S. (1999), 'Towards an Austrian perspective on the firm', *Review of Austrian Economics*, **11** (1), 77–97.

ISTAT (2004), 'Indicatori di contesto chiave e variabili di rottura', Istat annual report, www.istat.it/ambiente/contesto/infoterr/azioneB.html, 20 December 2006.

Kirzner, I. (1997), 'Entrepreneurial discovery and the competitive market process: an Austrian approach', *Journal of Economic Literature*, **35**, March, 60–85.

Krueger, N.J. and D.H. Brazeal (1994), 'Entrepreneurial potential and potential entrepreneurs', *Entrepreneurship Theory Practice*, **19**, 91–104.

Krueger, N.J. and P.R. Dickson (1994), 'How believing in ourselves increases risk taking: perceived', *Decision Sciences*, May/June, **25** (3), 385–401.

Lowe, R. (2002), 'Invention, innovation and entrepreneurship: the commercialization of university research by inventor founded firms', PhD dissertation, University of California at Berkeley.

McClelland, D.C. (ed.) (1961), *The Achieving Society*, Princeton, NJ: Van Nostrand.

McGrath, R.G. (1996), 'Options and the entrepreneur: toward a strategic theory of entrepreneurial wealth creation', *Academy of Management Proceedings, Entrepreneurship Division*, 101–5.

McQueen, D. and J. Wollmark (1991), 'University technical innovation: spin offs and patents in Goteborg, Sweden', in A. Brett, D. Gibson and R. Smilor (eds), *University Spin-off Companies*, Savage, MD: Rowman & Littlefield Publishers, pp. 103–15.

Mowery, D., R. Nelson, B. Sampat and A. Ziedonis (2001), 'The effects of the Bayh-Dole Act on US academic research and technology transfer', *Research Policy*, **30** (1), 99–119.

Normann, R. (ed.) (1977), *Management for Growth*, Chichester: Wiley.

OECD (2003), 'Turning science into business: patenting and licensing at public research organizations', Paris: OECD.

Radosevich, R. (1995), 'A model for entrepreneurial spin-offs from public technology sources', *International Journal of Technology Management*, **10** (7/8), 879–93.

Roberts, E.B. (ed.) (1991), *Entrepreneurs in High Technology*, Oxford: Oxford University Press.

Roberts, E.B. and D.E Malone (1996), 'Policies and structures for spinning off new companies from research and development organizations', *R & D Management*, **26** (1), 17–46.

Shane, S. (2000), 'Prior knowledge and the discovery of entrepreneurial opportunities', *Organizational Science*, **11** (4), 448–69.

Shane, S. (ed.) (2003), *A General Theory of Entrepreneurship: The Individual-Opportunity Nexus Approach to Entrepreneurship*, Cheltenham, UK and Northampton, MA, USA: Edward Elgar.

Shane, S. (ed.) (2004), *Academic Entrepreneurship: University Spin-off and Wealth Creation*, Cheltenham, UK and Northampton, MA, USA: Edward Elgar.

Shane, S. and S. Venkataraman (2000), 'The promise of entrepreneurship as a field of research', *Academy of Management Review*, **25** (1), 217–26.

Shaver, K.G. and L.R. Scott (1991), 'Person, process, choice: the psychology of new venture creation', *Entrepreneurship Theory and Practice*, **16** (2), 23–45.

Singh, R., H. Hills and G.T. Lumpkin (1999), 'Examining the role of self-perceived entrepreneurial alertness in the opportunity recognition process', presented at the 13th UIC/AMA Symposium on Marketing and Entrepreneurship Interface, Nice, 16 June.

Stiegler, G.J. (ed.) (1952), *The Theory of Price*, New York: MacMillan.

Streit M.E. and W. Gerhard (1992), 'Information, transactions and catallaxy: reflections on some key concepts of evolutionary market theory', in Ulrich Witt (ed.), *Explaining Process and Change: Approaches to Evolutionary Economics*, Ann Arbor, MI: University of Michigan Press, pp. 125–49.

Stuart, R. and P.A. Abetti (1987), 'Spin-off ventures: towards the prediction of initial success', *Journal of Business Venturing*, **2**, 215–30.

Tabachnik, B.G. and L. Fidell (eds) (2001), *Using Multivariate Statistics*, 4th edition, Needham Heights, MA: Allyn & Bacon.

Thursby J., R. Jensen and M. Thursby (2001), 'Objectives, characteristics and outcomes of university licensing: a survey of major US universities', *Journal of Technology Transfer*, **26**, 59–72.

Thursby J. and M.C. Thursby (2003), 'Are faculty critical? Their role in university–industry licensing', Emory Economics 0320, Department of Economics, Emory University (Atlanta).

Venkataraman, S. (1997), 'The distinctive domain of entrepreneurship research: an editor's perspective', in J. Katz and R. Brockhaus (eds), *Advances in Entrepreneurship, Firm Emergence and Growth*, vol. 3, Greenwich, CT: JAI Press, pp. 119–38.

Watson, W.E., L.D. Ponthieu and J.W. Critelli (1995), 'Team interpersonal process effectiveness in venture partnerships and its connections to perceived success', *Journal of Business Venturing*, **10** (5), 393–412.

Wickham, P.A. (ed.) (2001), *'Strategic Entrepreneurship: A Decision-Making Approach to New Venture Creation and Management'*, London: Prentice Hall.

Wright, M., S. Birley and S. Mosey (2004), 'Entrepreneurship and university technology transfer', *Journal of Technology Transfer*, **29**, 235–46.

Zucker, L., M. Darby and M. Brewer (1998), 'Intellectual human capital and the birth of US biotechnology enterprises', *American Economic Review*, **88** (1), 290–306.

11. Is There a Regional Equity Gap for Innovative Start-Ups? The Case of Germany

Michael Fritsch and Dirk Schilder*

INTRODUCTION

It is largely undisputed that spatial proximity between VC (venture capital) firms and the location of their investments should be important. The assumption underlying this conjecture is that spatial proximity may constitute a precondition for the formation of a VC relationship, and that it makes supervision of investments easier. This hypothesis implies that innovative firms in regions with no VC investment companies in the near vicinity may experience a serious disadvantage due to the poor availability of capital. This capital shortage could severely hamper their emergence and development. However, does this supposition that spatial proximity plays such a decisive role really hold? Based on an inquiry of VC suppliers in Germany, we cast serious doubt on the importance of spatial proximity in VC partnerships, especially in comparison to other types of financiers. We show that geographic distance does matter, but that its role is largely overestimated in the literature. Furthermore, we find evidence that regional proximity is less important for VC companies in comparison to other types of suppliers of smart capital, such as banks or business angels. These results provide evidence that a regional equity gap for innovative start-ups does not exist in Germany.

The literature offers several arguments that regional proximity between VC investor and financed firm is important. First, gathering of information about possible investments might be easier within a regional business community (Green 1991, p. 23; Doran and Bannock 2000). Second, the exchange of knowledge with the portfolio firms requires a certain amount of personal face-to-face contact and co-location (Gompers 1995, Lerner 1995). Third, more monitoring and advising conducted by the financiers leads to higher costs of distant investments (Mason and Harrison 2002a, Sorensen and Stuart 2001). This is especially important for VC investments as they focus on young and innovative companies that quite frequently call for acute involvement by the financier (Gupta and Sapienza 1992). For these reasons, it is concluded that VC companies should be located close to their possible investments. This leads to the assumption that the spatial distribution of VC companies and possible investments should show close correspondence. Therefore, a strong clustering of VC companies might lead to an undersupply of equity for innovative start-ups in regions where no or only few VC firms are present.

The chapter is structured as follows. First, we investigate the spatial distribution of VC firms and their investments in Germany (see next section). The section entitled 'Types of Smart Capital and Investment Behaviour' then provides an overview of the characteristics of the different types of financial institutions offering smart capital in our sample and the spatial proximity of their investments. In the subsequent section we then investigate the role of telecommunications for overcoming problems of spatial distance between VC suppliers and investments. Finally, we discuss reasons for the relatively low importance of regional proximity for VC investments in Germany and draw conclusions for policy as well as for further research.

THE SPATIAL DISTRIBUTION OF VC SUPPLY AND INVESTMENTS IN GERMANY

The spatial distribution of VC suppliers and investments on VC markets can provide a first indication of possible regional equity gaps. Several studies found a high degree of spatial clustering of suppliers and investments for the VC market in the USA on both the east and west coasts of the country (Sorensen and Stuart 2001, Powell et al. 2002, Florida et al. 1991, Leinbach and Amrhein 1987). The suppliers to the VC market in the UK are also highly clustered around London and the southeast part of the country, thus playing a dominant role (Mason and Harrison 1999, 2002a, Martin 1989, Martin et al. 2005). For the 'emerging' VC markets in continental Europe, for example France and Germany, Martin et al. (2002) also found a considerable degree of spatial concentration, but this concentration was not as pronounced as in the case of the USA or the UK.

The data from the German Private Equity and Venture Capital Association (Bundesverband Deutscher Kapitalbeteiligungsgesellschaften – BVK) confirm this result of a relatively low degree of spatial concentration. The VC suppliers are clustered in five regions: Munich has the lead with about 30 of the over 170 members of the BVK in January 2006. Frankfurt am Main is in second place with 27 VC suppliers (Figure 11.1).

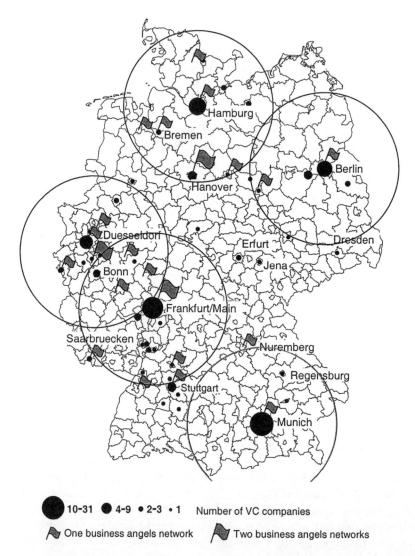

Number of VC companies
● 10-31 ● 4-9 ● 2-3 • 1

One business angels network   Two business angels networks

Note: Members of the German Private Equity Venture Capital Association and members of the German Business Angels Network Association as published online in January 2006.[1]

Figure 11.1   The Spatial Distribution of VC Firms in Germany (Symbol Size Shows Total Figures)

However, Berlin, Hamburg and the Rhine-Ruhr area (Duesseldorf, Cologne, Bonn) have around 20 VC suppliers each and several of the VC firms can also be found in various smaller locations. The spatial distribution of the German business angels networks[2], which are indicated by flags in Figure 11.1, is quite similar to the distribution of the VC firms. The circles in Figure 11.1 show a radius of 150 km around the most important VC centres in Germany. This is an approximation of a two-hour trip to reach a possible investment and indicates the accessibility of the regions (Mason and Harrison 2002b). Even though the vast majority of the country is covered by these circles, we still find considerably large areas in the middle and southwestern parts which could be threatened by a regional equity gap.

In order to assess the spatial concentration of the German VC industry, we calculated Gini coefficients for the regional distribution of the VC companies and for some measures of innovative activity[3] (Table 11.1). These measures of innovative activity, such as the number of innovative start-ups or the number of patents, point to locations of VC investment opportunities. The Gini coefficients clearly display a much stronger spatial concentration of VC companies as compared to the distribution of the indicators for innovative activity. These results indicate that the spatial clustering of VC firms in Germany is much more pronounced than the geographic concentration of innovative activity. This could be regarded as further indication of a regional undersupply of VC.

Table 11.1 Gini Coefficients for the Regional Distribution of VC Companies and Innovative Activity in Germany[4]

	Donaldson-Weymark Relative S-Gini Inequality Measures
Number of VC companies (BVK members)	*0.96*
Number of R&D-intensive start-ups (mean over the years 1990–2003)	0.45
Number of technology-intensive start-ups (mean over the years 1990–2003)	0.52
Number of knowledge-intensive start-ups (mean over the years 1990–2003)	0.60
Number of patents (mean over the years 1995–2000)	0.42

Rank correlation coefficients have been calculated (Table 11.2) in order to assess to what degree the spatial distribution of the VC companies corresponds to the location of their potential investment targets. These coefficients indicate some correspondence of the location of VC companies and the location of innovative start-ups. However, the values of the coefficients, although all statistically significant at the 1 per cent level, do not point to a dominant influence. The data indicate that the regional clustering of VC companies in Germany, though it is weaker than that of other countries, might lead to regional equity gaps in certain regions. Nonetheless, this is grounded on the assumption that spatial proximity is important for VC investments.

Table 11.2   Rank Correlation Coefficients for the Relationship between the Location of VC Companies and Potential Investment Targets

		1	2	3	4
1.	Number of start-ups (mean over the years 1990–2003)	1.00			
2.	Number of R&D-intensive start-ups (mean over the years 1990–2003)	0.89**	1.00		
3.	Number of technology-intensive start-ups (mean over the years 1990–2003)	0.91**	0.87**	1.00	
4.	Number of knowledge-intensive start-ups (mean over the years 1990–2003)	0.89**	0.82**	0.94**	1.00
5.	Number of VC companies (BVK members)	0.39**	0.36**	0.43**	0.43**

Notes:
Spearman and Kendall's rank correlation coefficients (Greene, 2003).
** Statistically significant at the 1% level

Unfortunately the data, which were obtained from the German Private Equity and Venture Capital Association, do not allow for identification of the location of the investments made by a specific VC company. For further analysis of the role of spatial proximity between VC firms and their portfolio companies we therefore use another database that entails a sample of this industry. This database is introduced in the next section.

TYPES OF SMART CAPITAL AND INVESTMENT BEHAVIOUR

The Database

The empirical in-depth analysis of the role of spatial proximity for VC in Germany is based on an interview survey that was carried out between September 2004 and September 2005. The survey consists of 75 personal interviews with managers who were actively involved in start-up financing. All interviews were based on a largely standardized questionnaire. Questions pertained mainly to investment behaviour, selection of investments, and monitoring and supervision of portfolio companies. Special focus was placed on the role of spatial proximity for the monitoring and advising with regard to an investment. We interviewed one manager per firm. The firms from the sample were located in diverse areas of Germany. The sample covers different types of financiers which offer money for innovative young companies. It contains 22 independent and corporate VC companies, 11 business angels, which are private individuals, 23 banks, 17 VC subsidiaries of banks and 12 public providers of equity. The firms in the sample can be regarded as representative of the respective types of financial institution; we are not aware of any bias in the sample.

In contrast to the data used in the previous section, the structure of the sample has two main advantages. First, it provides a detailed insight into the investment behaviour of the German VC suppliers. Second, since the survey is not solely limited to financial institutions which are specialized in VC, it allows us to analyse the heterogeneity of the market for so-called smart capital and compare different types of financiers. The term smart capital characterizes financial relationships between a provider of finance and new innovative businesses which are connected with pronounced reciprocal information flows between the financier and the financed company (Schäfer and Schilder 2006). Beyond equity investments with hands-on support, which is the typical element of VC, smart capital also encompasses credit financing offered by banks and informal VC investments by business angels.

Spatial Proximity of Investors and Investments

To demonstrate to what extent spatial proximity is important for VC investments, the interviewees were asked about the average share of investments in the following four spatial categories: at the same site, not at the same site but within a distance of 100 km, more than 100 km away but within Germany, and investments abroad. The results reveal great differences between the types of providers of smart capital in our sample (Figure 11.2).

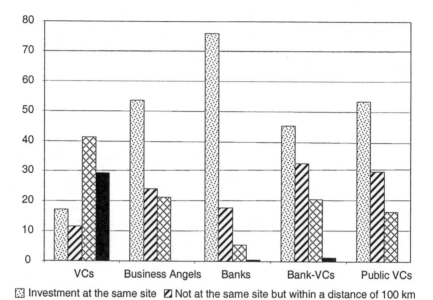

Figure 11.2   Average Share of Investments within a Certain Distance (%)

Banks, bank-dependent VC firms, public VC companies and Business Angels all have more than 75 per cent of their investments within a distance of 100 km. Thus, it can be assumed that these portfolio firms can be easily reached. In contrast, the independent VC investors in our sample have less than 30 per cent of their investments located within such a short distance but have spread their investments all over Germany and abroad. The high concentration of banks with investments in close proximity is, at least at first sight, rather astonishing because Schäfer and Schilder (2006) showed that banks typically offer a lower amount of consulting than VC companies. Hence, spatial proximity should be of relatively low importance for banks.

The high share of investments nearby can be explained by the banks' tight net of regional branches which makes investments in distant locations unnecessary. While the high share of investment within the region which we find for business angels may be caused by their limited amount of resources, the public VC companies are often limited in their regional focus by administrative or legal constraints.

The analysis shows that regional proximity is not an important issue for the German VC industry. The private VC firms have a particularly high share of their investments at a distance of more than 100 km. This indicates that the regional clustering of the German VC companies does not necessarily lead to a regional equity gap for innovative start-ups in certain German regions. However, the question of why regional proximity seems to be unimportant for the German VC industry still remains.

IS SPATIAL PROXIMITY SUBSTITUTED BY TELECOMMUNICATION?

One way of overcoming the problems associated with investment in distant locations could be intensive use of modern means of telecommunication that may make many of the personal meetings obsolete. This might particularly be the case for private VC companies because their investments are more often located farther away (see the previous section). If telecommunication works as a way to overcome the problems of geographical distance, the regional supply of VC will not suffer from the spatial clustering of VC firms.

Figure 11.3 shows the average frequency of contacts – personal and via telecommunication – between the investors and their portfolio companies per month. On average, financiers meet their portfolio companies once a month. The highest number of meetings (1.64 personal contacts per month) is found for the business angels and the lowest number (0.43 meetings) for banks. The average number of contacts via telecommunication differs much more between the types of financiers. While the private VC firms contact their portfolio companies via telephone or the Internet eight times a month, the banks have on average about 1.5 contacts via telecommunication. The average number of telecommunication contacts of the other types of financiers ranges between 2.3 and 4.2 contacts per month.

The results indicate that those types of financiers which have a relatively large share of investments located far away, particularly the private VC firms, have more contacts via telecommunication than investors with a pronounced regional focus. If telecommunication works as a substitute for personal contacts, then the number of personal contacts should be relatively low for those companies which have frequent contact with their companies by means of telecommunication.

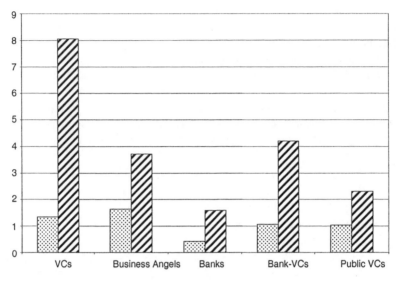

☷ Personal contacts ▨ Contacts via telecommunication

Figure 11.3   Average Number of Personal Meetings and Contacts via Telecommunication per Month

However, the correlation coefficients between the number of contacts via telecommunication per month and the number of personal meetings indicate a strong complementary relationship of the two modes of communication (Table 11.3).[5] Therefore, we can say that the obvious minor importance of regional proximity between the VC company and the portfolio firms (see the previous section) must have other reasons than the availability of measures of modern telecommunication.

WHY IS REGIONAL PROXIMITY INSIGNIFICANT FOR VC INVESTMENT?

Although we find an obvious clustering of VC companies and investments in Germany, our survey indicates that spatial proximity between the VC firm and the portfolio company does not play a dominant role. All of our interview partners agreed that regional proximity is definitely an advantage for VC investments, mainly due to lower costs and fewer problems of monitoring and advising. While none of the interviewees neglected the importance of monitoring and supervision of the portfolio companies on site, most of them stated that spatial proximity is not a dominant factor in this respect. With the exception of public VC companies, whose activities are mostly restricted to a specific region, none of the VC managers interviewed would reject a promising investment opportunity that is not located at the same site. The reasons for this are diverse.

Table 11.3   Rank Correlation Coefficients for the Average Distance to Investments and the Number of Contacts per Month

	Variable	1	2	3	4	5
1.	Share of investments at the same site	1.00				
2.	Share of investments not at the same site but within 100 km distance	-0.40**	1.00			
3.	Share of investments within Germany in more than 100 km distance	-0.62**	-0.04	1.00		
4.	Share of investments abroad	-0.46**	-0.17	0.22	1.00	
5.	Number of personal meetings per month	-0.18	-0.04	0.07	0.14	1.00
6.	Number of contacts via tele-communication per month	-0.34**	-0.06	0.26*	0.25*	0.72**

Notes:
Spearman and Kendall's rank correlation coefficients (Greene, 2003)
** Statistically significant at the 1% level
* Statistically significant at the 5% level; Number of cases: 75

First, the spatial structure of Germany is rather balanced and accessibility to any location within Germany is relatively easy – at least when compared to countries such as the UK or the US. Spatial distances are much smaller than in the US and a dense infrastructure for fast travel exists almost everywhere. Nearly all locations in Germany can be reached from the larger cities within a day and in most cases there are convenient possibilities for returning home on the same day. In conjunction with the findings from Mason and Harrison (2002b) for the informal VC market in the UK, many investment managers interviewed in our survey stated that they do not want to travel for longer than two hours to visit a company and that many locations in Europe can be reached by a two-hour plane trip. Therefore, the 150 km circumference adopted at the beginning of the chapter (Figure 11.1) does not appear to capture the two-hour rule indicated by the interviewees. In addition, other means of travel might be even better suited to accessing certain regions. A trip by train from Hamburg to Berlin, for example, which is a distance of almost 300 km, only lasts one and a half hours. Furthermore, to monitor and consult companies that are located far away some managers prefer staying several days on site, which causes the duration of travel to become less significant.

Second, the majority of the interview partners stated that a limited pool of promising investment opportunities was a main reason for searching for investments outside their resident region. They would finance companies located nearby if they existed. Therefore, if the mountain will not come to Mohammed, then Mohammed has to go to the mountain. Obviously, the main restriction for the German VC companies is the availability of promising investment targets, not the time and effort of monitoring and consulting. One of the VC managers that we interviewed said: 'Today is not the time to pick and chose in the regional sense if you want to earn money'.[6] This indicates that the main bottleneck hindering VC investments in Germany is not a lack of VC suppliers but rather the limited number of promising projects. As a consequence of the shortage of investment opportunities of a sufficient quality, only €21.5 billion out of the €54.2 billion under management by the members of the BVK was invested in companies in 2005.[7]

Third, the statements from the interviewees provide evidence that the VC companies use another measure to overcome the problems of distant investments: syndication. Syndication means that more than one financier invests in a portfolio company. If an investment is located far away, VC companies obviously try to get a syndication partner involved which is closely located to the financed firm. The VC firm that is located in close proximity to the investment then undertakes most of the monitoring and consulting of the portfolio company (see Fritsch and Schilder 2006a, 2006b).

CONCLUSIONS AND IMPLICATIONS

In this chapter we examined the role of spatial proximity for VC investments. The main part of the empirical analysis was based on a survey of 75 face-to-face interviews conducted with different types of financiers in Germany. This database enabled us to gain insight into the investment behaviour of VC companies and their attitude towards the importance of spatial proximity to portfolio companies. Furthermore, we could compare the results of the importance of regional proximity for different types of financiers offering smart capital.

The analyses clearly indicate that the importance of spatial proximity between the VC firm and its portfolio companies is widely overestimated in the literature. The VC companies in Germany, particularly the private VC firms, do not focus mainly on investments located nearby. Although telecommunication may be employed to overcome disadvantages of distance, it does not seem to play a dominant role. The reasons that we find for the striking unimportance of geographical distance for German VC providers are the balanced spatial structure that leads to good accessibility of most locations in the country as well as a lack of promising investment opportunities on site. Furthermore, we find evidence that VC companies use syndication to ease the monitoring and consulting of distant investments.

One main conclusion of our analysis is that the absence of VC firms in a region is not likely to be a bottleneck for innovative entrepreneurs in Germany. We cannot confirm that there are equity gaps in certain regions that represent a severe problem for innovative start-ups. At least from the perspective of the VC managers, the main bottleneck is the presence of promising investment opportunities. We cannot, however, completely preclude the existence of informational bottlenecks that prevent entrepreneurs and VC suppliers from meeting.

Our results lead to some important questions for further research. First, the role of syndication as a possible substitute for regional proximity in the VC industry should be more illuminated. Second, it would be rather interesting to compare the performance of investments on site with investments at considerable spatial distances to find out if proximity does indeed play an important role. Finally, additional research is desirable to find out if there is a regional equity gap or an information problem, especially from the viewpoint of entrepreneurs searching for VC.

NOTES

*   We gratefully acknowledge the financial support by the German Research Foundation.
1.   See www.bvk-ev.de/bvk.php/cat/4/title/Mitglieder and www.business-angels.de.
2.   Members of the German Business Angels Network Association (Business Angels Netzwerk Deutschland e.V.).
3.   See, for example, Fritsch and Slavtchev (2005, 2007) for a more detailed analysis.
4.   Data on innovative start-ups at the level of German districts (Kreise) is based on the Mannheim foundation panels at the Centre for European Economic Research (ZEW) in Mannheim. We are greatly indebted to the ZEW for making these data available.

5. A similar pattern of correlation coefficients can be found if they are calculated for each group of VC providers separately.
6. Translation from the German questionnaire.
7. German Private Equity and Venture Capital Association (2005).

REFERENCES

Doran, Alan and Graham Bannock (2000), Publicly sponsored regional venture capital: what can the UK learn from the US experience? *Venture Capital*, **2**, 255–85.

Florida, Richard L., Donald F. Smith and Elizabeth Sechoka (1991), 'Regional patterns of venture capital investment', in Milford Green (ed.), *Venture Capital: International Comparisons*, London and New York: Routledge, pp. 102–33.

Fritsch, Michael and Dirk Schilder (2006a), 'Does venture capital investment really require spatial proximity? An empirical investigation', Working Paper 07/2006, Technical University Bergakademie Freiberg, Faculty of Economics and Business Administration.

Fritsch, Michael and Dirk Schilder (2006b), 'Is venture capital a regional business? The role of syndication', Discussion Papers on Entrepreneurship, Growth and Public Policy #2506, Jena, Germany: Max Planck Institute for Research into Economic Systems – Group Entrepreneurship, Growth and Public Policy.

Fritsch, Michael and Viktor Slavtchev (2005), 'The role of regional knowledge sources for innovation: an empirical assessment', Working Paper 15/2005, Technical University Bergakademie Freiberg, Faculty of Economics and Business Administration.

Fritsch, Michael and Viktor Slavtchev (2007), 'Academic institutions and innovation in space', *Industry and Innovation* (forthcoming).

German Private Equity and Venture Capital Association (2005), *Statistics 2005*, Berlin.

Gompers, Paul A. (1995), 'Optimal investment, monitoring, and the staging of venture capital', *Journal of Finance*, **6**, 1461–89.

Green, Milford B. (1991), 'Preferences for US venture capital investments 1970–1988', in Milford Green (ed.), *Venture Capital: International Comparisons*, London and New York: Routledge, pp. 18–58.

Greene, William H. (2003), *Econometric Analysis*, 4th edition, New York: Prentice Hall.

Gupta, Anil K. and Harry J. Sapienza (1992), 'Determinants of venture capital firms' preferences regarding the industry diversity and geographic scope of their investments', *Journal of Business Venturing*, **7**, 347–62.

Leinbach, Thomas R. and Carl Amrhein (1987), 'A geography of the venture capital industry in the US', *Professional Geographer*, **39** (2), 146–58.

Lerner, Joshua (1995), 'Venture capitalists and the oversight of private firms', *Journal of Finance*, **50**, 301–18.

Martin, Ron (1989), 'The growth and geographical anatomy of venture capitalism in the United Kingdom', *Regional Studies*, **23**, 389–403.

Martin, Ron, Christian Berndt, Britta Klagge and Peter Sunley (2005), 'Spatial proximity effects and regional equity gaps in the venture capital market: evidence from Germany and the United Kingdom', *Environment and Planning A*, **37**, 1207–31.

Martin, Ron, Peter Sunley and Dave Turner (2002), 'Taking risks in regions: the geographical anatomy of Europe's emerging venture capital market', *Journal of Economic Geography*, **2**, 121–50.

Mason, Colin M. and Richard T. Harrison (1999), 'Financing entrepreneurship: venture capital and regional development', in Ron Martin (ed.), *Money and the Space Economy*, Chichester: Wiley, pp. 157–83.

Mason, Colin M. and Richard T. Harrison (2002a), 'The geography of venture capital investments in the UK', *Transactions of the Institute of British Geographers*, **27**, 427–51.

Mason, Colin M. and Richard T. Harrison (2002b), 'The barriers to investment in the informal venture capital sector', *Entrepreneurship and Regional Development*, **14**, 271–87.

Powell, Walter W., Kenneth W. Koput, James I. Bowie and Laurel Smith-Doerrs (2002), 'The spatial clustering of science and capital: accounting for biotech firm–venture capital relationships, *Regional Studies*, **36** (3), 291–305.

Schäfer, Dorothea and Dirk Schilder (2006), 'Informed capital in a hostile environment: the case of relational investors in Germany', Working Paper 03/2006, Technical University Bergakademie Freiberg, Faculty of Economics and Business Administration.

Sorensen, Olav and Toby E. Stuart (2001), 'Syndication networks and the spatial distribution of venture capital investments', *American Journal of Sociology*, **106**, 1546–88.

12. How Market Appraisal Affects Investments in Human Capital: Evidence from Austrian and Swiss Venture Capitalists

Carola Jungwirth

INTRODUCTION

Recent studies have shed light on the fact that human capital is a key driver of the investment strategies of venture capital firms. In fact, there appears to be a direct correlation between level of education attained by venture capitalists and successful investment strategy. For instance, it can be observed that venture capitalists with higher levels of education (Bottazzi et al. 2004), combined with awareness of more industry-specific knowledge (Jungwirth and Moog 2004, Dimov and Shepherd 2005), display more professional judgement in their investment activities. 'Professional' here refers to an early-stage and high-tech orientation in portfolio management that is often accompanied by a considerable specialization in an industry and/or a financing stage of the venture capital firm.

The US venture capital market represents the archetype of a professional approach in portfolio management. The majority of venture capital managers are assumed to be well educated, to own relevant industry-specific knowledge and to be specialized in one or a few high-tech industries and early financing stages (Dotzler 2001, Amit et al. 1998, Norton and Tenenbaum 1993). However, in Europe 'professional approaches' are still mixed. In the United Kingdom, for example, venture capitalists seem to be biased against high-tech and early-stage investments, whereas in Germany this type of project is more dominant (Martin et al. 2002, pp. 143–6). Furthermore, when evaluating the German-speaking venture capital market (Germany, Austria and Switzerland), considerable differences appear to exist between any given group of Swiss and Austrian venture capitalists and a group of German venture capitalists.

The former have only little specific knowledge and focus on 'later'-stage and 'lower'-tech projects, which can be clearly attributed to their lower propensity to invest in industry-specific human capital. The result is interesting because Germany, Switzerland and Austria are one cultural area[1] even if they differ in terms of geographical size and by the stage of development of the venture capital market. Overall, the German venture capital market is more developed and much larger than the other two (Becker and Hellmann 2003). Both market size and market development could cause these differences in human capital investments; therefore there are good reasons for this. For instance, demand in small markets could be too small to amortize investments in specific knowledge. On the other hand, delayed market development could be reflected in delayed learning and hinder appropriate investments in human capital. The objective of this chapter is to analyse to what extent market size and market development can explain the differences within the German-speaking region with respect to the willingness of venture capitalists to invest in specific intellectual capital opportunities.

This chapter is organized as follows. The next section discusses the potential effects of market size and market development on the venture capitalists' willingness to invest in human capital. The subsequent section presents a unique and hand-collected dataset. Venture capitalists from Switzerland and Austria answered a standardized questionnaire referring to structure, strategic choices and endowment with human capital, and subjective estimation of the market situation. The Swiss and Austrian markets are similar with respect to their geographical provinciality and their relatively late entrance into the venture capital business. Interestingly, they react quite differently to their market conditions. While Austrian venture capitalists seem to be rather frustrated by the low opportunities of the small market, Swiss venture capitalists act quite affirmatively; they invest much more in their human capital, try to specialize and go for internationalization. However, nationality does not appear to be a discriminating factor. The more a venture capitalist has invested in human capital, the more similar investment activities are for Austrian and Swiss venture capitalists. They invest more in early-stage and high-tech projects, co-operate more intensively and estimate the market situation as promising. That is the central result of this study.

APPRAISAL OF MARKET SIZE AND MARKET DEVELOPMENT AND THE WILLINGNESS TO INVEST IN HUMAN CAPITAL

Market Size

Adam Smith (1776) states that 'the division of labour is limited by the extent of the market'. Small markets do not offer enough demand for specialization, which is also true for venture capital markets where specialization will only take place if the demand for corporate financing is high enough, as in the case of biotechnology. The reason for this is that the costs of specialization are independent of the amount of portfolio enterprises the venture capitalists invest in. Therefore, only a high demand permits an amortization of the set-up costs of specialization (Besanko et al. 2000, pp. 117–22). Furthermore, a high demand is more likely in large markets and it supports the fact that market size should in fact influence the willingness of venture capitalists to invest in their human capital.

However, why should regional frontiers determine the size of venture capital markets? Capital can be invested elsewhere and regional frontiers should be meaningless. This is not true for venture capital, also called 'smart' capital, where regional proximity fosters a successful relationship between venture capitalists and portfolio enterprises (Zook 2002). Referring to distances, geographically small markets naturally have no problem, but they do have others. The narrow national borders also limit the amount of potential start-ups that compete for venture capitalists' money, for example. The number of potential start-ups is a prerequisite for successful investment activities for two reasons: first, because it allows venture capitalists to select the most promising projects; and second, it matches them up with appropriate projects. Nations like the United States, Germany, Switzerland or Austria can be understood as pools that comprise potential start-ups, projects and ideas that feed regional venture capital centres like the Boston region or Silicon Valley in the United States and the Munich or Frankfurt/Main region in Germany (Audretsch and Lehmann 2004, p. 21). Within these pools neither founders nor venture capitalists are perfectly mobile, even if both profit from short distances between each other. This explains the development of regional venture capital centres that are often near major universities (Audretsch et al. 2004).

However, fostering 'technopreneurship', venture capitalists are not always able to follow their projects because by leaving their region and/or country they lose a great deal of their idiosyncratic knowledge. Venkataraman (2004) refers to access to new ideas, role models, informal forums, region-specific opportunities, safety nets, access to large markets, and executive leadership. It is local knowledge that allows access to these resources. Therefore, to a considerable extent, the national market size determines the amount of potential projects to which venture capitalists have access.

Nevertheless, venture capitalists can influence market size by choosing a certain geographical focus; they can limit investments to their region, go national or even invest internationally. Going international, however, means that they have to syndicate with a lead investor monitoring the start-up on location. Considering all the problems of information asymmetries between an aware and an unaware partner, it can be said that they 'buy' international deals with considerable agency problems. Both Kuan (2005) and Jungwirth (2006) show that these problems of syndication can only be mitigated if venture capitalists do not cheat because they fear being cheated on during the next round of cooperation. Therefore, they have to be able to act as lead investor so that again the national market size is an important determinant. However, we acknowledge that the market size can be influenced by choosing a certain geographical investment focus.

In order to estimate the relative market size of Austria and Switzerland, some data are needed. Table 12.1 presents statistical data that allow a comparison of the size of the nation, venture capital market and the pool of potential projects of Austria and Switzerland. Aside from the markets we focused on, data were selected from Germany as a reference point within the German-speaking region, from the United Kingdom as the most established venture capital market in Europe, from mainland Europe, and from the United States as a general reference point.

The data demonstrate that national markets differ considerably concerning geographical and economic size, venture capital volume and potential for start-up projects. I abstain from building relative data (for example GDP per capita) because the absolute size of a nation's pool of resources and capabilities is important. After estimating the relative market size of the Austrian and Swiss venture capital markets, two points become evident. First, both markets are in fact small compared to Germany and the United Kingdom. Second, there is a considerable difference between Austria and Switzerland; the Swiss venture capital volume is nearly twice as large as the Austrian one. Nevertheless, it is a small market compared to Germany, the United Kingdom and the United States.

Market Development

Cohen and Levinthal (1990) refer to the need to have experience and knowledge, referred to as 'absorptive capacity', as a major factor in being able to learn. Therefore, existing knowledge cannot simply be used to improve a decision maker's strategy elsewhere. If the build-up of absorptive capacity is lost in a certain period, the development of the enterprise is eventually prolonged for many periods. The information from the environment cannot be 'absorbed' and no learning effects result from the experience of others within the same enterprise.

Table 12.1   Relative Market Size of Austria and Switzerland Compared to Other Markets

	Austria	Switzer-land	Germany	UK	Europe	USA
Geographical size						
Area (1000 km^2)[a]	84	41	357	244	4 113	9 631
Inhabitants (in millions)[b]	8.1	7.3	82.5	59.2	454	291
GDP[c] (in € billions)[d]	221	287	2 123	1 624	10 063	10 369
Size of the venture capital market						
VC invested without MBO (in € millions)[e]	114	212	1 035	3 464	10 691	19 432
Pool of potential start-up projects						
Patent applications in 2002 (in 1000)[f]	1.4	No data available	24.8	7.7	60.5	45.6
Citations SCI (in 1000)[g]	9	17	80	93	447	424
University degrees in S&T finished in 2000 (in 1000)[h]	8	No data available	80	126	556	439
Employees in S&T in 1999 (in 1000)	20	No data available	255	164	920	1 219

Notes:
a   Source: Federal Statistics Office Germany (2004), p. 24.
b   Source: Federal Statistics Office Germany (2004), p. 24.
c   GDP for gross domestic product.
d   Source: EVCA (2004).
e   Source: EVCA (2004).
f   Source: Federal Statistics Office Germany (2004), p. 122.
g   Source: own research in Web of Science, www.isinet.com/products/citation/wos/.
h   Source: European Commission (2003, p. 186).

Source: Author's own composition, but see notes.

Therefore, a lack of absorptive capacity can lead to a false estimation of what the market calls for. If the market calls for specialization but venture capitalists do not realize it, they will underinvest in human capital.

De Clercq et al. (2001) investigated the emerging Finnish venture capital market for the period 1994 to 1997. They were able to show that during that period venture capitalists were able to have the industry scope of their portfolio successively specialized. They also found evidence that less experienced venture capitalists had a time lag in these investment patterns compared to more experienced ones. They explained these results with delayed learning effects in the young but emerging Finnish venture capital market.

A similar situation could affect the Austrian venture capital market, which is well known for being 'still slightly behind when compared to other European countries' (EVCA 2004, p. 81). Peneder (1999) assumes that the traditional Austrian industry structure is responsible for this delay. Officials from the Austrian government and the Austrian Private Equity and Venture Capital Association (AVCO) estimate that the Austrian venture capital market has become more vigorous and is nearly as developed as the neighbouring venture capital markets (Peneder and Wieser 2002, Müller 2003), but we know from Cohen and Levinthal (1990) that a lack of experience in one period can affect strategic choices for periods to come. Therefore, path dependencies could be responsible for differences in investment behaviour today.

Even Switzerland is described by EVCA (2004, p. 241) as having 'lagged behind other similar sized countries such as Finland and Israel'. EVCA (2004) suggests that a lack of entrepreneurial spirit could be responsible for Switzerland's delay in strengthening its venture capital market, which is supported by studies focusing on a characteristic Swiss risk aversion (Hofstede 2001). However, things are not that simple. For instance, consider that Switzerland possesses capital far above the international average, but because of pension fund regulations, such as a current yearly minimum rate of return of 3.25 per cent, allocation of pension funds in the high-tech sector is limited. Therefore, venture capital has to be raised from private individuals, insurance companies and banks. Changes in legislation have been considered, but have not yet materialized (Volery et al. 2003).

HYPOTHESES

If differences in portfolio strategies of less-developed markets can be traced back to a lack of experience and knowledge, they should be mitigated in the long run. On the other hand, if market size does not lend itself to specialization, small markets will find their equilibrium on a low specialized level. High-tech investments will be rare because of a lack of knowledge. Both concepts could help to explain national and regional differences in market behaviour and to forecast the venture capital market development of a specific country or region. However, it will be hard to separate the two effects because the small markets are often less developed. Therefore, the focus of this chapter is to estimate the extent to which market development and market size affects the portfolio strategies of venture capitalists within a certain market.

To some extent, the question can already be answered. Data have shown that Austrian and Swiss venture capital markets are considerably smaller and less developed than markets in Germany, the United Kingdom and the United States. Furthermore, results of a previous study affirm expectations that Austrian and Swiss venture capitalists' investments are relatively low in human capital. OLS regressions show that an Austrian venture capitalist holds 26.5 per cent less specific knowledge than their German colleagues. This is significant on a 5 per cent level. A Swiss venture capitalist holds 8 per cent less but the second result is not significant. Consequently, both Swiss and Austrian venture capitalists also show a lower high-tech orientation than their German colleagues. For example, Austrian venture capitalists hold 14.5 per cent less high-tech projects in their portfolios, which is significant on a 10 per cent level, and Swiss venture capitalists hold 16.0 per cent less high-tech projects in their portfolios, which is significant on a 5 per cent level. Additionally, both Austrian and Swiss venture capitalists attend to less specialized portfolios holding 3 (Austria) and 3.4 (Switzerland) more industries in their portfolio than their German colleagues, respectively; which is significant on a 5 per cent level (Jungwirth 2006).

However, there are two problems with these results: First, as mentioned above, it is hard to assess whether market size or market development effects are responsible for that outcome. Furthermore, in spite of the same market conditions, portfolio strategies within the group of Austrian and Swiss venture capitalists vary considerably. The question is what method allows for differentiation between the two effects and explains the variations between venture capitalists. Gabszewicz and Grilo (1992) coined the term of 'heterogeneous beliefs', which explains why decisions made by equally informed individuals differ under the same market conditions. They assumed that beliefs about quality are heterogeneously distributed among individuals reacting rationally but differently. For the purposes of this study, I assume that 'heterogeneous beliefs' occur to venture capitalists in the following way. Austrian and Swiss venture capitalists know that their markets are small regarding access to venture capital as well as access to promising projects. However, it is not clear how they estimate this fact. For example, does small mean 'too small' or 'rather small'? The same holds for their assessment of market development. Does a delayed development mean 'too late' or 'promising'? The market assessment of each venture capitalist allows for an analysis of how beliefs about market size and market development influence investment activities. This consideration leads to the following testable hypotheses.

Hypothesis 1: Venture capitalists believing the market to have a certain potential for development show a considerably higher share of industry-specific human capital.

Hypothesis 2: Venture capitalists believing the market to be too small show a considerably lower share of industry-specific human capital.

DATABASE AND METHODOLOGY

Data

To test these hypotheses I generated a data set based on addresses provided by the Austrian Private Equity and Venture Capital Organization (AVCO) and the Swiss Private Equity and Corporate Finance Association (SECA). Between November 2004 and January 2005, 106 questionnaires were sent out via e-mail[2] and 58 fully completed questionnaires were returned, at a return rate of 54.7 per cent. Comparing the data with that from EVCA (EVCA 2004), AVCO (www.avco.at) and SECA (www.seca.ch) concerning the portfolio volume and the number of portfolio investments, the industry or investment-stage orientation, and the geographical activities, an assessment is made on the returns as representative of the population of venture capitalists in Austria and Switzerland.

Extensive data were collected by the standardized questionnaire on the venture capitalists' firm structure and investment focus, type of enterprises they attend, endowment with knowledge and experience, and their assessment of their home venture capital markets.

Firm structure and investment focus
I asked for data that reflected the size of the company (measured in number of employees, number of portfolio companies and volume of the portfolio), the company's development since foundation, the spatial focus of the company (regional, nationwide or international) and the governance structure (independent business or not). Concerning the investment focus of the venture capitalist, the question to what degree the venture capitalist was specialized in

an industry was asked. The responses were measured by the number of industries a venture capitalist invested in, ranging from investments in one industry, meaning they were more of a specialist, up to investments in seven or more industries, thus making them more of a generalist.[3]

Knowledge and experience to which the venture capital firm has access
The survey comprised information about education, defined by field of study and degree of education as well as experience of the employees and founders of the venture capital companies. Professional experience such as the industries in which they had obtained working experience was considered.

Assessment of the venture capital market
A group of statements refer directly to problems that deal with market size and market development. Thomas Jud, chairman of the AVCO, discussed all the statements with me and helped me to find items well known to all venture capitalists. Transferring the questionnaire to the Swiss venture capital markets, I asked SECA for support. They also approved the importance of the items. I will give an account of these items under 'operationalization' because they are essential in order to achieve accurate results from the analysis.

METHODOLOGY

The hypotheses in this study claim a relationship between market assessment and investment behaviour. In reference to Gabszewicz's and Grilo's (1992) heterogeneous beliefs, the hypotheses claim a direct and linear relationship between market assessment and investment behaviour, which was motivated in the theoretical part of the chapter. A multivariate OLS regression seems appropriate to analyse this relationship. Therefore, I test the influence of market assessment and some control variables on the dependent variables 'investments in human capital' (HCSPEC):

$$\text{HCSPEC} = \alpha + \beta_1 \text{ GOODPOTENTIAL} + \beta_2 \text{ TOOSMALL} + \beta_3 \text{ DUMMYREG} + \beta_4 \text{ DUMMYNAT} + \beta_5 \text{ DUMMYCORP} + \beta_6 \text{ DUMMYDEPEND} + \beta_7 \text{ AGEOFVCFIRM} + \beta_8 \text{ DUMMYAUSTRIA} + \varepsilon$$

I checked the model for linearity, multi-collinearity[4] and for heteroscedasticity (Wooldridge 2003) and found it valid, leading to meaningful results.

OPERATIONALIZATION

The next step is to operationalize the dependent, independent and control variables.

Dependent Variables

First, I refer to the willingness of venture capitalists to invest in their human capital. The variable is called HCSPEC. Venture capitalists' knowledge is categorized on the basis of information gathered about the higher education of the firm's employees and founders. If they only have a degree and/or experience in business administration or law, they are categorized as having 'general knowledge'. If they have degrees or experience in science or technology, they have 'specific knowledge'. In fact, most of the companies have a knowledge mix that is specified by a percentage grading of specific knowledge, that is, having two people with a Masters in Business Administration, one lawyer and one technical scientist within the team yields a share of specific knowledge of 25 per cent.

Independent Variables

The assessment of market size and market development is assumed to explain investment behaviour of venture capitalists. The bases for this assessment are the following items that were part of a set of items assessing the Swiss and Austrian venture capital market.

A. With its risk-taking and committed founders, the Austrian/Swiss market gives rise to a quick establishment of the venture capital market.
B. The Austrian/Swiss market contains many innovative projects an, therefore possesses a good potential for venture capital. (GOODPOTENTIAL)
C. With its tax and legal conditions, the Austrian/Swiss market supports the activities of venture capital companies.
D. The Austrian/Swiss market is too small to specialize in one or more industries. (TOOSMALL)
E. The Austrian/Swiss market is still in its infancy concerning venture capital.
F. The Austrian/Swiss market does not possess enough awareness of the function and advantages of venture capital.
G. The conditions for the economic use of new technological developments in the Austrian/Swiss market are inadequate.
H.   The Austrian/Swiss market has little potential for the high-tech projects,

since the innovative activities take place within the existing industrial structures.

While only one question was asked concerning the market size because the topic seemed to be clear, several items dealt with market development. However, a factor analysis reduced three items to one factor comprising size as well as development (C, D, E), while fast development and good innovation potential, bad conditions and low potential (with opposite signs) were reduced to another factor (A, B, G, H). One single item made the third factor (supportive market conditions, C). In all, the analysis offered three clearly distinguishable factors that comprised a very positive assessment of the market, a positive but reluctant assessment of the market, and quite a negative assessment of the market. Nevertheless, the factor analysis reveals that venture capitalists who are under the impression that the market is too small also believe the market is being developed too late. However, factor analysis does not help to separate the effects on market size and the effects of market development on investments in specific human capital. Actually, it should be said that this point refers to a general challenge of the study because venture capitalists frame the market situation differently. Nevertheless, the effort to separate both effects should be made, and therefore the original items (B and D) are used. Being measured on a Likert scale, variables can be handled as metric variables because they all displayed a normal curve of distribution. Again, the independent variables are: GOODPOTENTIAL to reflect the venture capitalists' assessment of market development, and TOOSMALL to reflect their assessment of the market size.

Control Variables

However, apart from market assessment many other factors probably exist which influence the investment behaviour of venture capitalists. Two very important variables try to map the actual market size of certain venture capitalists. A decrease in the chosen spatial investment focus results in a corresponding decrease in the ability to assess the actual market properly. Therefore, we controlled for geographical aspects. The regression encompasses whether a venture capitalist invests regionally (dummy variable DUMMYREG) or nationwide (dummy variable DUMMYNAT). In cases of regional or nationwide investment, international investments stand as the reference category for these dummies. Two dummy variables were built to differentiate corporate and another dependent venture capitalists because some evidence exists that institutional affiliation influences investments in human capital (Bottazzi et al. 2004). The reference category for both corporate and other dependent venture capitalists such as banks and governmental agencies is the class of independent venture capitalists. The questionnaire also asked whether the venture capital firm depends on a mutual savings bank, but no venture capitalist ticked this possibility. Therefore, I have only three institutional categories and the two I use are DUMMYCORP and DUMMYDEPEND. Another relevant factor independent of market experience should be the individual experience of a venture capitalist. The age of the venture capital firm can be used as proxy for experience (AGEOFVCFIRM). I also know that the Swiss and the Austrian venture capital markets differ regarding the amount of venture capital available. This seems to be an important influencing factor which makes controlling for country worthwhile (DUMMYAUSTRIA).

Table 12.2 sums up all dependent, independent and control variables.

DESCRIPTIVE RESULTS

This study focuses on two different countries, so it was important to determine whether significant differences exist in variable values between Austria and Switzerland (see Table 12.3). Results show considerable differences concerning investments in knowledge (HCSPEC). Swiss venture capitalists own considerably more specific human capital on average. Interestingly, I could not find such a strong difference in the 2003 study. I interpret this result as evidence of a difference in the development of the Austrian and Swiss venture capital markets since 2003. Upon comparison of Austrian and Swiss venture capitalists' market assessments, I also find significant differences concerning the item TOOSMALL. This result seems to prove that venture capitalists did indeed understand the meaning of the items. The Austrian venture capital market is smaller in size by about 50 per cent in terms of venture capital available. However, it also reflects the fact that Austrian venture capitalists choose a different spatial investment focus from the Swiss. While no Swiss venture capitalist limits their investment activities to regional projects, only a small share of Austrian venture capitalists invest internationally. Other significant differences result from the venture capitalists' status. While in many cases Austrian venture capitalists are dependent, Swiss venture capitalists tend to be independent. This can be assumed to reflect the stronger participation of the Austrian government in the venture capital market, which is well described in a qualitative empirical study by Müller (2003).

However, our central question is not to what extent Austria differs from Switzerland, but to what extent beliefs about market size and market development influence investments in human capital and portfolio management.

Table 12.2 Definition of Variables and Descriptive Statistics (N = 58)

Variables	Meaning	Measure	Medium	Standard Deviation
Dependent variable				
HCSpec	Share of specific human capital within the VC firm	Per cent, metric	28.06	29.56
Independent variables				
GoodPotential	Positive assessment of market development	Likert scale from 1 (I completely disagree) to 5 (I completely agree), metric	3.32	0.96
TooSmall	Negative assessment of market size	Likert scale from 1 (I completely disagree) to 5 (I completely agree), metric	3.73	1.23
Control variables				
DummyReg	VC investing with a regional focus	1 = Regional VC 0 = International VC	0.15	0.356
DummyNat	VC investing with a national focus	1 = National VC 0 = International VC	0.38	0.49
DummyCorp	Corporate VC	1 = Corporate VC 0 = Independent VC	0.06	0.23
DummyDepend	Other dependent VC	1 = Dependent VC 0 = Independent VC	0.15	0.36
AgeOfVCFirm	Age of the VC Firm, (2005 – Founding year of the VC firm)	Years, metric	8.02	6.44
DummyAustria	Austrian VC	1 = Austria 2 = Switzerland	0.52	0.50

Source: Author's own data 2005.

I expected that venture capitalists who believe the market to have a certain potential for development show a considerably higher share of industry-specific human capital, specialize in a few industries, attend to more high-tech projects within their portfolio, and invest in earlier stages. On the other hand, venture capitalists who believe the market to be too small should show a considerably lower share of industry-specific human capital, diversify over many industries, attend rather to 'medio' and low-tech projects within their portfolio, and invest in later stages. Correlation analysis revealed that venture capitalists assessing the market as too small invest less in human capital in later stages and hold more industries in their portfolio. Conversely, venture capitalists who believe the market is developing invest in earlier financing stages and hold fewer industries in their portfolio (all results significant on a 5 per cent level).

Table 12.3   T-Statistics Comparing Austrian and Swiss Data (N = 58)

Variables	Country	N	Medium	Standard Deviation	T-Value
HCSPEC	Austrian	29	16.59**	19.373	-3.355
	Swiss	25	41.36**	33.886	-3.229
GOODPOTENTIAL	Austrian	29	3.41	0.867	0.306
	Swiss	27	3.22	1.050	0.300
TOOSMALL	Austrian	29	4.17**	0.889	2.742
	Swiss	27	3.26**	1.375	2.628
DUMMYREG	Austrian	30	0.27**	0.450	2.960
	Swiss	25	0.00**	0.000	3.247
DUMMYNAT	Austrian	30	0.57**	0.504	3.338
	Swiss	25	0.16**	0.374	3.429
DUMMYCORP	Austrian	29	0.07	0.258	0.456
	Swiss	25	0.04	0.200	0.464
DUMMYDEPEND	Austrian	29	0.24*	0.435	2.125
	Swiss	25	0.04*	0.200	2.232
AGEOFVCFIRM	Austrian	30	7.77	6.548	-0.328
	Swiss	22	8.36	6.418	-0.329

Notes:
*** Significant at the 0% level
** Significant at the 1% level
* Significant at the 5% level

Source: Author's own analysis 2005.

RESULTS FROM REGRESSION ANALYSIS

Concerning investments in human capital (Table 12.4), I find that the assessment of the market as too small seemingly leads to lower investments in specific human capital. The size of the effect is quite considerable: one point on the Likert scale leads to a change in investments of nearly 6 per cent. As also expected, venture capitalists invest more in their specific human capital if they believe that the markets have good innovative potential. However, the second result is not significant. Interestingly, the spatial focus of investment activities does not influence investment behaviour at a significant level, even if descriptive statistics reveal a different result. Another result illustrates that corporate venture capitalists invest much more in specific human capital than independent venture capitalists.

Table 12.4   Regression: Investments in Human Capital

	Beta Value	Standard Default	T-Value
GOODPOTENTIAL	2.753	4.554	0.605
TOOSMALL	-5.644^t	3.288	-1.717
DUMMYREG	-6.803	15.217	-0.447
DUMMYNAT	-2.083	9.475	-0.220
DUMMYCORP	38.804*	15.877	2.444
DUMMYDEPEND	14.901	10.590	1.407
AGEOFVC	-0.577	0.638	-0.905
DUMMYAUSTRIA	-20.810*	10.264	-2.027
MODELFIT	$R^2 = 0.265$ (adjusted) $F = 3.069**$ $N = 46$		

Notes:
*** Significant at the 0% level
** Significant at the 1% level
* Significant at the 5% level
^{t} Significant at the 10% level

Source: Author's own analysis 2005.

Corporate venture capitalists often depend on an enterprise that wishes to observe the market development or to spin off its own innovative product developments (Campell et al. 2003). Therefore, it is not surprising that corporate venture capitalists own a considerable amount of specific knowledge. However, we know that many independent venture capitalists own a considerable share of specific human capital (Bottazzi et al. 2004) and we also know from Maula et al. (2005) that technical advice from corporate venture capitalists is only marginally better than from independent venture capitalists. Therefore, this result does not represent the average situation but refers to the low average share of specific human capital in this sample. The dummy Austria delivers the expected result that Austrian venture capitalists invest considerably less in specific human capital than Swiss venture capitalists. Regression results support Hypothesis 1 that beliefs about market size influence the propensity to invest in specific human capital. Nevertheless, these results do not support Hypothesis 2 that beliefs about market development affect investment behaviour.

DISCUSSION AND CONCLUSION

In this chapter I analysed whether and to what extent small market size and delayed market development would bar venture capitalists from specialization. The rationale behind this was that the demand in small markets is too small to amortize the investments in the specific stock of human capital. On the other hand, in delayed developed markets a lack of absorptive capacity deters venture capitalists from understanding adequately what the market calls for. Based on a former study, I knew that the Austrian and Swiss venture capital markets were small and had only recently developed. I also knew that the Austrian and Swiss venture capitalists invested less in human capital. However, I did not know how much of this investment behaviour referred to market size and to delayed market development. Another point was that variations between venture capitalists in the control sample were considerable. Therefore, it could be assumed that the objective market situation should not necessarily be critically relevant for investment behaviour but instead the crucial factor should be the subjective assessment of the market situation. The questionnaire asked some important items concerning market assessment of the Austrian and Swiss venture capital market that were taken as explanatory variables.

The results are instructive but ambivalent for two reasons. First, factor analysis revealed that venture capitalists jumble assessments about market development and market size so that items stating 'the market is too small' and 'the market is too young' are reduced to the same factor. Even if a thorough analysis of the item assessment revealed that the items are well understood by venture capitalists[5] I have to concede that 'too young' is not seen as a counterpart of 'too small' but put into the same category. Obviously, a relationship that is quite logical and clear for me is not necessarily so for venture capitalists.

Second, the strongest influence on investment behaviour is whether or not the venture capitalist is Austrian or Swiss. This is, in a sense, a strong support for our hypotheses. Starting from nearly the same investment behaviour at the beginning of 2003, differences in market size measured as venture capital available led to considerable differences in investment behaviour at the beginning of 2005. To ensure that national effects were not caused by non-discussed influence factors (for example tax regulations that punish high-tech investments), I compared venture capitalists with general knowledge and specific knowledge and found that national differences became less important. Austrian and Swiss venture capitalists possessing a high share of specific human capital behave similarly.

However, what can be said about the influence of market development and market size? At first glance market size seems to accelerate market development. However, another factor could distort the evidence. Switzerland is a financial centre and financial knowledge is deep-seated as a national resource. Therefore, it is not clear whether venture capital is provided because of intellectual capital or whether it fosters the accumulation of intellectual capital. Nevertheless, it can be shown that market size and market development play a major role in the investment behaviour of venture capitalists.

The limits of the study are obvious: dealing with 58 cases is a good number in relation to the Swiss and Austrian venture capitalists available but a small number for meaningful regression analysis. Nevertheless, the results are robust, as the specifications of different models illustrate. The next step should be a refinement of the regression analysis, which would produce more elaborate results using a linear probability model.

NOTES

1. 'Cultural' comprises here: same language, same university system, similar industry structure, same skill level, same risk propensity and so on.
2. All companies had e-mail access. However, I offered to send the questionnaire by e-mail, mail or fax to increase the response rate. Ninety per cent of responses were via e-mail. By offering two other options of sending back the questionnaire I was able to ensure that there was no response bias concerning the online survey technique.
3. I aggregated industries in seven fields, usually named by venture capitalists as typical investment fields, namely, bio-technology, computer software, medicine, electrical engineering, computer hardware, communication technology, Internet or e-commerce.

4. No correlation coefficient was higher than 0.502.
5. For example, comparing Austrian and Swiss venture capitalists' market assessments I find a significant difference concerning the item ENOUGHSUPPORT. The Austrian government actively fosters the venture capital market by supporting it with transaction cost-reducing services while the Swiss government acts reluctantly (Lüthy 2004).

REFERENCES

Amit, R., J. Brander and C. Zott (1998), 'Why do venture capital firms exist? Theory and Canadian evidence', *Journal of Business Venturing*, **13**, 441–66.

Audretsch, D. and E. Lehmann (2004), 'Universitäten als regionale Förderer der Wirtschaft?' *ifo Dresden berichtet*, 18–23.

Audretsch, D., E. Lehmann and S. Warning (2004), 'University spillovers: Does the kind of science matter?' *Diskussionspapiere der DFGForschergruppe*, Nr. 3468269275.

Becker, R. and T. Hellmann (2003), 'The genesis of venture capital: lessons from the German experience', CesIfo Working Paper No. 883, March.

Besanko, David, David Dranove and Mark Shanley (2000), *Economics of Strategy*, New York: John Wiley & Sons.

Bottazzi, L., M. Da Rin and T. Hellmann (2004), 'The changing face of the European venture capital industry', *Journal of Private Equity*, **7**, Spring, 26–53.

Campbell, A., J. Birkinshaw, A. Morrison and R. van Basten Batenburg (2003), 'The future of corporate venturing', *MIT Sloan Management Review*, Fall, 30–37.

Cohen, W.M. and D.A. Levinthal (1990), 'Absorptive capacity: a new perspective on learning and innovation', *Administrative Science Quarterly*, **35**, 128–52.

De Clercq, D., P.K. Goulet, M. Kumpulainen and M. Mäkelä (2001), 'Portfolio investment strategies in the Finnish venture capital industry: a longitudinal study', *Venture Capital: An International Journal of Entrepreneurial Finance*, **3**, 41–62.

Dimov, D.P. and D.A. Shepherd (2005), 'Human capital theory and venture capital firms: exploring "home runs" and "strike outs"', *Journal of Business Venturing*, **20**, 1–21.

Dotzler, F. (2001), 'What do venture capitalists really do, and where do they learn to do it?' *Institutional Investor*, 6–52.

European Commission (2003), *Third European Report on Science and Technology Indicators*, Luxembourg.

EVCA (2004), *Annual Survey of Pan-European Private Equity and Venture Capital Activity*, Brussels.

Federal Statistics Office Germany (2004), *Statistical Yearbook 2004*, Wiesbaden.

Gabszewicz, J. and I. Grilo (1992), 'Price competition when consumers are uncertain about which firm sells which quality', *Journal of Economics and Management Strategy*, **1**, 629–49.

Hofstede, G. (2001), *Culture's Consequences, Comparing Values, Behaviors, Institutions, and Organizations Across Nations*, Thousand Oaks, CA: Sage.

Jungwirth, Carola (2006), *Wissensabhängige Strategiewahl in der Venture-Capital-Industrie. Eine theoretische und empirische Analyse*, Wiesbaden: Gabler.

Jungwirth, C. and P. Moog (2004), 'Selection and support strategies in venture capital financing: high-techs or low-techs – hands-off or hands-on?' *Venture Capital: An International Journal of Entrepreneurial Finance*, **6**, 105–23.

Kuan, J. (2005), 'The role of hostages in establishing venture capital networks',

Discussion Paper, Stanford University, jwkuan@stanford.edu, 21 April 2005.

Lüthy, Lukas (2004), 'Staatliche Förderaktivitäten bei der Venture Capital-Vergabe', Diploma thesis, Wirtschaftswissenschaftliche Fakultät, Universität Zürich.

Martin, R., P. Sunley and D. Turner (2002), 'Taking risks in regions: the geographical anatomy of Europe's emerging venture capital market', *Journal of Economic Geography*, **2**, 121–50.

Maula, M., E. Autio and G. Murray (2005), 'Corporate venture capitalists and independent venture capitalists: what do they know, who do they know, and should entrepreneurs care?' *Venture Capital: An International Journal of Entrepreneurial Finance*, **7**, 3–19.

Müller, Richard (2003), 'Österreichische Beteiligungskapitalnetzwerke', Diploma thesis, Wirtschaftswissenschaftliche Fakultät, Universität Zürich.

Norton, E. and B.H. Tenenbaum (1993), 'Specialization versus diversification as a venture capital investment strategy', *Journal of Business Venturing*, **8**, 431–42.

Peneder, M. (1999), 'The Austrian paradox: old structures but high performance?' *Austrian Economic Quarterly*, **4**, 239–47.

Peneder, M. and R. Wieser (2002), 'Der österreichische Markt für Private Equity und Venture Capital 2001', *WiFo Monatsberichte*, **10**, 661–7.

Smith, Adam (1776), *An Inquiry into the Nature and Causes of the Wealth of Nations*, reprinted from the original London edition (1994), Munich: Idion.

Venkataraman, Sankaran (2004), 'Regional transformation through technological entrepreneurship', *Journal of Business Venturing*, **19**, 153–67.

Volery, Thierry, Georges Haour and Benoit Leleux (2003), *Global Entrepreneurship MonitorBericht 2003 zum Unternehmertum in der Schweiz und weltweit*, 2003 Swiss Executive Report, St Gallen: University of St Gallen.

Wooldridge, Jeffrey M. (2003). *Introductory Econometrics. A Modern Approach*, Mason, OH: Thomson/South Western.

Zook, Matthew A. (2002), 'Grounded capital: venture financing and the geography of the Internet industry', *Journal of Economic Geography*, **2**, 151–77.

Index